Notable British Trials Series No. 84

TRIAL OF

ISRAEL LIPSKI

EDITED BY

M.W. Oldridge

LONDON
MANGO BOOKS

First edition published 2017 (Hardcover)
This edition 2019 (Softcover)

Copyright © M.W. Oldridge, 2017, 2019

The right of M.W. Oldridge to be identified as the author of this work has been asserted in accordance with the Copyright, Designs & Patents Act 1988.

All rights reserved. No part of this book may be reprinted or reproduced or utilised in any form or by any electronic, mechanical or other means, now known or hereafter invented, including photocopying and recording, or in any information storage or retrieval system, without the prior permission in writing of the publishers.

ISBN: 978-1-911273-20-2 (hardcover)
ISBN: 978-1-911273-58-5 (softcover)
ISBN: 978-1-911273-21-9 (ebook)

Notable British Trials imprint ©William Hodge & Company (Holdings) Ltd
Used with kind permission.

Published by Mango Books
www.mangobooks.co.uk

Notable British Trials Series No. 84

TRIAL OF
ISRAEL LIPSKI

EDITED BY

M.W. Oldridge

Israel Lipski
© *The National Archives*

FOREWORD.

A History of the Notable British Trials Series

Messrs William Hodge and Company, of Glasgow and Edinburgh, have in the press, ready for early publication, an interesting series of Notable Scottish Trials, comprising most of the 'causes celebres' of last century. The first volume of this series, *The Trial of Madeleine Smith*, will appear on 4th October, and will be followed at short intervals by volumes containing the trials of the City of Glasgow Bank Directors, E. M. Chantrelle, and others. Each book deals exhaustively with its subject, and is edited by a well-known lawyer, and the series, when complete, should form a most valuable collection. In *The Trial of Madeleine Smith*, all the letters from the accused to her lover that have appeared in previous editions of the trial are given, along with many that are now published for the first time. A facsimile of one of her letters and a specimen of L'Angelier's handwriting also appear, while a view of the trial, sketched when it was actually in progress, forms one of the interesting illustrations in the book. The price of each volume of the series will be 5s net.[1]

In this manner, in an Aberdonian newspaper, in the early autumn of 1905, the birth of a new series of Notable Scottish Trials was announced. Within a few days, advertisements ran to announce that the first instalment in the series would be edited by A. Duncan Smith ('Advocate, Edinburgh'), and that the book itself would be a handsome object: 'Demy 8vo, Cloth, Gilt Top, 400 pp., with Several Illustrations'.[2]

A glowing review of *Trial of Madeleine Smith* (now shorn of its definite article) appeared in *The Scotsman* on 9 October. The anonymous reviewer found the book to be 'of supreme interest', and a balance had been struck between the thrill of the case – 'her trial reads like a romance' – and the 'educative' and 'considerable historic value' of introducing it to a new readership. 'It is approaching half a century since the beautiful and fascinating Madeleine Smith was placed in the dock of the High Court of Justiciary in Edinburgh,' the reviewer reflected, and some of the (often inadvertent) luminaries of trials gone by were becoming 'mere names of vague import' as memories began to fade. An early indication of the ambition of the Notable Scottish Trials project could be derived from a list of future titles, including, in the words of the reviewer (and in addition to the trial of the directors of the City of Glasgow Bank and the Chantrelle case, already noted), '*Dr Edward W. Pritchard, Jessie*

---

1 *Aberdeen Press and Journal*, 18 September 1905.
2 *Dundee Courier*, 27 September 1905.

Lipski.

M'Lachlan, Charles Soutar (Dunecht Mystery), The Dynamitards, J. W. Laurie, The Glasgow Cotton Spinners, and *Alfred J. Monson*'.[3] Not all of these volumes would appear – Soutar, the Dynamitards and the Cotton Spinners were put aside – and, as time went by, alternative titles were found. Deacon Brodie, Captain Porteous and James Stewart were all waiting to find their way into green cloth.

Trial of the City of Glasgow Bank Directors and *Trial of Dr Pritchard* were issued in late 1905 and early 1906 respectively; *Trial of Eugène Marie Chantrelle* followed in June. Four volumes of the fledgling series had therefore been produced, and the responses of the book reviewers had been consistently positive. 'Messrs William Hodge & Co., Glasgow, are doing distinct service not only to the legal professional, but also the general public by the publication of Notable Scottish Trials' was the view of the *Dundee Courier*; the *Arbroath Herald* awaited *Trial of James Stewart* 'with something like impatience' – but not for long, as the book was published in 1907.[4] This encouraging reaction continued as new volumes were issued. Clement King Shorter, of *The Sphere*, wrote that he 'rejoice[d] particularly' in the series, and described *Trial of Deacon Brodie* (1907) as 'a presentation of manners and customs of the end of the eighteenth century in Scotland that no amount of ordinary fine writing could secure to us'.[5] For the *Illustrated London News, Trial of A. J. Monson* (1908) was 'much more interesting than a police novel'.[6]

Notable Scottish Trials had, therefore, been a great critical success for its publishers, Hodge & Co., especially bearing in mind that the series was – according to legend, at least – 'founded as a hobby' by its general editor, Harry Hodge.[7] This gentleman, the son of the founder of the company, was no stranger to success. Schooled at Glasgow and Leipzig, he followed his father in providing – alongside the publishing arm of the company – shorthand writing services in the Scottish courts, 'acting in that capacity', as his obituary tells us, 'at the famous trial of Oscar Slater in 1909'. He was a man of 'particularly wide interests', one of the chief among these being music. 'A number of his compositions for pianoforte were published in this country and in Germany, and he was president of the Edinburgh Music Club,' we hear. 'He owned a harpsichord which was believed to be the only one of its type in Edinburgh, and at one time played the double bass in the Scottish Orchestra' (the harpsichord was also 'reputed to be one of the finest extant and used by Mozart in his visit to

---

3   *The Scotsman*, 9 October 1905.
4   *Dundee Courier*, 24 February 1906; *Arbroath Herald*, 28 June 1906.
5   *The Sphere*, 16 February 1907.
6   *Illustrated London News*, 4 April 1908.
7   'Notable British Trials and War Crimes Trials', William Hodge & Company Ltd., 1954.

Foreword.

London'.)[8] Hodge was studiously modest about his musical achievements, and 'protested he could not play'; likewise, 'while disclaiming to be a linguist, he had many friends on the Continent with whom he conversed and corresponded in their language'. Self-effacement was the default position for this 'kindly, debonair' man.[9]

Not unreasonably, *The Scotsman* wondered at the nature of the polymath – 'it was surely odd to find a musician a criminologist' – but Hodge's criminological credentials were impeccable. 'Such eminent jurists as the late Earl of Birkenhead and Sir Marshall Hall' recognised his authority, and 'admitted him as one of the very few early members to the exclusive "Crimes Club"'.[10] He even stamped his mark on the legal history of the Falkirk region in July 1906, for an offence committed just as Eugène Marie Chantrelle was making his appearance in the static court of a volume of Notable Scottish Trials:

> At Falkirk Sheriff Court today, Harry Hodge, printer and publisher, Murrayfield, Edinburgh, was charged with having during the night of the 10th-11th June, and between Polmont and Linlithgow Bridge, travelled in his motor tri-car without exhibiting a white light. Mr Hodge did not appear. His agent in pleading guilty on his behalf, said his client had driven a motor car for a good number of years, and had not committed this offence wilfully. He went in his motor car from Edinburgh to Stirling on a visit to friends. On leaving Stirling, he had two white lights in front, although he only required one. On the way between Stirling and Falkirk one of the lights went out, and on examination he found that the bottom of the lamp had fallen out. The other light was still burning. When he passed through Polmont at ten minutes to eleven the light was out, but he did not light it as he meant to stop at Linlithgow, which was four miles further on. It was then he was stopped by the police. Mr Hodge had no intention of driving without lights, and he was altogether the victim of circumstances. The Fiscal said this was the first case of the kind in the district. The Sheriff imposed a modified fine of £1.[11]

Even Hodge's musical endeavours seemed to possess the characteristic values – the absence of complication, of pretence, and of self-importance – which would distinguish the Notable Scottish Trials series, its general editor, and its successors.

> Some interesting pianoforte compositions by an amateur musician well-known in Edinburgh and Glasgow, Mr Harry Hodge, include a cleverly developed

---

8   *The Scotsman*, 11 December 1947; 16 December 1947.
9   *The Scotsman*, 16 December 1947.
10 *The Scotsman*, 16 December 1947.
11 *Edinburgh Evening News*, 2 July 1906.

Lipski.

'Toccatina' (London: J. & W. Chester). By the same composer, and published by Breitkopf & Härtel, Leipzig, there are also 'Variations on an Original Theme in G minor', and 'Allegro', a 'Gavotte', a 'Waltz', and a transcription of the Prelude to John Sebastian Bach's Violoncello Suite in E major. All of these pieces present a happy combination of matter of a nature to reward the attention of a good pianist, with an absence of the technical difficulty which might serve to discourage one of more modest attainments.[12]

But with this mention of successor series we have already jumped ahead of ourselves.

*

From the earliest volume, *Trial of Madeleine Smith*, the general production values and format of the Notable Scottish Trials series were established. In each book there was, as described above, a verbatim account of the trial – or as near as could be had to it; there was a chronology of the main events; there were appendices of related material; and there were illustrations, frequently showing the chief players in the legal drama – the advocates (according to the nomenclature in the Scottish law) and the judges – alongside the defendants (in Scottish proceedings, the 'panel'), and so on. There was also an introduction to the case written by the editor, and the first three volumes were shared between three editors: the aforementioned A. Duncan Smith; William Wallace ('M. A., Sheriff-Substitute, Campbeltown'), the editor of *Trial of the City of Glasgow Bank Directors*; and William Roughead.[13] Roughead's public debut as a writer had taken the form of a half-serious book of poetry which might have contended for the crown then being vacated by William McGonagall, but Harry Hodge's commission suited him better, even if he did miss out on Madeleine Smith – his greatest love in the Scottish criminal canon, and a subject to whose mystery he would return several times in later volumes of true crime writing. His exalted place in the historiography of crime is assured, and, where he is concerned, the reader is encouraged to seek out anything they can, with the possible exception of the early poems. His introduction to *Trial of Dr Pritchard* showed that his distinctive narrative voice was already established – learned, careful, purposeful, and exhibiting touches of intimacy and feeling from which other authors may have shied away. Examples abound. 'Now,' he writes of Pritchard's mother-in-law, 'Mrs Taylor, though a strong and healthy old lady for her seventy years, had, unfortunately, contracted the habit of taking a preparation of opium, known as Battley's Sedative Solution. She commenced to use this medicine as

---

12   *The Scotsman*, 20 August 1906.
13   *Aberdeen Press and Journal*, 20 November 1905.

Foreword.

a remedy for the neuralgic headaches from which she suffered, and the practice had so grown upon her as to enable her to take with impunity considerable quantities of that drug.'[14] We get, with Roughead, not just the details, but a sense of the joy of telling the story, and an idea of what can be achieved by subtlety and understatement. No doubt Mrs Taylor's habit had indeed 'grown upon her', perhaps more so than her son-in-law ever did. Roughead, to a greater extent than anyone else, defined the creative role of the editor within the Notable Scottish Trials series – and, for we have caught up with ourselves now, its successor series.

Clement Shorter, the founder of *The Sphere*, was, as we have seen, an early champion of the Notable Scottish Trials books, and in his column of 2 March 1907, he began to yearn for an English counterpart series.

> I would willingly read of the trial of Wainwright, the poisoner, whom some of us only know through the essay by Mr Oscar Wilde; of Thurtell, whom we know from references in George Borrow, in Carlyle, and in many another quarter – only the other day that clever and prolific writer, 'Dick Donovan', wrote a novel upon it – above all of Müller, who somewhere in the sixties created a fever of excitement through England by murdering a Mr Briggs in a railway carriage. That trial is known to the present generation only by an amusing reference by Mr Matthew Arnold. There are great possibilities in a series of this kind if only they have such good introductions and so many interesting notes as are to be found in Mr Hodge's series.[15]

Two of Shorter's three wishes would soon come true. By late 1909, Harry Hodge had formulated plans to launch a parallel series, bound in red cloth, to commence with *Trial of Franz Müller*, edited by H. B. Irving. (Shorter's tastes had changed by this time, and he now announced that 'of English murder trials the ones that most interest me are those of Müller, Dr Dodd, and Lord Ferrers, who killed his valet'.[16]) In fact, the Notable English Trials series reached the bookshelves for the first time with J. B. Atlay's *Trial of the Stauntons* in March 1911; *Trial of Franz Müller* followed two months later. Again, the reception was enthusiastic, and *The Scotsman*, turning its eyes to the south, remarked that the new series 'promises to be as successful as its forerunner'.[17] In October 1911, the

---

14 Roughead, W. (ed.), *Trial of Dr Pritchard*, Edinburgh: William Hodge & Company, 1906), 27.
15 *The Sphere*, 2 March 1907.
16 *The Sphere*, 6 November 1909. Dr Dodd, as had the Dynamitards and others, flickered into and out of the consciousness of the publisher in about 1928, when a volume in his name was advertised as 'in preparation' in Trial of the Duchess of Kingston. The volume, which never appeared, was due to be edited by Eric R. Watson and W. Teignmouth Shore.
17 *The Scotsman*, 22 May 1911.

Lipski.

publication of *Trial of Simon, Lord Lovat of the '45* created another connection between the original series and its successor. His lordship – a Scotsman whose thoughts about the contested monarchy had shifted – was tried in England under English law, and beheaded in public in 1747. His trial was, uniquely, published in both series – in the green covers of Notable Scottish Trials, and in the red of Notable English Trials.

By the end of the 1910s, anyone in possession of a complete collection of Notable Scottish Trials and Notable English Trials had a considerable criminological library. A few cases of particular interest can be selected: for example, *Trial of William Palmer* (1912) had been a popular volume in the latter series, illuminating a case which changed trial procedures in England – these were the sorts of cases which were 'notable' in their truest sense, although why Palmer was not accorded his professional designation in the title of the book is not clear – the best answer seems to be that some doctors were (as Pritchard had been), and some were not. *The Tatler* – another periodical founded by Shorter – said that *Trial of Mrs Maybrick* (1913), featuring an introduction by H. B. Irving which played the turning ball of the Maybrick case with a very, very straight bat, 'should be eagerly read'.[18] The *Pall Mall Gazette*, however, regretted the missed opportunity for some combative hitting, speculating that Irving had been inhibited by the fact that 'Mrs Maybrick is still living'.[19]

Whether this was truly the cause of Irving's cautious approach to his introduction to the case we cannot know, but the risk of libel suits had certainly affected, or would affect, Hodge & Co. once or twice. Covering cases from long ago was a natural way to avoid complications of this sort – nobody was going to sue over anything in *The Annesley Case* (1912), another early component of the Notable English Trials series, and one whose title deviated from the usual pattern somewhat. But the Maybrick case was a controversy of recent years. Occurring in 1889, it spotlighted a wrongful conviction, a misuse of executive authority at the Home Office, and a judge with indications of dementia. Mrs Maybrick herself had only been released from prison in 1904 after an ordeal to which she should never have been subjected. The balance between covering, on the one hand, trouble-free cases from the depths of history and, on the other up-to-date trials, especially ones which were 'notable', was a difficult one to strike. Defendants acquitted in 'notable' trials were apt to dislike seeing their names on the spines of books in bookshops. In 1931, after an extensive trial in Bodmin, a lady going under the name of Sarah Ann Hearn had (probably) bluffed her way to an acquittal in a serial poisoning case. Graham Brooks, who had recently

---

18 *The Tatler*, 29 January 1913.
19 *Pall Mall Gazette*, 4 February 1913.

Foreword.

edited *Trial of Captain Kidd* (1930) – a safe subject from long ago – wrote to the Director of Public Prosecutions asking to see the official paperwork in the Hearn affair. The Director wrote to Hodge & Co. asking whether Brooks had been 'authorised by your company to undertake this work'. The recipient – perhaps Harry Hodge, although the initials are difficult to read – annotated the letter in pencil: 'No!'[20] Brooks's instincts may have been right, although his methods may have left something to be desired: Mrs Hearn's trial would have been an interesting and significant addition to the growing canon, but one senses that the possibility of legal action may have been a deterrent to its publication. For his part, Brooks never edited a trial for Hodge & Co. again.

In 1913, another deviation from the established style of the series occurred with *Eugene Aram: His Life and Trial*, edited by Eric R. Watson. In this example, as Shorter pointed out, 'you have no adequate report of this trial, which took place in 1759'. Still, Watson had constructed his story piecemeal, 'picking up a trifle here and a trifle there', and had overthrown the idealised view of Aram which had been created by 'Thomas Hood's poem, Bulwer Lytton's novel, and the play associated with Sir Henry Irving'. 'The only point at which the romance touches the truth,' Shorter reported, 'is in the fact that the murderer was executed fourteen years after the murder, and he did not give himself up through contrition as poetry and fiction would lead us to assume, but was "found out"'. Shorter's delight in the series was unaffected by this variation from their usual format, and he continued to describe them in thrilled terms: they were 'so much more exciting than half the novels published, with the additional advantage that everything in these books actually happened'.[21]

Back in Scotland, new volumes in the Notable Scottish Trials series had begun to appear at greater intervals. *Trial of Mrs M'Lachlan* – another triumph of editorship by William Roughead – had emerged in 1911, but after four more years no further contributions to the series had been made. Certain developments in 1914, however, made it necessary to prepare a second edition of *Trial of Oscar Slater*, the first edition of which had published in April 1910, and edited – naturally – by Roughead. Experienced true crime readers ought to know already that Slater had been convicted by majority verdict of the murder, in December 1908, of Marion Gilchrist in Glasgow, and that the case against him had been, at least in some of its aspects, troubling. Roughead had, by his own bashful description, 'expressed no opinion regarding the accused's guilt or innocence' in the first edition, but 'attention was directed to some unsatisfactory features in

---

20 Kent State University Libraries: Jonathan Goodman Papers: Box 22, Folder 30
21 *The Sphere*, 26 July 1913.

the evidence for the prosecution'.[22] We should turn to Roughead himself, and to his postscript to the 1915 second edition, in which he picks up the story.

> On 21st April 1910, a verbatim report of the trial was published in the present series; on 21st August 1912, appeared Sir Arthur Conan Doyle's booklet, *The Case of Oscar Slater* ... Actuated by the firm belief that Slater was unjustly convicted Sir Arthur Conan Doyle expressed his views in a pamphlet, written in a popular manner and published at a popular price, basing his examination of the facts upon the printed report. Under such distinguished auspices and in a form so convenient the circumstances became more widely known, and the attention of many who otherwise would have had no interest in it was directed to the subject. ... Altogether the little book is a capital bit of special pleading, and must have dismayed those confiding folk who regard juries as immune from error; but one wishes that the author had entrusted the investigation of the case to his friend Mr Sherlock Holmes, who could not only have confounded the prosecution but would infallibly have unmasked the murderer.[23]

Without really meaning to, Roughead's first edition of *Trial of Oscar Slater* had brought a doubtful case to the attention of the era's most zealous populariser of ideas both legitimate and eccentric. It so happened that, in the matter of Slater, Sir Arthur was on the right track. There were other developments along the way, but, by 1914, the demand for an investigation into the police's handling of the evidence against Slater was overwhelming. An inquiry was held, but, even after it reported its findings to the Secretary of State for Scotland, the official line, described in the House of Commons on 17 June 1914, was that 'no case was established that would justify me in advising any interference with the sentence'.[24] In July, however, a detective who had expressed concerns about the suppression of evidence favourable to the prisoner – and who was later found guilty of 'communicating to a person who is not a member of the Glasgow Police Force ... information which he had acquired in the performance of his duty and copies of documents from official records' – was dismissed from his occupation. But what, if not his sincere misgivings about the security of the verdict against Slater, could have motivated the detective to break the line? 'He stood to lose,' Roughead commented, 'and in fact lost everything – prestige, place, and pension'.[25]

In Roughead's view, 'if the evidence taken at the inquiry had been before the

---

22 Roughead, W. (ed.), *Trial of Oscar Slater* (Edinburgh: William Hodge & Company, second edition, 1915), lix.
23 Roughead, *Trial of Oscar Slater* (second edition), lviii-lix.
24 Roughead, *Trial of Oscar Slater* (second edition), lxii.
25 Roughead, *Trial of Oscar Slater* (second edition), lxx.

Foreword.

jury, they must have given the accused the benefit of the doubt'.[26] The anxieties that had existed after the trial were multiplied by the outcome of the inquiry; the detective had been hung out to dry, as the saying goes; but the Secretary of State had decided on a course of inaction, and, scandalously, Slater was not released from confinement until 1927. Later editions of *Trial of Oscar Slater* moved through the gradual developments in the case, and Roughead himself – quietly staying the course – appeared at Slater's belated appeal.

Trial of Oscar Slater exemplified the potential influence of Hodge and Co.'s series, but it was neither the mission of the series nor a practicable ambition to systematically unearth and examine miscarriages of justice. Of rather less gravity was the minor storm cooked up by Filson Young in 1920. His *Trial of H. H. Crippen* – another 'doctor' divested of his professional denomination in Hodge & Co.'s title, although Crippen's 'medicine' was on the fringes of orthodox scientific practice – appeared in the Notable English Trials series, and it looked unlikely to provoke controversy. The defendant in the main case – the eponymous Crippen – had been found guilty and executed. The defendant's girlfriend, the semi-pseudonymous Ethel le Neve, was extant but living in anonymity; perhaps she would not risk a return to the spotlight even if she read the book and objected to it. The reputation of the defendant's wife, however, was rather there for the taking, she having had nothing further to say since Crippen had poisoned her, or shot her, or perhaps both, and segmented her ready for burial in his basement in 1910. Young characterised the unfortunate Cora Crippen as a dominant and readily-antagonised narcissist, and one Richard King, writing in *The Tatler*, found himself charmed by Young's portrayal:

> The more I read about Mrs Crippen the more I understand why Crippen murdered his wife. She must have been an utterly impossible woman, hopeless alike as wife, companion, and as individual. You understand this all the more vividly after reading Mr Filson Young's interesting account … Strangely enough, one finishes reading the story of the trial with a sneaking sympathy for the murderer, who, in his love for Miss le Neve and in his unselfishness on her account, seems to possess a certain grandeur very rare among murderers.[27]

That paragraph is probably better left alone, since to unpick it would be to give it a dignity it does not deserve. Suffice to say, nothing published prior to 1920 is known to depict Cora in the florid and derogatory way that Young did – so it is quite unclear what Richard King thought that he had been reading. Cora's friends wrote to the newspapers to contest Young's misrepresentation

---

26   Roughead, *Trial of Oscar Slater* (second edition), lxx.
27   *The Tatler*, 10 March 1920.

of her, but subsequent secondary works have more or less universally followed Young's unjustified lead. The rehabilitation of Cora's personality has only begun recently, driven by the comprehensive historical endeavours of Nicholas Connell.[28]

In 1921 – although the book is dated 1920 on the colophon – *Trial of Thurtell and Hunt* was published, edited by Eric R. Watson. With this, Clement Shorter's second wish came true, several years after the publication of *Trial of Franz Müller* had granted him his first. Wainewright the poisoner – to give the more usual spelling of his surname, restoring the *e* omitted by Shorter in his 1907 article and in spite of his professed enthusiasm for the case – would never figure in the red cloth of Notable English Trials. And, indeed, the series itself closed at this point, fusing unobtrusively with its Scottish counterpart under the new, unified banner of Notable British Trials.

*

From 1921 onwards, the green cloth of the Notable Scottish Trials series would grace no new volumes. In sixteen years, the series had grown from a parochial concern, with its books published and distributed in Scotland and covering Scottish legal affairs, to one with a Sassenach sibling and nationwide recognition (indeed, overseas editions were also licensed, appearing under other publishers' names and sometimes in blue cloth). The new appellation matched the increased sense of ambition and the greater reach of the series.

Perhaps appropriately, the first product of the Notable British Trials series was a reprint of A. Duncan Smith's *Trial of Madeleine Smith* (eventually, most of the volumes in the original Notable Scottish Trials series would be reprinted as Notable British Trials, including a revised third edition of *Trial of Oscar Slater* in 1929). Chasing Madeleine into print were *Burke and Hare*, another product of the prolific Roughead, and the first Scottish case in the series to appear only in the red cloth of Notable British Trials. New volumes were now retailing from booksellers at 10s 6d – more than twice the original cover price – and, although Roughead found it 'personally regrettable', *Burke and Hare* was forced into two editions: one general edition which omitted 'the elaborate judgements delivered in the proceedings taken against Hare subsequent to Burke's trial', and an enlarged edition, 'limited to 250 copies', with the Hare material included.[29] Roughead said that the post-war 'conditions in which books are produced must be blamed, rather than excess of subject-matter or the

---

28   Connell, N., *Doctor Crippen* (Stroud: Amberley, 2013).
29   Roughead, W. (ed.), *Burke and Hare* (Edinburgh: William Hodge & Company, third edition, 1948), preface to first edition; *Aberdeen Press and Journal*, 21 June 1921.

Foreword.

intemperance of the Editor'.[30] A revised edition published in 1948 replicated the limited edition, copies of which are extremely difficult to trace.

The execution of Edith Thompson for the murder of her husband, which had occurred at Ilford in 1922, brought the Notable British Trials series face to face with another controversial case. This time, the volume on the trial – *Trial of Frederick Bywaters and Edith Thompson* (1923) – was entrusted to Filson Young, and, in an echo of his work on the Crippen trial, his characterisation of Mrs Thompson attracted criticism. One reviewer considered that he had 'rather lost his head' about her. 'He pictures her as belonging to "the class of influencing, compelling, driving, beckoning women, who have power over men, and, through them, over the world."'[31] From this, it hardly seems as if Young was persuaded that the hanging of Mrs Thompson was an injustice from every angle except legal formality, but yet this was his argument, and the *Yorkshire Post* observed that he had 'reversed the usual verdict of the general public as to the relative guilt of the two criminals'.[32] Bywaters, infatuated with Edith, had killed Percy Thompson, perhaps believing that she had encouraged him to do so in her escapist love-letters. Filson Young's interpretation challenged the norm, and presented Bywaters not as a 'young boy led away by a wicked and immoral woman', but as a 'well-developed and fully ripened man at twenty, who had spent many years at sea, and who had seen and sampled life in all its aspects in ports where restraints upon vice were neither strong nor encouraged'.[33] Young's recalibration of the roles of Bywaters and Thompson certainly resonated with those who had begun to consider the execution of women, in particular, to be morally wrong.

The role of women in society was, as everybody knows, changing rapidly at this time. It is true to say, though, that, except for their appearances in the witness box, or, in one or two examples, in the dock, women had been largely omitted from Notable British Trials and its predecessor series up to this point. Editorships had typically been allotted to legal professionals (although Young, and to some extent Irving – who abstained from legal work from the moment he qualified to perform it – were exceptions), and this policy by itself militated against women's opportunities. Not until 1922 was the first woman called to the English bar.

A shift in the balance, however, was heralded by the publication, in 1927, of another edition of *Trial of Madeleine Smith*. This one was edited by F. Tennyson Jesse, a remarkable character whose exemplary literary credentials prepared

---

30   Roughead, *Burke and Hare* (third edition), preface to first edition.
31   *The Scotsman*, 24 December 1923. Mrs Thompson's thirtieth birthday would have followed two days later.
32   *Yorkshire Post*, 28 November 1923.
33   Ibid.

her perfectly for the case in hand. The *Illustrated London News* considered it 'appropriate that this record of a woman's trial (on a charge of poisoning an inconvenient lover) should be edited by a woman who is also a skilful dramatist'.

> Miss Tennyson Jesse diagnoses Madeleine's mental make-up in the light of modern manners. 'Nowadays [she says] Madeleine would have had various outlets for the violence of her personality. She would have become a business woman, or gone on the stage, or lived in a bachelor flat and had love-affairs, without the end of the world having resulted. In the 'fifties none of these solutions was available. ... In the late war she would have driven an ambulance, had sentimental little affairs with wounded officers, been thoroughly competent and completely occupied.'[34]

Who can fail to be charmed by Tennyson Jesse's imaginative indulgences here? There was plenty of Madeleine's character in Tennyson Jesse's – vivacious, extravagant, complex and somehow disordered. Writing introductions to Notable British Trials was an extension of her personality: Susannah Clapp, reviewing Joanna Colenbrander's *A Portrait of Fryn*, summarises Tennyson Jesse as 'alternately brisk and gossipy, chatting about stray cats, about Old Bailey murder trials, about Noel Streatfeild being accosted by a French tart in Bond Street,' but, beyond this, she was sufficiently sensitive to her environment to clutch at the Zeitgeist when it fluttered past.[35] Madeleine Smith, in Tennyson Jesse's radical, thoughtful re-conception, was a modern, liberated woman living in an antiquated, illiberal age.

Notable British Trials had never been stuffy – academic, yes, but never stuffy. Still, Tennyson Jesse's literary knowhow instantly propelled her into the top rank of editors, and she went on to edit several further volumes, among which *Trial of Rattenbury and Stoner* is her masterpiece: a stunning piece of writing in any genre, let alone true-crime-by-way-of-legal-analysis. The reader should seek it out at all costs.

Other women subsequently joined the Notable British Trials roster, some not long after Tennyson Jesse's pioneering *Trial of Madeleine Smith*. Helena Normanton, the second woman admitted to the bar in England after the implementation of the Sex Disqualification (Removal) Act of 1919, edited *Trial of Alfred Arthur Rouse* in 1931, and some of her source materials are stored today in the Women's Library at the London School of Economics. Winifred Duke, a somewhat neglected figure now, took on three volumes, including one which was probably made possible only by the death of its subject. *Trial of*

---

34 *Illustrated London News*, 18 June 1927.
35 Clapp, S., '"You are my heart's delight"' in *London Review of Books*, Vol. 6, No. 10, 7 June 1984.

Foreword.

Harold Greenwood, published in 1930, described the case of a solicitor who, ten years earlier, had been found not guilty of poisoning his wife. Acquittals were, as we have seen, uncertain territory for editors of Notable British Trials, but Greenwood's demise (under the name of Pilkington) obviated any legal concerns. Duke herself was a talented writer, and her book *Six Trials*, published by Victor Gollancz in 1934, was her *tour de force*, reviewing the cases of Greenwood and Sarah Ann Hearn (the latter very agnostically, since libel was still feared), observing William Herbert Wallace, and considering the case of Dr Philip Cross, who had, at one time, been the subject of a volume 'in preparation' in the Notable British Trials series, to be edited by P. J. O'Hare. *Six Trials* may be read alongside the canon of Notable British Trials, bound to the series by its author, and addressing some cases which could easily have appeared within the series itself. In addition to Tennyson Jesse, Normanton and Duke, Letitia Fairfield, a barrister and doctor, edited the 1953 volume *Trial of Peter Barnes and Others (I.R.A. Coventry Explosion)*, and *Trial of John Thomas Straffen* (1954), the latter in partnership with Eric Fullbrook.

In 1930, with the publication of H. L. Adam's *Trial of George Chapman*, the Notable British Trials series (and its predecessors) reached a milestone of fifty volumes, published at the rate of two a year. However, from this point until its demise in 1959 – twenty-nine years ahead – the rate at which new volumes were produced would drop by nearly half. One reason for this may have been the arrival of competitor series, in particular the Famous Trials series published, in blue cloth with a propensity to fade to uglier shades of green and yellow, by Geoffrey Bles, and under the general editorship of the crime writer George Dilnot. The *Illustrated London News*, noting the publication of *Trial of Jean Pierre Vaquier* and *Trial of John Donald Merrett* in the Notable British Trials series, also noted in the same column the publication of *The Trial of Norman Thorne* and *The Trial of Thomas Henry Allaway* in Bles's series.[36] All these volumes were available at the same price, 10s 6d, and the format of the Famous Trials series was not very different to that of the Notable British Trials series: introduction, trial, appendices, and so on. There was occasionally some crossover between the series: Helena Normanton, for example, had edited *The Trial of Norman Thorne* for Bles before editing *Trial of Alfred Arthur Rouse* for Hodge & Co.; H. Fletcher Moulton, who had edited *Trial of Steinie Morrison* for Hodge & Co. in 1921, would edit *The Trial of Alexander Campbell Mason* for Bles in 1930 (his introduction to the case is superb). Once, there was direct competition – Bles published *The Trial of Alfred Arthur Rouse* (edited by Sydney Tremayne – the pseudonym of Sybil Taylor) in May 1931, a month ahead of

---

36 *Illustrated Police News*, 13 July 1929.

Lipski.

Normanton's similarly-titled volume for Hodge & Co. In the end, the Famous Trials series ran to a little over a dozen volumes, crammed into four years in the late 1920s and the early 1930s, before it ceased to exist. Notable British Trials had seen it off, but at what cost?

Seeking to repackage the wealth of material which was, by then, in their possession, Hodge and Co. published *The Black Maria* in 1935 – a so-called 'Criminals' Omnibus' collecting, for a journey through the underbelly, the introductions from fifteen of the volumes of the Notable British Trials series and its predecessors. The book was produced as a joint venture with Victor Gollancz, and retailed at 8s 6d: a wider reading public was obviously expected to enjoy the observations of Tennyson Jesse, Roughead and so on, without troubling themselves about the minutiae of the trials themselves. Little could go wrong with this scheme, at least from a critical angle, and Roughead's introduction to *Trial of Mrs M'Lachlan*, H. L. Adam's introduction to *Trial of George Chapman*, and Donald Carswell's introduction to *Trial of Ronald True* – all of which are required reading – find themselves neatly arranged in a book which is still available relatively cheaply through second-hand retailers.

Another opportunity to reframe the Notable British Trials back catalogue arrived after the war. The paperback revolution invited the further distillation of introductions for the convenience of the reader, and Penguin's Famous Trials series – this evocative formulation having fallen out of usage in the thirties – set out onto the popular paths which *The Black Maria*'s lamps had begun, some years before, to illuminate. The first cheap volume – two shillings only – collected the introductions to the volumes discussing Madeleine Smith, Oscar Slater, Dr Crippen and Dr Palmer, and established a format which would be used with minor variations across ten paperback volumes – some of those published in the Sixties being especially attractive with their stylised cover art. Old copies are typically easy to come by.

Harry Hodge died in 1947, but the Notable British Trials series lived on without him; his son, James Hodge, assumed the general editorship. Old editions were reissued, and new editions, including *Trials of Evans and Christie*, edited by F. Tennyson Jesse in 1957 – 'Notable British Trials Series: Vol. 82', as the (rather uninspiring) dustjacket noted – were published. Evans and Christie's dingy, post-war, kitchen-sink milieu distinctly contrasts – at least in this reader's mind – with the quainter ambience of some of the earlier volumes, but, as ever, long-term contributors such as Jesse, the personal commitment of the Hodge family and the unswerving formatting ensured that lines of continuity were easily visible. And yet, with the publication in 1959 of the eighty-third volume – *Trial of August Sangret*, edited by Macdonald Critchley, and retailing

Foreword.

at 18s – the project shuddered to its sudden conclusion. No further additions were made to the Notable British Trials series, and, to judge from the tenor of remarks made in a 1954 sales catalogue (such as 'the trials now published by William Hodge and Company, Ltd., now approach the century mark'), the cessation of the series may not have been long anticipated. Fifty-eight years have now passed since the last volume was produced.

This attempt to assess the impact and value of the Notable British Trials series is probably overdue. As a publishing phenomenon, its success was built on its clear vision and its sense of purpose. In 1905, *Trial of Madeleine Smith* defined a format and a style which did not change because they did not *need* to change. Harry Hodge may have treated the series as a hobby, and he may have been 'more concerned to produce a worthwhile book than with the money profit he might secure', as *The Scotsman* put it after his death, but the professionalism of the enterprise shone through from volume one to volume eighty-three.[37] The benign philosophy behind the series, as articulated in the catalogue – 'A *Notable British Trial* is neither a "camouflaged thriller" nor a legal text-book. The book's value to the lawyer, historian and medical man is beyond dispute, and sensation and human interest certainly abound, but its greatest attribute lies undoubtedly in its interest for the ordinary member of the community, that wide range of society commonly called the general public.' – had held up for more than fifty years. Hodge & Co., in a moment of deserved self-congratulation, noted that the series had 'come to be regarded by many people as one of the greatest British publishing ventures of the twentieth century'. To judge even from this brief survey of its history, it is difficult to disagree.

With the volume you are holding now, Mango Books are proud to revive the Notable British Trials imprint, and especially pleased to acknowledge the kind permission of Laurence Hodge and William Hodge & Company (Holdings) Limited. We hope that new volumes in this series will be true to the objectives and achievements of their distinguished predecessors.

---

37   *The Scotsman*, 16 December 1947.

Notable British Trials Series No. 84

TRIAL OF
ISRAEL LIPSKI

EDITED BY

M.W. Oldridge

CONTENTS.

Foreword i
Introduction 1
Leading Dates. 45

THE TRIAL —

FIRST DAY — FRIDAY 29th JULY 1887.

Opening Speech for the Prosecution. 49

George Bitten	50	Dinah Angel	90
Isaac Angel	54	Leah Levy	91
Philip Lipski	57	Rachel Rubenstein	92
Simon Rosenbloom	60	Samuel Spiers	93
Richard Pittman	66	Harris Dywein	94
Annie Pittman	73	William Piper	100
Mark Schmidt	73	Arthur Sach	104
Isaac Schmuss	76	Alfred Inwood	106
Steva Tartakowski	80	Charles Peters	108
Leah Lipski	81	William Piper [recalled]	109
George Bitten [recalled]	89	Thomas Warwick	110

SECOND DAY — SATURDAY 30th JULY 1887.

David Final	112	Thomas Redmayne	127
Henry David Smaje	116	Charles Moore	128
David Final [recalled]	118	Hannah Lyons	130
John William Kay	120	George Bitten [recalled]	131
William Dobree Calvert	125		

Closing Speech for the Prosecution 132
Speech for the Defence. 132
Charge to the Jury. 133
The Verdict. 134

Appendices. 135
Index. 203
Notable British Trials Series. 209

LIST OF ILLUSTRATIONS.

Israel Lipski	*Frontispiece*	
Scene of the crime: Batty Street	*facing page*	10
The lock and bottle containing poison	"	14
Israel Lipski's clothes and Miriam Angel's nightdress	"	14
Mr Harry Poland QC	"	50
Mr Charles Mathews QC	"	56
Mr Justice James Fitzjames Stephen	"	66
Isaac and Jane Angel	"	202
Isaac Angel	"	202

ISRAEL LIPSKI.

INTRODUCTION.

I.

If the celebration of Queen Victoria's jubilee was expected to be the centrepiece of the summer of 1887, then Israel Lipski was the ghost at the feast, arriving late, ambiguous in the spotlight. Over the course of eight weeks, he emerged from nothing, retreated into nothing, and meanwhile wrote himself into the criminal – and the political – history of his time, achieving the whole thing from the respective confines of his hospital bed, police custody, and a prison cell. Even after his conviction for an offence of horrifying properties, there were those who insisted that his personality, and even his physique, could not be matched to the actions attributed to him.

The facts, as far as they went, were these: on the top floor of a three-storey house in Batty Street, in the translucent East London district of St George in the East, lived Lipski. On the floor below him there were two rooms, and in one (at the back) lived Mrs Rachel Rubenstein and Mrs Leah Levy; and in the other (at the front) lived Mr Isaac Angel and his wife Miriam. On the ground floor, occupying rooms both back and front, lived Mr Philip Lipski (who was the son of the aforementioned Mrs Rubenstein), his wife Leah, and their children – seven of them, the eldest being fifteen years of age. The downstairs Lipskis were not relations of the one at the top of the house, but he – Israel Lipski – had lived with Philip and Leah Lipski for some time. They were his *de facto* landlord and landlady, first at Batty Gardens, and then just around the corner at 16 Batty Street. In fact, every room at 16 Batty Street was a sort of sub-let.

Lipski's prior history was more difficult to pin down. He was understood to have parents, back home in Poland, and perhaps even brothers and sisters. One newspaper article, by-lined by someone describing themselves in modest terms as 'One who Knows Him', gave a romanticised account of a daring flit across national borders and militarised zones, but it was impossible to know how accurate this story was.[1] Besides, the tale cut both ways. Lipski had been his parents' lifeblood – they 'became poor', and, worse, 'were becoming poorer and poorer', but he had decided that conscription into the armed forces was no life for him, and he escaped to England. Youthful disinhibition? A yearning for

---

1 See Appendix XVI.

Lipski.

adventure overseas? Or, perhaps, an act of selfishness, performed not to spite his parents, but *in* spite of their economic misfortunes? He arrived in London under the name of Israel Lobulsk, and later changed it to that of his host family.

It is worth considering some of the factors which might have influenced this decision. Philip and Leah Lipski's eldest child (Fanny, the fifteen year old) had been born in St George in the East in early 1874, and both Philip and Leah – with a decade and a half of experience behind them – spoke satisfactory English. The Lipskis were, to use a word which is still not quite gone from the dialectic of immigration, quite well *integrated* into British life, or, at least, London life as it was played out in St George in the East – of which more shortly. The other characteristic of the Lipskis was that, alongside their integration, they retained a distinct Jewish cultural identity. In February 1887, Philip had testified before coroner Wynne Baxter at the inquest into the deaths of seventeen people in a crush at the Hebrew Dramatic Theatre on Prince's Street (now Princelet Street), in Spitalfields. He had not been at the theatre at the time of the disaster, but, as the *Evening Standard* put it, 'his brother-in-law's name, Rubinstein [*sic*], had been mentioned' at an earlier hearing, and Philip wanted to stick up for him. Marks Rubenstein, the brother-in-law in question, was the owner of a rival dramatic club, and had been accused of threatening to engage a gang of hooligans to vandalise the Prince's Street theatre. (Inspector Frederick Abberline, a policeman made famous by his work on the Jack the Ripper case in 1888, wrote a report to the Lord Chamberlain about one of Rubenstein's prior complaints about the place.[2]) Hebrew drama was not the least important of the cultural signifiers of East London's Jewish population. Israel Lobulsk may have become Israel Lipski in part because the Lipski family represented, to him, a viable, healthy vision of immigrant life, recognising and – to some extent, for they were very far from rich – enjoying the advantages of the twin cultures in which they existed. His adoption of their surname may have been a tribute, or an incantation; a prayer for similar happiness, or social inclusion.

The international backdrop was certainly not so optimistic. Behind the vast numbers of Jewish immigrants to England in the late nineteenth century were the urgent motive forces of pogroms and persecution in Eastern Europe. Lloyd P. Gartner estimates that 120,000 Jewish people arrived in England between 1870 and 1914; William Fishman cites Charles Booth's calculation that there were over 42,000 Jewish residents of St George in the East, Whitechapel (which lay immediately to the north) and Mile End (to the north-east) by 1887, and a competing estimate (formulated by the secretary of the Jews' Temporary

---

2   *Evening Standard*, 5 February 1887.

Introduction.

Shelter) of just over 32,000 Jewish residents in Tower Hamlets by 1888.[3] Jewish social services were well organised and thorough, providing a safety net for the many who arrived in London with (perforce) nothing, but the persistent levels of immigration caused some tensions among the indigenous population: populism – then, as now, a safe philosophical harbour for those seeking not to understand the predicaments of others – fanned the flames of anti-semitic feeling. Martin Friedland, whose admirable book, *The Trials of Israel Lipski*, is the key secondary text where Lipski is concerned, observes that anti-Jewish uprisings (emulating those occurring on the continent) were forecast in 1886 by Joseph Laister, a man of apparently unenviable politics, and given oxygen by the inscrutable fiat of the editor of the *Pall Mall Gazette*:

> … the foreign Jews of no nationality whatever are becoming a pest and a menace to the poor native-born East-ender. They oust him out of all the decent habitation and greatly lower the standard of living, as well as the general moral tone. …[4]

Laister's letter ostensibly presented the 'Judenhetze' which was supposedly 'brewing in East London' as a social trauma to be avoided, but nobody could have failed to notice that, between its measured lines, it was drooling at the prospect of an English pogrom. At an official level, however, agitation of this sort frequently failed to penetrate. In the early years of the twentieth century, the perpetrators of the Houndsditch Murders – those who survived the Siege of Sidney Street, at least – were prosecuted for their offences; they were political refugees from the Baltic, but they were dealt with, properly, as criminals, and were not made to serve as scapegoats for the kneejerk abandonment of deeply-held and humane social values. No doubt the Jewish population in the Victorian East End could sometimes have wished for the authorities to exhibit a more understanding attitude towards them (this was certainly the wish of the Bengali population of Tower Hamlets in the 1970s, arriving in East London after the war in Bangladesh to face a climate of neo-fascism in the streets and institutionalised apathy in public offices), but, in general, Gartner determined, the average Jewish immigrant at the end of the nineteenth century might nonetheless have 'regarded England as a free country' in which 'Jews enjoyed civil and political rights'. At the very least, bearing in mind the violence occurring there, Russia was 'infinitely worse'.[5]

After immigration came employment. Jewish arrivals knew that they 'would have to work extremely hard to earn very little', and the rooms and workshops

---

3 Gartner, 30; Fishman, 131.
4 *Pall Mall Gazette*, 18 February 1886, cited in Friedland, 131.
5 Gartner, 27-28.

Lipski.

in which they laboured were often injurious to their health.[6] Sweated trades – in which workers were paid poorly for long hours of work in what Gartner calls 'extremely insanitary conditions' – were already a scandal by the mid-1880s.[7] Setting foot back in Batty Street, for our brief look around the Jewish East End is now almost over, we see, at number 1, Mr Moses, a vestmaker, in interview with Charles Booth. It is 18 April 1888 – a little after Lipski, and a little before Jack the Ripper, that other awful embodiment of chronic want in the East End – but close enough for our purposes. Booth takes up the story:

> A middle aged man, apparently in a good way of business and with little to worry him. He took me into his workshop which is a brick building in the yard lighted by four windows in the roof. The shop, which was about 30 feet long, was evidently too small for Mr M's trade & he had enlarged it by the addition of a wooden erection between the brickwood of the shop & the house. In this extension of the shop, 7 out of the 8 females in the place were working.

There were nine men on site, in addition to Mr Moses and the eight women, and they worked 'from 8 a.m. to 9 p.m. (both sexes) but did not work on Saturday or Sunday'. These long hours, Booth went on, ventriloquising Mr Moses,

> were the great evil of the trade, but were necessary as the men wanted such high wages. ... He thought that there was not much to complain about in the trade. A good workman could always earn good wages. It was the bad & inefficient workmen who could not get work.

Booth, reverting to his own voice, knew better – 'Mr M is evidently a prosperous man and I should think he was making a good thing out of his work' – but we see enough here to begin to appreciate the precarious economic situation of the immigrant craftsman (or craftswoman).[8] Earning a living was an arduous ordeal, and there was always someone willing to work for a little less. Sydney and Beatrice Webb, who were engaged in the same sort of emergent sociological analysis as Booth, noticed the ambition of the Jewish worker: 'he will accept the lowest terms rather than remain out of employment; as he rises in the world new wants stimulate him to increased intensity of effort, and no amount of effort causes him to slacken his indefatigable activity'.[9] Of course, there was nothing else for it – every personal resource was devoted to the campaign to establish and maintain a financial foothold.

---

6   Gartner, 27.
7   Gartner, 68.
8   London School of Economics, Booth Archive: BOOTH/A/19.
9   Cited in Gartner, 65.

Introduction.

Let us leave Mr Moses and his workers there, and pass down the road again to number 16 – a house denuded of its glitter, with Mrs Levy's jewels in pawn, and Mrs Lipski's, and Israel Lipski's gold stud, and his silver watch ...[10]

II.

The first sighting of Israel Lipski on the morning of Tuesday 28 June 1887 was at about 6.30 am. Philip Lipski, who had to be at his factory in Spitalfields by seven o'clock, spotted him in shirtsleeves and shoeless in the yard behind the house, searching under a table for a piece of iron piping ('belonging to me', as Philip pointed out). Israel returned upstairs without finding it, and Philip, after saying his prayers, left for work, closing the street door behind him.[11]

Isaac Angel, inhabiting the front room on the first floor with his wife Miriam, had departed for his own workplace – a boot-riveting enterprise on George Street, in Spitalfields – at 6.15 am, leaving Miriam in bed. There had been a little inconsequential conversation between them before Isaac's departure. Miriam was pregnant, and it was her custom to wake later than her husband, and to go to the nearby house of his mother, Mrs Dinah Angel, for breakfast. 'Sometimes at half past eight, sometimes at nine,' Dinah remembered. 'Not often later.' Isaac closed the bedroom door behind him before setting off down the stairs and into the street. The bedroom key was in the lock, on the inside, but the door was not locked.

Other members of the household began to rouse themselves. Mrs Lipski was awake by 8.30 am, and hurrying her older children off to school; she encountered Israel Lipski in the kitchen – the second of the downstairs Lipskis' rooms, the back parlour. He was, by now, fully dressed, wearing a coat and hat, and he asked her to fetch his morning coffee. Mrs Lipski left the house to obtain some hot water, and, fifteen minutes later, Mrs Levy – one of the first-floor lodgers – looked out of the street door, seeing Mrs Lipski returning from her excursion to Backchurch Lane, coffee pot in hand. Mrs Rubenstein found her way downstairs at some point between 9.30 am and 10.00 am: while Mrs Lipski and Mrs Levy went shopping in Petticoat Lane, she was put in charge of Mrs Lipski's younger children, one of whom – probably either Louis or Morris – wriggled away from her, and cavorted in the yard ('I was afraid it had run away,' she remarked). When the crisis was over, Mrs Rubenstein spent a little time sitting in the street. Her eyesight was very poor, but her resolve was unimpaired: at about 10.00

---

10   TNA:PRO HO 144/201/A47465/87.
11   TNA:PRO CRIM 1/26/5.

Lipski.

am – the timings are not precise – she deterred Samuel Spiers from entering the house, although all he wanted was to collect some boots which Miriam Angel had undertaken to repair for him.

Meanwhile, the top floor had been a small hive of haphazard activity. In the week of the jubilee, Lipski had left his job at Marks Katz's factory, where he was a maker of umbrella sticks, apparently because the wages were insufficient, especially during the seasonal downturn in the trade. Truly, money must have been tight. Lipski was engaged (re-engaged, in fact, since 'the engagement was broken off for a time') to be married to a young lady named Kate Lyons, whose mother, Hannah, was the sister of Mr Katz's wife, Sarah.[12] This relationship was close enough to give Lipski a kind of moral stake in the business, and there were other employees – one of whom we will meet shortly – who had stayed on although they had no similar personal investment in the business or its owner. Perhaps on Hannah's advice (although the source – 'One who Knows Him' – is not a reliable one, and her own testimony gives no indication of it), Lipski had decided to set up on his own, in his bedroom. Cottage industry of this sort was not uncommon in the East End, but one wonders whether the venture was really a step too far for Lipski. In a seasonal business which was then in the doldrums, based in a room which was not properly adapted to the purpose, he can hardly have hoped to acquire commissions lucrative enough to make a decent living. The start-up costs alone were prohibitive, and the downstairs Lipskis had hiked his rent from two shillings to five shillings a week to reflect the fact that his bedroom was now a factory. Lipski himself had borrowed twenty-five shillings from Hannah Lyons on Monday 27 June, and this stood in addition to a previous loan of £1. Bumping into Mrs Lipski in the kitchen at 8.30 am on Tuesday 28 June, when he asked for his coffee, he had also implored Mrs Lipski to lend him five shillings, saying that he was ashamed to return to Mrs Lyons for more. Costs were spiralling: even before the most recent benefaction of Mrs Lyons, Lipski had already paid out somewhere in the region of £2 (perhaps more) for requisites – tools, raw materials, and so on – and he had not yet fitted out the extemporary workshop to his satisfaction. He also intended to employ no fewer than four staff.[13]

The first of these to arrive at their new second-floor workplace was Simon Rosenbloom. Like Lipski, Rosenbloom had previously been an employee of Marks Katz; indeed, Lipski had met Rosenbloom on Saturday 25 June, and had persuaded him to leave Katz's workshop and to join him in the new bedroom-factory in Batty Street. Rosenbloom, responding favourably to the promise of

---

12 *Pall Mall Gazette*, 20 August 1887.
13 TNA:PRO HO 144/201/A47465/80.

Introduction.

regular remuneration, agreed to do so, and, at 7.00 am on Tuesday 28 June, he knocked on the street door. His new employer – Lipski – appeared in shirt sleeves and bare-footed, opening the door from the inside, and together they went to Lipski's room and began to work. Rosenbloom's task was to file horn handles.

Before long, Lipski realised that additional resources were required. He put on his boots, a coat, and a hat, and left, telling Rosenbloom that another man would arrive to help with the filing, and that that man – like Rosenbloom, who was using the only one in the room – would need a vice to hold the handles in place. He also determined that a sponge would be needed for varnishing: a boy was expected to arrive to perform that part of the job. Rosenbloom was thus left in the room by himself, and Lipski made the short journey to Backchurch Lane, where he visited the shop of Mark Schmidt. This was a general dealership – an 'old iron shop', according to the definition given in the 1891 census – and the proprietor, who had been in England for some years and sometimes went by the Anglicised appellation of Smith, had been a stickmaker himself. He opened at 7.00 am, and Schmidt estimated that Lipski went there at 8.00 am, but, again, the timings are not precisely known. Lipski asked Schmidt to show him some vices, but he baulked at the asking price, and departed without purchasing one. As he left, he asked Schmidt what time Mr Lee's oil shop opened. The oil shop stood at 96 Backchurch Lane, next door to Schmidt's premises. 'Half past eight,' Schmidt said.[14]

Lipski returned to Batty Street, and told Rosenbloom that the shop was shut. This comment had the potential to mislead – Schmidt's shop had been open for an hour, and Lipski had turned down the vice because he had quibbled over the price. He had not mentioned the sponge to Schmidt. Rosenbloom watched apparently without remark as Lipski then went 'up and down the stairs' – for what reason is not known. Rosenbloom was pressing on with his work, but Lipski was not assisting.

At – he thought – 8.00 am, Richard Pittman arrived. This was the varnishing boy, the son of a bone-boiler, a thirteen year old who would testify to being sixteen and whose mother thought that he was fourteen, who cried while giving his evidence in court, and whose memory of events became more uncertain the more anybody explored them. Pittman could write his own name in neat cursive script, having attended at least a couple of local schools in his younger days, but he was now part of the workforce, and, in common with Rosenbloom and Lipski, he had been on the payroll at Katz's factory in Watney Passage.

14   TNA:PRO CRIM 1/26/5.

Lipski.

On the evening of Wednesday 22 June, Lipski had approached Pittman while the latter, in his own words, was 'playing about Chapman Street', near his home. Apparently keen to leave his position with Katz, Pittman agreed to go to work for Lipski, and, on the incentive of 'a shilling and your breakfast', not to mention wages of 'five shillings a week, and a shilling rise every three months', he went to Batty Street on the morning of Thursday 23 June. He had spent Thursday, Friday (an abbreviated working day of two hours) and Monday helping Lipski to fill his room with tools and materials.[15] Now, on the Tuesday morning, he saw Rosenbloom at the vice; the tiny factory was up and running, but its owner was absent.

In fact, Lipski appeared soon afterwards, saying that he was going out again to purchase a sponge (by Rosenbloom's recollection; Pittman thought he mentioned a vice). Either way, this left Rosenbloom and Pittman alone in the workshop, and Pittman entertained himself – and annoyed Rosenbloom – by hammering 'at the place where all the tools were'. Pittman would later claim that Rosenbloom told him to get on with his work, but Rosenbloom remembered Pittman 'doing nothing', and he reasoned that this was because Pittman did not have a sponge to work with – there was no work for Pittman to do, and he hammered things in his idleness. We see small examples of Pittman's weakness as a witness: nothing quite tallies, and while some of his evidence later proved to be, *prima facie*, interesting to the Home Office – in theory, it blew Lipski's version of events to smithereens – it was soon realised that *everything* that Pittman said was equally problematic. At risk of labouring the point, Pittman swore that he had not seen Rosenbloom before the morning of 28 June, which, by itself, seemed strange, since they had both been employed at the same workshop by Mr Katz; but later, when Inspector John Tunbridge of the Metropolitan Police questioned him about Rosenbloom's dress sense, Pittman said, complaisantly, 'I worked at the same place as Rosenbloom two or three months. Rosenbloom usually wore a neckhandkerchief and no collar …'[16] And so it went. Pittman said that he had known Lipski for a month before 28 June, but Lipski had worked for Katz for much longer than a month – Pittman can hardly have known Rosenbloom for longer than he had known Lipski. But then Pittman claimed not to know Rosenbloom at all – but then he knew how he dressed … The tangle of Pittman's childlike evidence was impossible to unravel: 'No reliance should be placed on the boy's story,' wrote one of the Home Office mandarins, reviewing the evidence.[17] At (perhaps) about 8.50 am,

---

15   TNA:PRO CRIM 1/26/5.
16   TNA:PRO HO 144/201/A47465/80.
17   TNA:PRO HO 144/201/A47465/16.

Introduction.

Pittman heard the landlady calling up the stairs to Lipski – 'Come down and have your coffee!' – and, when she called a second time, he replied, in the absence of his new employer, 'He ain't here'. But the timings are unreliable; and, besides, we are getting ahead of ourselves.

At (he thought) about 8.15 am, although it may well have been a little later, another new employee, Isaac Schmuss, found the street door of 16 Batty Street standing open, and, as he went inside, he encountered Lipski, who was on his way out. The previous afternoon, Lipski had hired Schmuss, selecting him from a line-up of potential workmen who had gathered at Schmidt's shop, which operated as a sort of informal labour exchange for the Jewish community. (Another labourer, named Tartakowski – giving Lipski a scarcely-affordable complement of four – had been hired at the same time, but he had not kept his arrangement to meet Schmuss at Schmidt's shop on the morning of Tuesday 28 June, and so Schmuss, after waiting for a short period, had proceeded to his new workplace alone.) Lipski directed Schmuss to the second floor, promising to set him to work when he returned. Schmuss went upstairs and into the workshop, where he saw Rosenbloom and Pittman. He stayed only a few minutes, passing a few words with Rosenbloom, whom he had not previously met, before concluding that there was little chance of getting enough work at Lipski's bedroom factory. Accordingly, he left, heading for breakfast at his lodgings on Oxford Street (behind the London Hospital), where he spent the morning with his landlord, Nathan Rabinowitz, Rabinowitz's wife, and another lodger named Lewis.[18]

Pittman's stomach was also rumbling, and much was made of the sequence in which he and Schmuss left Lipski's room. Pittman and Rosenbloom both thought that Schmuss was the first to leave – although, typically, Pittman's evidence on the subject was not delivered without confusion. Schmuss thought that Pittman was the first to leave; and, if so, he and Rosenbloom were placed in the room together, unobserved, for a period estimated by Schmuss as 'about a minute's time, not more'. These statements are not to be taken uncritically – indeed, they were tested over and over again – but we must hold them in mind if we are to understand what follows. Let us conclude our consideration of the movements of Lipski's employees by following Pittman home, where, at about 9.15 am, his mother gives him breakfast, which he takes about a quarter of an hour to eat, and then out into the street, where, by his own admission, he spends a quarter of an hour playing 'a little game', and then back to Batty Street – a walk of about a quarter of an hour – and back up the stairs to the workshop,

---

18   TNA:PRO HO 144/201/A47465/117b.

Lipski.

where, at about 10.00 am, he finds Rosenbloom, alone, exactly as before, filing handles on the vice.

III.

So much for the scene at Batty Street. Let us now follow Lipski. He encounters Schmuss at the door of the house, and sends him up to the room. Schmuss goes upstairs, and Lipski leaves.

Back to Backchurch Lane, and to Matthew Lee's oil shop at number 96, where the manager, Charles Moore, was running behind time. The shop should have been open for business already. The bell of the nearby school rang: 8.50 am. At 9.00 am, 'cool and composed', into the shop came Lipski.[19] Speaking in English, he asked for a pennyworth of *aqua fortis* – nitric acid.

Moore looked up at him. 'What do you want it for?' he asked.[20]

Lipski said that he was a stickmaker, and Moore noted that the creases in the sleeves of the customer's coat were 'full of dust as if he had been filing wood'.[21] Lipski handed over a discoloured bottle with a dirty label adhering to it.[22] Moore filled it halfway up – an ounce of nitric acid in a two-ounce phial. He told Lipski that the substance was poisonous. He put a cork in the bottle. Lipski took the bottle, and left the shop.

He was seen once more, by Thomas Warwick, who lived opposite 16 Batty Street at number 19, where he occupied the front parlour and worked on boots and shoes. Warwick said that the sighting occurred at about 8.45 am – before the school bell heard by Charles Moore – but he must have been incorrect, and he admitted that he did not return from breakfast until after 9.00 am. He saw Lipski going into 16 Batty Street, through the front door, hat and coat on, and carrying 'a little small parcel, very small'. The parcel itself is a mysterious entity in the case. Lipski contended that he had planned to go to Petticoat Lane 'to buy some sponges from the hawkers', having realised that those from Moore's shop would be more expensive. He also stated that he had bumped into a hawker at 'the Whitechapel end of the Commercial Road' – not far from Batty Street and Backchurch Lane – from whom he bought a shilling's worth of sponge, and who was loosely described as 'an old man of about sixty, with a beard'. It was also said that 'a man answering this description has been seen selling sponges,

---

19　*Pall Mall Gazette*, 17 August 1887.
20　Ibid.
21　TNA:PRO CRIM 1/26/5; TNA:PRO HO 144/201/A47465/76.
22　*Pall Mall Gazette*, 17 August 1887.

Scene of the Crime: Batty Street

from The Police Encyclopedia, Vol III (1914)

Introduction.

but he is a foreigner, speaking English most imperfectly, and says he recollects nothing of the matter'.[23]

A note in the Home Office files on the case gives a few additional details: 'Lipski says on the morning he purchased from a hawker two large pieces of sponge in a paper bag'.[24] But two large pieces of sponge in a paper bag do not sound like 'a little small parcel, very small'. The sponges themselves were never seen again – if they ever existed.

Nor was Lipski seen at large after this – he did not return to his workshop; indeed, he would never set foot there again. There was a pause in Batty Street; the absence of something.

Over in Grove Street, the absence of Miriam Angel had begun to make Dinah, her mother-in-law, anxious. Miriam had not arrived for breakfast, and no explanation had been forthcoming for this deviation from her usual routine. Dinah resolved to investigate, and, at about 11.00 am, she went to Batty Street to make enquiries. She let herself in through the front door, and went up the stairs to the first floor. She stood at the door to her daughter-in-law's room. She knocked.

'Miriam?'[25]

There was no answer, and the door did not open.

Mrs Lipski was downstairs. 'You go up and help,' she said to Mrs Levy.[26] Mrs Levy joined Dinah on the landing, and then went up a few more stairs towards the second floor; here, there was a little internal window, looking from the staircase into Miriam's room. The pane was covered with a muslin cloth, but still one could see *something* through the material. Mrs Levy peered at Miriam's outline on the bed. Something was wrong.

Mrs Lipski arrived on the landing, and between the three of them, knees and hands against the door, they burst into the room. Miriam was on the bed, on her back, with her hair disarranged, and her head tilted to one side. From her mouth flowed a trickle of yellow fluid, and her right eye was blackened, and her right temple bruised. There were stains, yellow like the liquid which had run from her lips, on her neck and her hands. She was exposed from the chest down, with her legs apart. William Piper, a surgeons' assistant practising at 100 Commercial Road, on the corner with Batty Street, was urgently summoned to the scene. He saw that Miriam was dead, and, having moved her head and her arm in his attempts to check for signs of life, he returned her to her original position. When

---

23 TNA:PRO HO 144/201/A47465/14.
24 TNA:PRO HO 144/201/A47465/117e.
25 TNA:PRO CRIM 1/26/5.
26 Ibid.

Lipski.

he decided to clear the room – which now contained not only the three ladies, but also Rosenbloom, who had dashed downstairs from the workshop when he heard the commotion; and Harris Dywein, a passer-by and an acquaintance of Miriam's who had run upstairs from the street; and 'perhaps another man', as Piper recalled (possibly a man named Diomed, who 'keeps a little shop near') – he discovered that the door could not be locked from the outside.[27] The bolt was shot, and the key was standing in the lock, on the inside. Piper went back into the room, turned the key to retract the bolt, removed it, stepped outside again, and placed the key in the lock, turning it to deploy the bolt. The bolt did not fit perfectly into its casing, but the door held. Mr Piper, keeping the key in his possession, went for the assistance of the doctor.

IV.

These were the strange, disjointed and unhappy circumstances leading up to the discovery of the crime, and they were surpassed only by what followed.

With the arrival of Dr John Kay – Piper's superior – at a quarter to twelve, the small throng of people once again spilled into the room containing the corpse. More people had gathered outside the building, in the street – indeed, this number was swelling all the time – and some had even taken positions in Mrs Levy and Mrs Rubenstein's room, across the landing, to watch proceedings. Kay believed, taking a rough estimate from the temperature of the body, that Miriam Angel had been dead for three hours. The stains on her body were indicative of nitric acid. The hunt was now on for clues, and, at Kay's instruction, Harris Dywein removed a few articles from under the bed to see whether a bottle could be found there. 'Is there anything underneath the bed?' asked Kay.

Dywein stooped down. 'There is something underneath the bedstead,' he replied.

'Go and see what it is,' said Kay.

Dywein lay on the floor of the room, and reached out underneath the frame of the bed. He touched something. A hand.

'I think there is a body here,' Dywein said.[28] One wonders whether he could have been quite so cool about this new discovery, but this, at least, was how he remembered it.

Kay pulled the bedstead away from the wall and lifted the feather bed cover, which had partially fallen into the little space to the side of the bed. 'Why,' he

---

27 TNA:PRO HO 144/201/A47465/85.
28 TNA:PRO CRIM 1/26/5.

Introduction.

said, looking into the now-uncovered space, 'it is a man!'

A second victim of the acid, perhaps – but this one was apparently still alive. The heart beat, and the eyes were slightly open, but the man, pallid, in his shirt-sleeves, was unconscious, and did not respond when Kay touched his cornea. A slap brought him back to his senses, and the eyes widened. The police were now in attendance, and PC Arthur Sach 389H and PC Arthur White 155H lifted the man to his feet, holding him up by the window. The man, White remembered mournfully, 'looked round the room, and also at the woman who was lying dead on the bed', and swooned again (it is interesting to note that Dr Kay disagreed, saying that there was no swooning at this point). The man did not speak, although Dr Kay, jumping to conclusions, supposedly said, 'You see what you have done, and what did you do it for?' Kay's examination of the man's body revealed that the soft tissues of his mouth had been burned by acid, but 'not so much as the woman'. There were also 'a few trivial scratches on his arms – not recent – they were scabbed over – on the front of both arms'.[29]

Dr Kay – a dogmatic fellow, scarcely admitting uncertainty about what happened even in retrospect – glanced over at Simon Rosenbloom. He had re-entered the room with the doctor, having been one of the advance party who had attended the body during Piper's initial examination of it. Now, Kay observed, Rosenbloom 'turned ghastly white'. The man retrieved from underneath the feather bed cover was – of course – Israel Lipski, Rosenbloom's mercurial employer of, by this time, something approximating five hours. Kay studied Rosenbloom, 'and I noticed no stains on his hands or clothes of nitric acid'.[30] By contrast, Lipski's coat was shortly discovered in the room, and found to be extensively burned by acid.

The order was given to remove Lipski to the police station at Leman Street. This journey, short though it was, was not going to be easy. The stairway leading down to the front door was dark and narrow, and, looking from the window, Kay saw the street filled with 'a howling mob – I have heard it estimated at two thousand'.[31] When Lipski was removed from the room, with PC Sach holding one arm, PC William Kean 237H the other, and PC White behind, the spectators in Mrs Levy and Mrs Rubenstein's room 'tried to make a rush at him and shouted in Yiddish'. White 'knocked two or three of them back, and kept them back'. Down the dark staircase, Kean missing his footing and falling down two steps. And then outside, where, White recalled, 'we tried to get him along, but as the mob increased we found great difficulty in getting along, and I

---

29 TNA:PRO HO 144/201/A47465/85.
30 Ibid.
31 Ibid.

Lipski.

suggested that we should put him in Mr Kay's surgery till I could get a cab'. The atmosphere was febrile, and 'one of the constables had to draw his truncheon to keep the mob back'. There was some disagreement about the extent to which the mob were successful in their attempts to injure the prisoner. Kay – ever the amateur moralist – said that the women in the crowd were 'as bad as the men', but he saw the police resisting the popular attempt to 'drag [Lipski] away … he never fell on the pavement – he might have been knocked against the wall of the street'. Sach reported that 'no one touched him [Lipski]' in the street, despite efforts to do so, 'except myself and the other constable'. White recalled that some members of the crowd 'took hold of his [Lipski's] hair and one or two kicked him on the legs'. Sanctuary was only reached in the quietness of Dr Kay's surgery, and even then the trip to the police station was still to be negotiated.[32]

Back in Miriam Angel's room, the hunt for the receptacle in which the nitric acid had been transported was now on. Harris Dywein – perhaps hoping that his role in the matter was at an end following his discovery of the unconscious form of Lipski – was nonetheless the one to spot it. The bottle, an uncorked two-ounce phial, appeared from within the folds of the feather bed. Dr Kay collected it, secured the room, and returned to his surgery. Lipski had survived the short walk to the corner of the street without injury, except for two abrasions, one on each elbow, which Dr Kay had not noticed during the impromptu examination at 16 Batty Street. Kay was 'certain' – and he seemed to become more certain as time went on – that the abrasions had been caused by the attentions of the mob. 'They *were*,' he insisted, with emphasis, 'because I saw him before and after'.[33]

V.

We now follow Lipski from place to place, but he is not our guide – not yet. He still said nothing, vouchsafed nothing. PC White hailed a cab on Whitechapel High Street, returned with it to Dr Kay's surgery, and, with the aid of his colleagues, delivered Lipski to Leman Street Police Station (PC Sach volunteered to cling to the exterior of the cab, while White and Kean travelled inside, with the prisoner). They carried Lipski into the charge room, placed him on the floor, and put pillows under his head. The divisional surgeon, George Bagster Phillips – another individual thrust into the spotlight of history by the Jack the Ripper murders of 1888 – was sent for by telegraph, and, since it was feared that some acid may remain in the prisoner's stomach, an emetic

---

32 TNA:PRO HO 144/201/A47465/85.
33 Ibid.

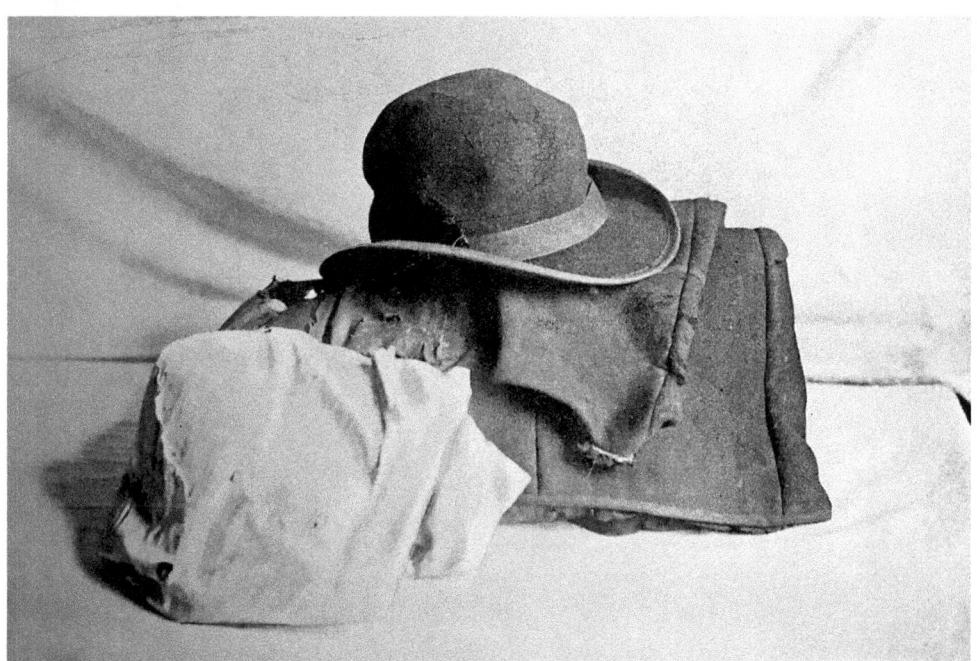

Top: The lock and bottle containing poison
Bottom: Lipski's clothes and Miriam Angel's nightdress

from The Police Encyclopedia, Vol III (1914)

Introduction.

consisting of warm water and mustard was administered.[34] The prisoner was not sick. Phillips, upon his arrival, ordered another emetic (which proved to be as useless as the first one), and sent Lipski on to the London Hospital by ambulance. There, Thomas Redmayne, the doctor working in the receiving room, administered the stomach pump, which, despite the resistance of the patient, achieved what the emetics had not.

By about a quarter past two, Lipski had been admitted to Holland ward.[35] PC White, nearing the end of his rotation, asked the prisoner for his name. 'He shook his head,' White recalled, 'and motioned for paper. This was given him, and he wrote down, *Lipski*.' His faculties were returning. Whereas he had been partially insensible, but responsive to stimuli, at the police station, he was now capable of understanding and responding to language. At a quarter to three, Dr William Calvert thought that he was 'all right – I mean, he was intelligent. He put out his tongue, opened his mouth, when I told him.' Sister Harrison, a kindly nurse, asked Lipski whether he was warm enough, and Calvert noted that 'he answered her in English'.[36]

Some time that afternoon – she thought it was around two, but Sister Harrison and PC White both thought that it was nearer three – Kate Lyons arrived at the hospital with her mother. 'We saw Lipski in bed,' Kate remembered.

> He appeared to be very composed. He spoke to me in Hebrew, which I understand, and said that he had been assaulted, and as well as I could make out mentioned the name of Plotski, which I knew referred to Rosenbloom. He asked me to telegraph home to his father. I told him I did not know the address and could not understand it. He said he would write the name and address if I got a piece of paper. I got some paper and was going to him with it when the nurse said I must not speak to him any more until the doctor had seen him. I asked him what it was to telegraph to his home and he said, 'Six shillings'. I asked my mother if she had any money; she said no. I asked Lipski if he had any. He said, 'There must be some in the pocket of my trousers, if they have not taken it out'. I asked the nurse if she would give me the trousers to take the money out, and she said no.[37]

Kate had got the message. 'She spoke out very loudly,' Sister Harrison recalled, 'so that all in the ward could hear, something to the effect that Lipski had been assaulted'. Lipski was on the counterattack. Kate may have been unable to send the telegraph – because her mother's funds had already been drained by Lipski – but now she willingly became the mouthpiece for her injured fiancé's

---

34 TNA:PRO HO 144/201/A47465/85.
35 TNA:PRO HO 144/201/A47465/80.
36 TNA:PRO HO 144/201/A47465/85.
37 Ibid.

Lipski.

exculpatory theory. She made her way to the police station. Lipski, she said, wished to make a statement.

Inspector David Final of H Division went to Lipski's bedside, accompanied by a translator, Henry Smaje, and took a statement in these terms:

> At seven a.m., a man working for me came. He asked me for work. I told him to wait. I would buy a vice for him so as he could work. I went to purchase a vice. I went to the shop but it was too soon. As I was going along, I met another workman whom I knew at the corner of Backchurch Lane. I went back; the shopkeeper wanted four shillings. I offered him three shillings. He would not take it. I returned and came into the passage and I saw the man that I met in Backchurch Lane. He asked me, 'Will you give me work, or not?' I said, 'Go to the workshop. I am going to get my breakfast. Then I will give you work.' I then told my landlady to make some coffee. I then told a man (meaning the first man) that called at seven a.m. to fetch some brandy. I then went to the yard. I went upstairs to the first floor. I then saw both these men. I saw them open a box. They took hold of me by the throat and threw me to the ground, there – on the ground – opened my mouth, and put in some poison, and said, 'That is the brandy'. They got my hands behind me and asked me if I had any money. 'I have got no more than the sovereign that I gave you to get the brandy with.' He then asked, 'Where is your gold chain?' I said, 'It is in pawn'. They said, 'If you don't give it to us, you will be as dead as the woman'. They put a piece of wood in my mouth. I struggled; they put their knees against my throat. One said to the other, 'Don't you think he is quite dead?' The reply was, 'He don't want any more'. They then threw me under the bed and there I lay for dead.
>
> Question: Do you know who those two men are? Answer: I know one who formerly worked with me.
>
> Question: Do you know his name and where he lives? Answer: His name is Simon. I don't know where he lives.
>
> Question: Do you know anything of the other man? Answer: I don't know him. He is a stranger to me.
>
> Question: Is his name Simon Rosenbloom? Answer: I can't say.
>
> Question: Do you know if Simon lives in Philpot Street? Answer: I think so. I have nothing further to say.

In this way, the two competing narratives in the case – on the one hand, that of Lipski; and, on the other, one might say, that apparently set out by all the evidence and all the other witnesses – were established before sundown on the day of Miriam Angel's murder.

Introduction.

VI.

Lipski was eventually charged with the murder of Miriam Angel upon his discharge from hospital, on 2 July 1887. By this time, the inquest into Miriam's death was complete, coroner Wynne Edwin Baxter having steered the investigation efficiently through two sittings at the St George in the East Vestry Hall. Seventeen witnesses were heard, but Lipski, who remained under police guard in his hospital bed, was not one of them. In his absence, the jury found a verdict of 'wilful murder' against him.

The committal hearings before the magistrate, by contrast, were a protracted affair. With a few exceptions, the witnesses were those who had already testified at the inquest, and three hearings took place at the Thames Police Court, on 9 July, 16 July and 22 July. The Treasury had taken up the case, prosecuting for the Crown, and Mr Francis Sims presented the prosecution's evidence. Lipski had also found legal representation in the form of a barrister, Mr Gerald Geoghegan, instructed by Mr John Hayward, an elderly solicitor of limited repute operating from offices on King Street, near the Guildhall. At the end of the third day, when the evidence for prosecution had been given, Lipski, who was described by the *Illustrated Police News* as a 'slimly-built man, clean-shaven, and boyish-looking', stated that he was 'not guilty' and that he had 'no witness to call here'.[38] The case was sent to the Old Bailey for trial, and preparations for the next sessions, which were due to begin in a few days, were now commenced.

Much is made of the superficial weaknesses of Lipski's legal team, and this view is not without some justification. As far as anyone can tell, Hayward was a long way from the cutting edge of his profession: a jobbing solicitor crashing suddenly into the limelight of a controversial murder trial at the age of something like sixty-four. His selection of barristers was, it is often thought, an eccentric one, ungoverned by relevant experience. The energies of the aforementioned Geoghegan, to whom we will return shortly, were supplemented by the doubtful forensic talents of Mr A. J. McIntyre, Q.C., a seasoned commercial lawyer who was not entirely unknown in the criminal courts, but whose last appearance had apparently been in 1883, the one before that in 1881, and the one before that in 1873. Like Hayward, McIntyre's *curriculum vitae* hardly seemed to prepare him for the professional demands of a murder case. Martin Friedland, the author of *The Trials of Israel Lipski*, sees reasons to believe that McIntyre's health was failing – McIntyre was older even than Hayward.[39]

Geoghegan, meanwhile, is depicted by Friedland as a chaotic alcoholic.

---

38 *Illustrated Police News*, 9 July 1887; TNA:PRO CRIM 1/26/5.
39 Friedland, 30.

Lipski.

Here, of course, the modern researcher has the advantage. Friedland wrote his book more than thirty years ago, and was unable by his own endeavours to locate the sort of information that is now available to anyone with anything more than a casual interest in the matter from the comfort of his own living room. To take one example, Geoghegan did not, as Friedland said, die intestate. In fact, he left his estate – which was, admittedly, not a spectacular one – to his unmarried sister. The point is a little pedantic, but it alters the reader's understanding of the problems which, Friedland says, beset the defence team. Geoghegan was more functional than Friedland thought. Between 1878 and 1902 (the year of his death), Geoghegan appeared in at least 955 cases at the Old Bailey. Ninety-four of these – nearly ten per cent of the total – were homicide trials, and, of these, he acted for the defence in all but four. Between 1881 and 1893, he never appeared in fewer than forty-six Old Bailey cases in a calendar year: in 1887, the year of Lipski's trial, he appeared in something in the order of fifty-three cases (including eight homicide cases), which was only between three and four cases short of his annual mean average over this peak period. (He appeared in sixty-five cases in 1888; a further fifty-five in 1889; and a career-high ten homicide cases in 1890, among an annual total of forty-seven.) All these statistics omit any periods spent in the lower courts (as he had represented Lipski at the Thames Police Court), and any cases heard away from the Old Bailey. Friedland's critical characterisation of Lipski's legal team has some support, but one finds oneself disagreeing with him on particular points. It is no longer possible to conform unconditionally to his view that it was 'not at all unlikely that Geoghegan started drinking' before Lipski's case began, and that he was 'not in a fit condition to handle the Lipski case' by the time the trial began.[40]

In view of all of this, Friedland's hypothesis about the apparently counterintuitive appointment of McIntyre – that he was 'probably brought in at the last moment because Geoghegan was unable to conduct the case owing to alcohol' – cannot be easily sustained. There are more natural, pragmatic explanations for Hayward's choice: in one, Hayward simply discovered that McIntyre was available at short notice (for time was indeed running short, with only a week between the conclusion of the committal hearings and the beginning of the trial); in another, he considered McIntyre to be the best man for the job, preferring him to other barristers. McIntyre himself can have had little doubt about his own capacity to perform the work, since lawyers are, in the interests of fairness, required to return briefs which lie beyond their professional expertise. As Friedland observes, it is true to say that Geoghegan

---

40   Friedland, 30-31.

Introduction.

practically vanished during the trial itself, taking 'no active part in the case', and that McIntyre assumed all the live forensic work in the well of the court – but he also accepts that McIntyre made no complaint about Geoghegan's unobtrusive contribution to the defence effort. McIntyre told a newspaper that Geoghegan 'always works his cases up thoroughly well', and this seems to have been Geoghegan's designation – to listen, to prepare questioning sequences, to ensure that the brief was fulfilled by McIntyre in cross-examination.[41] This sort of division of responsibilities was not unusual. Both Mr Basil Watson and Mr J. P. Valetta sat silently through the 1903 trial - covered in this series as NBT 44 - of Samuel Herbert Dougal, leaving the delivery of the defence argument to Mr George Elliott; Mr R. F. Graham-Campbell, one of the three prosecution barristers in the case, also refrained from taking an 'active' part, and nobody has yet suggested that all three were incapacitated by substance misuse. Equally, it is not at all clear whether Mr Richard Muir adopted an 'active' role in the 1899 trial of Louise Masset (forthcoming in this series); or, indeed, whether Mr Arthur Hutton, working in the shadow of Lord Coleridge, took an 'active' part in Ms Masset's defence (beyond two interruptions to the judge's summing-up). The *Times* reported that a third barrister, Mr W. Bovill Smith, was also briefed to defend Ms Masset, but his 'inactivity', we might say, was almost certainly total.[42] It is difficult to make any critical inferences about the state of Geoghegan's health from the fact of his silence during the Lipski trial.

No similar mysteries lay at the heart of the Treasury's choice of barristers. Mr Charles Mathews and Mr Harry Poland were senior figures, veterans of such notable cases as those of Christiana Edmunds and Percy Lefroy Mapleton (in Poland's example; forthcoming in this series, for the latter case), and (in Mathews's) the *Mignonette* cannibalism affair. Equally illustrious appointments lay before them. On the bench sat Mr Justice James Fitzjames Stephen, another luminary of his era, and a man whose reputation, just two years later, was to come under severe pressure as a consequence of his clumsy handling of the trial of Florence Maybrick (see NBT 17). Significant doubts were expressed about Mr Justice Stephen's mentality during that affair – but none were expressed during the trial of Israel Lipski, and the surviving documentation does not suggest that the judge's powers were already failing him.

On Friday 29 July – following a two-day period of grace, requested by Geoghegan 'to give him further time to prepare his defence', as Friedland puts it – Israel Lipski was brought from his cell in Newgate Prison, positioned in the dock at the Old Bailey, and asked whether he was guilty or not guilty of

---

41   Friedland, 158.
42   *Times* (London), 19 December 1899.

Lipski.

the murder of Miriam Angel. He replied that he was not guilty, and so the trial began.

VII.

Of course, we are now amazed – and probably appalled – by the celerity of things. In a world which moves more quickly than ever, we are accustomed to the paradox that the wheels of justice often turn slowly. It was not so in Victorian England. Miriam Angel had been killed – in a horrible fashion – only a month and a day before the commencement of the criminal trial of the man accused of killing her. The trial itself occupied two days: the reader can see what transpired in the pages following this introduction. The jury retired to consider its verdict at 4.43 pm on the afternoon of Saturday 30 July 1887, and returned to announce its findings eight minutes later. By about five o'clock, Israel Lipski had been sentenced to death; he listened to the judge's words 'with apparently great earnestness', and defiantly told the court interpreter, Mr Karamelli, that he was innocent of the crime, but he was escorted back to Newgate to await execution.[43] In the usual course of things, this would follow after three Sundays had elapsed. The date fixed for Lipski's hanging was Monday 15 August.

Why had Lipski lost his case? A modern reading of the trial suggests a few reasons – and others have been suggested along the way: let us consider them. In the first place, the defence had no room for manoeuvre. Lipski had given his statement to the police on the afternoon after the murder, and he had never resiled from it, despite the fact that it failed in some parts to account for the physical evidence left at the scene of the crime. Even the possibility of attributing the deficiencies of the statement to mental stress, pain or confusion seemed to be eliminated by the very deliberate manner in which Lipski went about securing the attendance of Inspector Final at his bedside (via the medium of Kate Lyons). He could have waited until the police arrived, in their own time, before committing himself to a particular narrative – instead, he nailed his colours firmly to the first available mast. This was a mistake. McIntyre, reflecting on the case afterwards, regretted that his hands had been tied by the specific allegations which Lipski had made in his statement. His brief – as described, afterwards, by Hayward, the solicitor – had been to emphasise that nobody had heard Miriam Angel cry out: this was, as Hayward put it 'wonderful', since any 'conversation in the ordinary way in Mrs Angel's room' could be 'distinctly heard in the room in

---

43   *Pall Mall Gazette*, 1 August 1887.

Introduction.

which Simon [Rosenbloom] was at work'.[44] But nor had Lipski cried out when, as he stated, he was thrown to the floor after being accosted by Rosenbloom and Schmuss. McIntyre said that Hayward's point was made 'as strongly as possible', but 'Lipski's not hollering if attacked made it difficult to lay stress on noise'.[45] Either Lipski's story was a true one, and accurate in its details, or it was a lie; and, if it was a lie, there could be only one reason why he had lied about what had taken place. Even if McIntyre managed to do a little damage to the prosecution's case in cross-examination, this was little use unless the uncertainty happened to coincide with Lipski's statement. On the prosecution's part, the fact that Miriam had not screamed was relatively easily explained – the 'tremendous' blow to the right eye and temple, which left a large bruise – 'blood was effused and the muscle lacerated' – was 'such as would stun a woman'.[46] She had had no opportunity to raise the alarm: but, by Lipski's own description, he had.

In other examples, Lipski's statement was, if anything, even more unhelpful to his lawyers. Some of it was untouchable – how could McIntyre and Geoghegan hope to substantiate the allegation that Lipski had had a wooden stick inserted into his mouth? No wooden stick was found. It was true to say that an abrasion was discovered at the back of Lipski's palate, but this was neatly (and plausibly) attributed by Dr Calvert to the application of the stomach pump. Lipski changed his mind after his conviction, telling his solicitor that the wooden stick was not a wooden stick but a steel bar, but there was no sign of a steel bar either, so this hardly improved the correlation between his statements and the facts of the case.[47]

Then there was the unlikely conspiracy itself. Lipski – faltering on Schmuss's name in his original statement, but leaving no doubt whom he meant – placed Rosenbloom and Schmuss in occult collusion. How plausible was this? Rosenbloom stated that he did not know Schmuss, Schmuss that he did not know Rosenbloom. They did not agree on the question of whether they were left alone after Richard Pittman, the hammering boy, departed for his breakfast, but Schmuss, who thought that they were (if only for a minute), never changed his story, even though to deny it would have struck against the credibility of Lipski's narrative. Indeed, neither Schmuss nor Rosenbloom ever behaved in a manner which suggested that they had anything to hide. Schmuss departed for Birmingham shortly after the murder, for his landlord, Rabinowitz, had

---

44   TNA:PRO HO 144/201/A47465/14.
45   TNA:PRO HO 144/201/A47465/117a.
46   TNA:PRO CRIM 1/26/5.
47   TNA:PRO HO 144/201/A47465/117e.

Lipski.

suggested that he may be able to find work there with a Mr Lieb, a cigarette maker. Schmuss journeyed there without ostentation, took lodgings at 42 Gough Street, and began working as a maker of slippers, first at 22 Inge Street, and then at 126 Suffolk Street.[48] Whenever he was required to return to London to give testimony – and to attend meetings at the Home Office, of which more later – he did so without complaint. Beyond Lipski's statement and the unsophisticated, sub-evidential statement of Richard Pittman (who appeared to believe that, since Rosenbloom and Schmuss spoke the same language, they must, therefore, have known one another), nothing tied Schmuss to Rosenbloom, or *vice versa*. Let us leave to one side the undoubted facts that their clothing was tested in a laboratory and discovered to be free of acid stains, despite the struggle in which Lipski said that they had been engaged, and that neither of them had been known to buy any acid; still, nobody reading the paperwork in the case can believe that these two men – though they appeared in the same fantasy – were anything other than the unlucky, honest victims of a self-serving slander.

So it was that Geoghegan and McIntyre, handicapped in their task from the very beginning, struggled to break down the edifices of the prosecution's case in court. But perhaps other factors – procedural, rather than forensic – were involved? One line of reasoning, tentatively nudged forward by Friedland, held that Mr Karamelli's interpreting was, as 'many persons later said', not of an adequate standard, and that Lipski was therefore unable to follow the evidence.[49] Karamelli himself wrote to a newspaper – which one will become clear – to clarify that he was 'checked and followed' by the judge, one barrister from each side, and two members of the jury, 'who all spoke German and understood the witnesses'.[50] McIntyre seems to have thought that Karamelli was 'not very good', but he added that there was 'nothing to complain of' and 'no suggestion of any wrong translation'.[51]

One other possibility presented itself. Had the judge, as Friedland puts it, been 'grossly unfair in stressing the "lust" theory' during his summing-up, before the jury retired to deliberate?[52] Mr Justice Stephen confessed to his own anxieties about this subject. The prosecution were not required to say why Lipski might have entered Miriam Angel's room; but his object was generally held to be either 'lust' – that is, rape – or theft. We know what Godfrey Lushington, a senior civil servant in the Home Office, made of the competing explanations:

---

48   TNA:PRO HO 144/201/A47465/88.
49   Friedland, 34.
50   *Pall Mall Gazette*, 17 August 1887.
51   TNA:PRO HO 144/201/A47465/117a.
52   Friedland, 204.

Introduction.

> The object might have been either to steal a few clothes and pawn them ... or to ravish the woman from having seen her through the window. The question is not very material, for from either point of view the after acts might be the same.
>
> For if he entered the rooms only to steal, and then, finding the woman had discovered him, killed her, he might have gone on to ravish the body, or have prepared to ravish it when he was interrupted.
>
> The theory of stealing is the more probable, because it is free from the difficulty which attaches to that of lust, *viz* that Lipski must have known that if he ravished Mrs Angel, he could not escape detection, and his only chance would be to run away from the district.
>
> The theory of stealing has also this to support it. It is clear that Lipski wanted money, because he tried to borrow 5/- of Mrs Lipski, and just starting business for the first day he must have been anxious to provide the necessary tools lest the men should leave him for want of them. This may explain the falsehood he told about having failed to buy a vice because the shop was not open. The shop was open at 7.00, and he went there only once, and refused to buy the vice because it was too dear.[53]

This analysis raised interesting questions – not least among them the possibility, as Friedland observes, that Lipski may have been, or sought to be, a necrophiliac – but the judge had come at the matter from a slightly different angle. In a letter to the Home Secretary, Mr Justice Stephen reported that he had come to regret the phrasing of one part of his summing-up:

> I now come to the remarks which suggest themselves in the comparative general probability of the two stories. First, as to motive. I do not on full reflection think that much can be said on this subject. Lust and robbery are the only conceivable motives. I think each is about as likely to have actuated one man as to have actuated two. At the trial I suggested that if lust was the motive, it was more likely to have actuated one man. But, on reflection, I am disposed to think that no reliance might be placed on any speculation of this sort. Someone did commit a murder for some reason or other.[54]

The Times had reported Stephen's remark in its coverage of the case in broadly similar terms – 'His Lordship pointed out that it was more probable that passion was the motive for the crime, and that if that were so it would rather be the act of one man than two' – but other newspapers omitted the observation from their own accounts, which (perhaps) goes to show that, among everything else that was said, this particular observation was not universally considered to

---

53 TNA:PRO HO 144/201/A47465/117e.
54 TNA:PRO HO 144/201/A47465/17.

be of the utmost relevance.[55] The extent to which it might have influenced the jury, however, could not be known.

Friedland considers Stephen's remark to be one of the most profound reasons for believing Lipski's conviction to be unsafe. He says that the statement 'effectively took the case out of the hands of the jury' and that 'an appeal court today would, I think, quash the conviction'.[56] One wonders. Dr Kay, testifying before the coroner on 29 June, had identified a substance located in Miriam Angel's vagina: it 'looked like semen'. He also noticed 'no marks of violence around the private parts, or the thighs, or the genital parts whatever'. He returned to the inquest two days later to report that he had placed the substance under a microscope: 'There are no spermatozoa. Had there been any, I could have proved it was semen. It might be semen. I agree with the remark of a text book that the semen even of a healthy young man varies much and is scarcely ever twice alike, so that the absence of spermatozoa is no proof that the matter is not semen. There is no other test.'[57] During his examination of Dr Kay at the Old Bailey, Mr Poland decorously veered away from the subject, apparently leaving his observation hanging, incomplete:

> On the lower part of the body, you saw no signs of violence? — Yes.
>
> No signs of recent connection? — No.
>
> You saw some discharge. That was the natural ... What was the date of the post mortem?

Either way, there was no evidence before the jury to show that Lipski – or anyone – had raped, or attempted to rape, Miriam Angel. If they were to dispense with the 'lust' theory on this basis, then Mr Justice Stephen's remark, unhelpful as it was, ought, if anything, to have steered the jury *towards* Lipski's case, rather than away from it. The guilty verdict was returned in spite of the judge's remark, rather than because of it.

It is also possible to make the argument that Stephen was right – which is not the same thing as saying that he was right to make the remark at all. In 1886, the year before the Lipski affair, roughly 270 guilty verdicts were handed down by Old Bailey judges trying cases of theft. In about seventy-two per cent of these cases, there was a single defendant; there were two or more defendants in the remaining twenty-eight per cent of cases. By contrast, there were guilty verdicts in just over eighty cases of sexual offending (not including bigamy – a slightly different matter) tried at the Old Bailey over the same period. Of

---

55   *The Times* (London), 1 August 1887.
56   Friedland, 204.
57   TNA:PRO CRIM 1/26/5.

these, about ninety per cent featured a single defendant; about ten per cent featured two or more defendants. This is only a guideline, and not a good way to inform the decision-making processes of juries; but it appears that Mr Justice Stephen's remarks may not have been far from the statistical truth of the matter. Criminals working in collaboration *were* more likely to commit thefts, rather than sexual offences – although criminals were more likely to work alone than with other people in both of these areas of the law. It may – perhaps – be argued that Stephen's undoubtedly regrettable remark was neither prejudicial to the interests of the defendant, nor generally incorrect.

The forensic and procedural objections to the conviction of Israel Lipski were therefore insufficient to compel the Home Secretary, Mr Henry Matthews, to interfere with the process of law. Lipski was in the condemned cell, waiting for mid-August to roll around. Could something – anything – spring him from his fate? It may be that the establishment thought not. But the first sign of what was to follow appeared in the *Pall Mall Gazette* on 1 August 1887:

> The result of the trial of Lipski leaves several points unsettled. Was the door of the murdered woman's room locked or not? The whole matter hinges on that. The landlady is not sure that it was. And the solicitor for the defence raises a good point this morning by the inquiry where the second ounce of nitric acid came from, as two were apparently employed and Lipski only bought one. The case is one which calls for consideration at the hands of the authorities before the death sentence is enforced.[58]

This was the shot in the distance, over the rooftops of Whitehall. The armada was coming in.

VIII.

The editor of the *Pall Mall Gazette*, in 1887, was W. T. Stead, and few more complicated personalities could have been found in London at the time. Simultaneously, he was swashbuckling and impetuous, passionate and inflexible, inspiring and maddening, genuine and disingenuous. He had been the driving force behind the 'Maiden Tribute of Modern Babylon' affair of 1885, bringing his innovative journalistic techniques to bear against a society in which the sexual abuse of children was tolerated without consequence. Anchoring himself in the vibrant space between investigative journalism and gonzo journalism long before either of those terms existed, he served a prison sentence for 'unlawfully

---

58   *Pall Mall Gazette*, 1 August 1887.

taking Eliza Armstrong, aged thirteen, out of the possession and against the will' of her parents, just to prove that the corrupt mechanisms about which he was writing actually worked in real life.[59] Sacrifices such as these were rationalised as the inevitable side-effects of undertaking campaigns of social importance, but the fact that sensation sold newspapers had not gone unnoticed by Stead's counterparts in other London publications. Michael Diamond quotes the *Standard*: 'So far as ordinary people can judge from the flaunting posters, the roaring newsboys, the successive editions, the elaborate advertisements which characterise sales of this sort of literature at the present day, the philanthropic crusade of the agitators has been worked on a strictly commercial basis. The sewer that runs underground may need cleaning; but the zeal that makes a handsome profit by turning it into the street will hardly be appreciated.'[60]

It remained to be seen whether Stead's vigilante approach to journalism was informed by careful ratiocination and the diligent selection of investigative topics, or whether it was an opportunistic shoot-out, coming to the boil whenever the newspaper's circulation flagged. Suitably, since the character of the paper mirrored the complexities of its editor, there seemed to be aspects of each approach. Stead would reproduce irresponsible correspondence from readers such as Joseph Laister, quoted above, apparently without considering its socially harmful effects. Friedland says that 'many Jews in the 1880s considered the *Pall Mall Gazette* to be anti-semitic'; publishing material such as Glaister's and warning against the 'Judenhetze brewing in East London' can hardly have been expected to nurture any alternative perception.[61] Still, it seems that, at heart, Stead had no particular grudge with Judaism. Instead, he had a grudge with the establishment in general, society at large, the Unionist Conservative administration as a whole, and Catholicism in particular. These predispositions were given full rein with the appointment, in 1886, of the Catholic, Conservative, unionist Henry Matthews to the position of Home Secretary. Matthews became the target of Stead's vehemence – this was not just day-to-day sensation-rousing with virtuous financial results; this was a premeditated policy decision. Harry Poland, reflecting on the Lipski case, made a similar observation. 'I don't say that Stead took all the trouble he did because Matthews was a Roman Catholic,' he said, 'but he took a lot'.[62]

---

59   See Old Bailey Proceedings Online (www.oldbaileyonline.org, version 7.2, 14 April 2017), October 1885, trial of Rebecca Jarrett, William Thomas Stead, Sampson Jacques, William Bramwell Booth and Elizabeth Combe (t18851019-1031).
60   Diamond, 115-116.
61   Friedland, 131.
62   Bowen-Rowlands, 206.

Introduction.

Hayward, Lipski's solicitor, had submitted his first petition for clemency to the Home Office on 6 August 1887, passing it through the hands of several members of Parliament who recommended the appeal to Matthews (see Appendix II). Both the questions raised by the *Pall Mall Gazette* – whether the door to Miriam Angel's room had been locked, and whether one ounce of nitric acid was sufficient to account for all the damage to Miriam Angel, Lipski's coat, and so on – were likewise raised, *inter alia*, in the petition. The Home Office reassured itself that there had indeed been enough acid in Lipski's phial to inflict the corrosion and injuries seen on the persons, items and floor of the Angels' room. Dr Thomas Stevenson, a Home Office analyst working at Guy's Hospital, experimented with some acid of his own: 'Although the burning [of the coat] was extensive, on fitting the burnt patches together I found that no very large quantity of the fabric had actually disappeared. I have produced an equal effect by applying half an ounce of nitric acid to a similar coat. I am of opinion that half an ounce of a strong corrosive acid might amply suffice to produce all the results met with on Lipski's coat' (see Appendix V).[63] This left the other half-ounce for everything else. At the London Hospital, Dr Calvert's was a dissenting voice – on 8 August, he told Hayward that he had 'examined the prisoner's coat at the trial, and I consider it would take an ounce of nitric acid to produce the damages and stains which I saw upon the coat' – but his position was a qualified one. 'As I have made no experiment,' he admitted, 'I cannot speak positively to this'.[64]

The question of the locked door appeared to be a slightly trickier one. Mrs Lipski, the landlady, had told the court that she herself had not tried the door, so – as the *Pall Mall Gazette* suggested – she could not be sure whether it was really locked, or just stiff. The lock itself was an eccentric, poorly-fitting arrangement, and Mrs Lipski accepted that the key, standing in the lock on the inside, could be touched, but not turned, by someone outside the door, through a small hole. That Isaac Schmuss had once been a locksmith had not escaped Hayward's notice. But the evidence of Dinah Angel, who could not open the door, and William Piper, who found the bolt shot when he went into the room to examine the body (the door having been burst open by the combined efforts of Mrs Angel, Mrs Levy and Mrs Lipski), was not susceptible to serious challenge. Hayward met with Mr Justice Stephen – panging with insecurity following his unwise words to the jury – on 8 August, and pushed the theory that the key might have been turned 'by some one of the party who pressed into the room, one of whom was Rosenbloom; and it is possible, though hardly likely, that he

63 TNA:PRO HO 144/201/A47465/26.
64 TNA:PRO HO 144/201/A47465/23.

might have turned the key'.[65] Even if one considered it fair, as the *Pall Mall Gazette* did, to gloss Mrs Lipski's careful evidence in such a way as to suggest that she was no longer 'sure' that the door was locked, Hayward's point about Rosenbloom – subtly turning the key so as to suggest that Lipski had locked himself into the room – was nothing more than improbable conjecture. There was no evidence for it, and the available evidence led to the opposite conclusion.

Mr Justice Stephen described himself as 'favourably impressed' by Mr Hayward, but their meeting would later become the subject of some controversy.[66] The assignation had apparently taken place at Stephen's instigation, and Hayward considered the opportunity to meet a judge to be a rare privilege for an unremarkable solicitor: 'Never,' he glowed, 'in the whole course of my experience had I heard of a judge sending for a solicitor in this way before'.[67] But headway was there none. Stephen, deploying his execrable informal handwriting style for the occasion, fired off a seventeen-page letter to the Home Secretary, giving an account of their discussion, but articulating the unchanged view that 'the difficulties attendant on the theory of the guilt of Rosenbloom and Schmuss are to my mind very great'.[68] Hayward, as much as his barristers (against the quality of whose work he now protested: 'It was scandalous, and I don't care who knows it'), was hamstrung by the obligation to conform to the details of Lipski's statement.[69]

What was needed was additional firepower – something to break the unworkable stranglehold of Lipski's description of events, and to project the activities of those working for his reprieve into a stratosphere of new and compelling information. With Hayward's encouragement – if he needed it at all – and apparently courtesy of an introduction from the editor of *Society*, Stead rolled his cannons onto the lawn of the Home Office, and took aim (see Appendix X). From the moment the case truly began to engage him – with the clock ticking down before Lipski's scheduled hanging – he stopped at nothing to implicate Matthews in a miscarriage of justice; for those around Matthews, collateral damage was an occupational hazard. Stead threw his immense resources at the problem of Lipski's guilt and innocence, and, for the first time, Hayward found himself in a position to test the prosecution's evidence. If there had been an inequality of arms at the Old Bailey, now – with the trial long since over – the balance had begun to shift to the advantage of the defence.

The way Hayward now told it, his 8 August meeting with the judge had

---

65   TNA:PRO HO 144/201/A47465/17.
66   Ibid.
67   *Pall Mall Gazette*, 13 August 1887.
68   TNA:PRO HO 144/201/A47465/17.
69   *Evening News* (London), 17 August 1887.

Introduction.

had revelatory significance. 'Mr Justice Stephen, who tried Lipski, and whose summing-up contributed not a little to his conviction,' boomed the *Pall Mall Gazette*, in its fifth edition of 12 August, 'has since been converted, and is aghast at the prospect of hanging a possibly innocent man'. Hayward told Stead that Stephen's 'anxiety, his agony of mind almost ... were obvious'. It would, said Stephen, 'be a terrible thing ... to hang this man, when in reality he may have been half killed by the real murderers, who by that means endeavoured to hide their guilt' He wished Hayward success in his appeal to the Home Office and, as Hayward was leaving, he encountered Stephen's clerk. 'The governor is terribly worried about it,' said the clerk. 'I've never known him so bothered about a case all the forty years I've been with him'.[70]

There was plenty more – the article itself is reproduced below as Appendix VIII – but this disclosure by itself was enough to cause anxiety in the Home Office. Mr Justice Stephen, when he was made aware of the allegation, wrote everywhere – to his wife, to the Home Office, to the *Times* – decrying (to his wife) 'the vile Stead ... the liar'.[71] The story was what we would now call fake news. As a *reductio ad absurdum*, Stephen targeted the allegation against Philip Dyke, his clerk. Dyke had not been with him forty years: 'Why, in 1847 I had not gone up to Cambridge and Dyke cannot have been seven years old'.[72] (Indeed, we can see Dyke in the 1881 and 1891 censuses, aged, by his own estimation, thirty-six and forty-five.) Nonetheless, the pressure was instantly on.

One final remark about the *Pall Mall Gazette* article of 12 August. Its conclusion was a masterpiece of misleading swagger. Hayward, the newspaper wrote, 'could not and would not permit one word' of his interview with Mr Justice Stephen to be published; its content was 'confidential', and Hayward had only discussed them with journalists 'to induce us to call attention to the case of the doomed victim'.[73] It is hard to think of anything sillier – but Stead, being Stead, seized the opportunity to inject himself, and the plural voices of his conscience, into the story.

> When Mr Hayward left, the editor of this journal was placed in one of those difficult positions in which all the commonplaces of ethics seem to point one way and paramount and imperious duty in another. To save Lipski – to prevent a judicial murder of the most aggravated kind, one way lay open, and only one way. Publish the fact that Mr Justice Stephen is, to say the least, haunted by a terrible doubt as to whether Lipski is not as innocent as the poor woman for

---

70   *Pall Mall Gazette*, 13 August 1887, reprinting copy from the previous evening's late edition.
71   Friedland, 123.
72   Friedland, 124.
73   *Pall Mall Gazette*, 13 August 1887.

whose murder he is to be hanged, and his execution becomes morally impossible.

But then the conversation was private, the interview confidential. We were in precise terms interdicted from using it. If we published it, Mr Justice Stephen might be very angry. Mr Hayward would fall into disgrace, and we should have to face the odium of a breach of confidence. 'You have no right to use a private conversation.' 'If you don't, an innocent man will be hanged.' 'You may ruin Mr Hayward.' 'But save Mr Hayward's client.' 'And no one will trust you any more.' 'Well, when a life is at stake they had better not tell me anything that would save that life and expect me to keep it secret.'[74]

The formal innovation can be appreciated – for here we approach something approximating gonzo journalism years before Tom Wolfe and Hunter S. Thompson – without endorsing the arrant fiction of the article's premise.

On the morning of Sunday 14 August, with the sound of the *Pall Mall Gazette*'s bombardment ringing in his ears, Mr Justice Stephen telegraphed to the Home Office from Salcombe, in south Devon, where he was on holiday. He advocated a 'respite of one week with intimation that reprieve is not to be expected – this would remove any impression of haste from public mind & give Hayward opportunity of answering Stephenson [*sic*]'.[75] (Thomas Stevenson's work on the acid was ongoing, and his latest report had been received at the Home Office on 11 August – see Appendix VI.) Mr Matthews must have recognised that Stephen was correct. The execution of Israel Lipski could not be allowed to look like an act of convenience for a Home Secretary who was under fire from the press. The respite went out to the governor of Newgate Prison, to Mr Hayward, and to a host of newspapers and news agencies later the same day.[76] It is this decision to which Fenton Bresler referred in his book, *Reprieve: A Study of a System*, when he wrote that Matthews had 'bungled' the case.[77] Indecision had taken over; but Lipski had another week to live.

IX.

The re-imagined timeline gave Stead and Hayward opportunities to reload, and to fire again. Liberated from the story which Lipski had told, they now sought to undermine the case against the prisoner in any way they could – this was 'trial by journalism', a weapon of last resort for deployment when

---

74   *Pall Mall Gazette*, 13 August 1887.
75   TNA:PRO HO 144/201/A47465/44.
76   TNA:PRO HO 144/201/A47465/38.
77   Bresler, 133.

Introduction.

conventional methods such as 'trial by due process' had failed to bear the desired results. A second petition from Hayward – arriving at the Home Office on 13 August, in the wake of the previous evening's splash in the *Pall Mall Gazette* – established new reasons to believe that there was more to the defence case than had originally met the eye. There had been, Hayward said, an attempted robbery at 16 Batty Street on the morning of the murder, and two boxes of clothing and pawn tickets belonging to Mrs Lipski and Mrs Levy 'had been forced open and the contents thereof disarranged by someone making a hasty search therein'.[78] This put the Home Office and the police to work again. Inspector Tunbridge of the Criminal Investigation Department saw Mrs Lipski's box, which had a broken catch, on 15 August, noting with suspicion that 'although it is now nearly two months since the catch was broken, still no attempt had been made all this time to secure it'.[79] Nor was anything missing. It was concluded that the box, if indeed it really had been broken on the morning of the murder, had been damaged by 'the crowd standing on it in order to see what was going on'.[80]

One part of Hayward's renewed petition was presented in the form of a convenient premonition. He now understood that 'evidence is forthcoming that the nitric acid was sold to a man not at all corresponding with the description of the prisoner and that 2ozs were sold & not 1 oz as alleged'.[81] This prophecy was fulfilled on 18 August in – where else? – the *Pall Mall Gazette*, which had got hold of 'the signed deposition of Mr M. Buchner, chemist, of 149 Houndsditch'.[82] The symbiotic relationship between Hayward and Stead can be seen most vividly in this example. The solicitor's efforts were driven, and influenced, by the newspaper's coverage of his efforts; which in turn inspired the newspaper to help him to identify further juicy and money-spinning revelations. Mr Buchner's first statement – made to Hayward, and handed in at the Home Office at lunchtime on 18 August – is given in Appendix XII. The delay between its advertisement in the petition and its arrival with the Secretary of State is a matter of wonder, and perhaps not a factor operating in its favour as evidence; nonetheless, the *Pall Mall Gazette* crowed its triumph in newsprint:

> If this evidence be true, a final blow is given to the case of the prosecution. The bottle spoken of … corresponds to the bottle found in the murdered woman's room; but the man who brought it to Mr Buchner's shop was certainly not Lipski. Whoever else the man may be, that is certain. Lipski is fair and slightly built; the

---

78 TNA:PRO HO 144/201/A47465/117.
79 TNA:PRO HO 144/201/A47465/87.
80 TNA:PRO HO 144/201/A47465/117e.
81 TNA:PRO HO 144/201/A47465/117.
82 *Pall Mall Gazette*, 18 August 1887.

Lipski.

owner of the bottle was dark and square built.[83]

But Mr Buchner, for whatever his qualities as a responsible chemist, had not sold the acid which killed Miriam Angel. It had been known to the Home Office since Stevenson's report of 11 August that the bottle detected in Miriam's room had held 'an adulterated article, containing sulphuric and nitric acids in the proportion of two parts nitric acid to three parts sulphuric acid'.[84] Charles Moore's 'nitric acid' – the same batch used to fill Lipski's bottle on the morning of the murder – turned out, on analysis, to be an 'adulterated article' in the same proportions. This strongly suggested that Moore's shop was the place of origin of the acid used to kill Miriam. Buchner's nitric acid, in the meantime, was found to be a pure supply, traceable to a wholesaler in Southwark.[85] Despite the *Pall Mall Gazette*'s excitement, the idea that Buchner's evidence could unseat the prosecution case stumbled on the qualification which the journalist had smuggled into the start of his declamatory paragraph. 'If this evidence be true' … It was not.

One more thing needs to be said about Stevenson's evidence to the Home Office. Friedland writes that, 'Stevenson's crucial report that the acid was precisely the same as the acid sold by Moore was *not* given to Hayward. The Permanent Under-Secretary, Godfrey Lushington, specifically notes on the file … "Dr Stevenson's report is not to be communicated to Hayward."'[86] He also states that 'the crucial decision not to give the chemist's report to Hayward was inexcusable, causing Hayward to pursue a dead-end, one the Home Office knew to be exactly that'.[87] But the meaning of Lushington's remark is not so easy to divine. Mr Justice Stephen, following up his telegram of Sunday 14 August with a rushed letter, advised Lushington that he 'should inform H[ayward] of Stephenson's [*sic*] evidence so that he might show if he could that the nitric acid of commerce is really a mixture of nitric & sulphuric acid', and Lushington, even if one assumes that he had a predisposition towards upholding the verdict of the court, would have had no remit to withhold any evidence germane to the case from Mr Hayward.[88] But the fact is that Hayward had already received at least the gist of the 'adulterated article' report (on 12 August) describing the composition of Moore's acid, and this explained that the acid obtained from Moore's batch and the acid found on Lipski's coat, on the clothes of Miriam

---

83 *Pall Mall Gazette*, 18 August 1887.
84 TNA:PRO HO 144/201/A47465/33.
85 TNA:PRO HO 144/201/A47465/93.
86 Friedland, 142.
87 Friedland, 204.
88 TNA:PRO HO 144/201/A47465/55.

Introduction.

Angel and on the bottle produced at the trial was all separable into a mixture of nitric and sulphuric acids, and all in the same forty-sixty proportion (see Appendix VI). It is also true to say that another memo, dated 16 August and written 'by Mr Lushington's desire', instructed one of the more junior civil servants in the Home office 'to inform Hayward that upon analysis it appeared that the acid which was found on [the] prisoner's coat was found to be more sulphuric acid than nitric acid, and that a similar result was obtained from analysis of the so-called nitric acid at Messrs Moore'.[89] It is difficult to know why this information would need to be provided to Hayward again, since he was apparently in receipt of it already. But, even so, Friedland's assertion that 'if Hayward had received Stevenson's report, he might not have pressed Buchner's evidence so strongly' cannot be right.[90] Buchner's evidence – finally presented by Hayward to the Home Office on 18 August, after all the foregoing letters, reports and memos had been written and actioned – was a long shot, and, as far as anyone knows, he made no attempt in advance to discover whether Buchner's acid was an 'adulterated article' in the way that Moore's was. The Home Office commissioned the experiment that determined that Buchner's acid had no part in the murder of Miriam Angel. Hayward was in possession of the facts he needed, but he was trying anything.

So, too, was the editor of the *Pall Mall Gazette*. An interview of the usual dubious nature with Harris Dywein elicited the 'fact' that 'Rosenbloom has lost twenty-four pounds in weight since the murder', and Harry Poland told the jovial and unreliable Ernest Bowen-Rowlands, some time later, that Stead, who was always conscious of his commercial interests, had put the claim on a poster, viewable by anyone passing by a newspaper boy in the street (Poland misremembered the amount of weight which Rosenbloom had supposedly shed, thinking that it was 'a stone', rather than nearly twice as much).[91] Strange things were happening: Buchner, the chemist, was besieged by journalists ('I have had no end of reporters round'), despite the immateriality of his evidence, and he wondered at the rapidity with which his version of events was being transmitted and republished (see Appendix XIII).[92] Kate Lyons, Lipski's fiancée, was similarly in demand. Inspector Andrew Lansdowne, of Scotland Yard, was 'engaged nearly two hours before I could get an interview' with her.

> She told me that she had been so hunted by representatives of the press and private enquiry agents that both her friends and herself had decided not to see

---

89 TNA:PRO HO 144/201/A47465/33.
90 Friedland, 142.
91 *Pall Mall Gazette*, 17 August 1887; Bowen-Rowlands, 206.
92 TNA:PRO HO 144/201/A47465/93.

anyone. Yesterday, she said, her place of business was watched by two men wishing to take her portrait for the *Pall Mall Gazette*, and it was only when her employer sent out another young woman, whose portrait these men sketched as that of Miss Lyons, that they could be got rid of.[93]

Isaac Schmuss was similarly harassed. He had been called back from Birmingham to answer to some quite unsubstantiated allegations made by Emil Barsuch, one of the labourers who would frequent Mark Schmidt's shop. (Unsurprisingly, the allegations, which suggested that Schmuss had been untruthful when testifying to his movements on the day of Miriam Angel's murder, were presented in the *Pall Mall Gazette*, which noted without much concern for the credibility of its article that Barsuch had 'just come out of prison, where he served a few days for some petty theft'.[94]) Barsuch and Schmuss were invited to confront one another at the Home Office on 17 August, and Schmuss made effective work of demolishing Barsuch's story; Henry Matthews and Mr Justice Stephen, overseeing the encounter, came to believe that Barsuch's evidence was not factual.[95] On 18 August, Barsuch told Inspector Final that 'Mr Hayward has paid my passage to go to America. He has brought me some clothes, which I am now wearing.' He later amended his account: 'My brother in New York has paid my passage. Hayward has the ticket. I was to have sailed this morning. Hayward promised to change the ticket, and I have not seen it since. Hayward has only paid me my travelling expenses – about four shillings – perhaps more.'[96]

But if evidence damaging to the case against Lipski could not be bought, perhaps it could be extracted by deception and menace. Schmuss returned to Nathan Rabinowitz's house for a few days after the meeting at the Home Office, and, at about 1.00 pm on 20 August, he received an unexpected visit.

> A boy with a cab called at 60 Oxford Street, where I live, and said, 'You are wanted at once by the Queen's Counsel'. I did not want to ride because it is my Sabbath. I got in the cab and was driven to Liverpool Street. A man got in the cab and told the boy to go to the office. I was then taken in the cab to a house in Houndsditch.
>
> I went into a room and an old man was there who said, 'Can you speak English?'
>
> I said, 'No'. Then a person who could speak German came in and asked me for the name of the man I worked for in Birmingham. I said, 'I don't know. I have

---

93 TNA:PRO HO 144/201/A47465/86.
94 *Pall Mall Gazette*, 17 August 1887.
95 TNA:PRO HO 144/201/A47465/117f.
96 TNA:PRO HO 144/201/A47465/90.

Introduction.

not worked there long.'

He said, 'Do you know Barsuch? Did you tell Barsuch that you saw Lipski and Simon [Rosenbloom] in the room where the murder was?' I did not tell him anything at all.

He asked me, 'Where did you get the money to go to Birmingham?'

I replied, 'I was working in the Goswell Road and saved the money'.

He asked me, 'Do you know that Lipski is to be hanged on Monday?'

I said, 'I don't know'.

'Perhaps you can help us so that Lipski is not hanged?'

Then the old man gave me a shilling and let me out. I did not want to take the shilling. I did not take it. I saw Mrs Lipski, the landlady at 16 Batty Street, there. The old man said, 'I will come home to you to speak to you,' as I would not speak to him.[97]

There were clear signs that the Jewish community of East London were divided by their feelings about the case. Friends were turning against one another, and disagreements were rife. Some of these, at least, had to be investigated. Rumours spread, many of the least credible variety. Far from the least compelling was that propagated by a gentleman named Maurice Marcolescu, who alleged that his lodger, 'a man named Tartakowski ... had said to him that he had received fourteen shillings to go the police court as a witness against Lipski, and had stated that Schmuss had remained in London ten days after the murder, whereas he had only remained two or three; and that if anybody were to give him twice as much he would go as a witness for Lipski so that he should not be hanged'.[98] Tartakowski's roommates – three men named Leib, David and Schacher – all told similar stories about him, but Tartakowski objected to this characterisation of his involvement in the case.

I have never said the words they accuse me of saying. ... When I said at the police court that Schmuss stayed here in Whitechapel eight or ten days, I told the truth. I received fourteen shillings from the Old Bailey for my expenses as a witness. I have received money from no other person for going as [a] witness in Lipski's case.[99]

No further evidence was available, and, despite their honest efforts, the police could find no proof that Tartakowski had ever announced himself as either

---

97   TNA:PRO HO 144/201/A47465/116.
98   TNA:PRO HO 144/201/A47465/90.
99   Ibid.

Lipski.

a witness for hire or the purveyor of false testimony. The allegation appears to have been cooked up between Marcolescu and Tartakowski's roommates, perhaps out of spite, or simply to rid themselves, in a particularly nasty way, of a tenant and cohabitee of whom they had already tired.

Over in Watney Passage, Simon Rosenbloom had returned to work for Marks Katz. 'My husband is a stickmaker,' Sarah Katz told A. K. Stephenson, the Treasury solicitor, on 18 August. '[The] prisoner and Rosenbloom formerly worked for him, and Rosenbloom does still.'[100] Mr Katz had, in fact, re-employed Rosenbloom 'the week after' the murder.[101] One is forced to speculate about how Kate Lyons might have felt about this: Rosenbloom had been re-employed by her uncle, although he, Rosenbloom, was the man whom her fiancé – now the inhabitant of the condemned cell – had accused of the murder of Miriam Angel. It certainly looks as if the Katz family had very little confidence in Lipski's self-proclaimed innocence.

X.

'Dare we hang Lipski?' The *Pall Mall Gazette* concluded a week of innuendo, false claims and chicanery with a casual swipe at the personality of its editor's political nemesis. 'Mr Matthews's mind must be fact-proof indeed if it does not admit the introduction by this time of an element of doubt into the case.' There had been lively exchanges in the House of Commons (see Appendix XV), and, as the *Pall Mall Gazette* reported, 'a memorial from members of Parliament to the Home Secretary protesting against the execution of Lipski … has now been signed by 109 members'.[102] By the evening of Saturday 20 August, however, it was still impossible for Matthews to justify interfering with Lipski's sentence. Lushington wrote to Hayward to advise him that no commutation of Lipski's sentence would be forthcoming; Hayward described himself as 'sick at heart when I think that in a few hours he will be no more'.[103]

And yet Matthews and Mr Justice Stephen sat it out at the Home Office through Sunday, too. The uncertainty which had provoked the respite continued to unsettle them, and they continued to consider the matter. Lipski would be hanged early on Monday morning. They had less than twenty-four hours – closer to twelve – to act, if action was called for.

Then, unexpectedly, Lipski's confession arrived from Newgate.

---

100 TNA:PRO HO 144/201/A47465/90.
101 TNA:PRO HO 144/201/A47465/80.
102 *Pall Mall Gazette*, 19 August 1887.
103 Friedland, 166-167.

Introduction.

I, Israel Lipski, before I appear before God in judgment, desire to speak the whole truth concerning the crime of which I am accused. I will not die with a lie on my lips. I will not let others suffer even in suspicion for my sin. — I alone was guilty of the murder of Miriam Angel. I thought the woman had money in her room. So I entered, the door being unlocked, & the woman asleep. I had no thought of violating her, & I swear I never approached her with that object, nor did I wrong her in this way. Miriam Angel awoke ~~while I was~~ before I could search about for money & cried out, but very softly. Thereupon, I struck her on the head, & seized her by the neck & closed her mouth with my hand, so that she should not arouse the attention of ~~all~~ those who were about the house. I had long been tired of my life. I had bought ~~some aqua fortis of Mr Moore~~ a pennyworth of *aqua fortis* that morning for the purpose of putting an end to myself. Suddenly I thought of the bottle I had in my pocket. I drew it out, & poured some of the contents down her throat. She fainted, & ~~seeing~~ recognising my desperate condition, I took the rest. The bottle was an old one which I had formerly used & it ~~which I [obscured] the oilman~~ was the same as that which I had taken with me to the oil shop. The quantity of *aqua fortis* I took had no effect on me. Hearing the voices of people coming up stairs, I crawled under the bed. The woman seemed already dead. ~~From~~ There was only a very short time from the moment of my entering the room until I was taken away. In the agitation I ~~partly~~ also fainted. I do not know how it was that my arms became abraded. I did not feel it & was not aware of it. As to the door being locked from the inside, I myself did this immediately after I entered the room, wishing not to be interrupted. — I solemnly declare that Rosenbloom & Schmuss knew nothing whatever of the crime of which I have been guilty, & I alone. I implore them to pardon me for having in my despair tried to cast the blame upon them. I also beseech the forgiveness of the bereaved husband. —

~~I acknowledge the justice of the sentence which has been passed upon me.~~ I admit that I have ~~[obscured] rightly and fairly dealt~~ had a fair trial and acknowledge the justice of the sentence that has been passed upon me. I desire to thank Mr Hayward for his efforts on my behalf, as well as all those who have ~~shown me such~~ interested themselves in me during this unhappy time.

~~A gold stud, wh~~ ~~The above is written by Mr Singer at my re~~ This confession is made of my own free will, & is written down by Mr Singer at my request.

May God comfort my loving father & mother, & may He accept my repentance & my death as an atonement for all my sins![104]

It is impossible to know whether Matthews would have offered a commission in the absence of this confession. Friedland quotes from one unreliable source – clipped years after the event by the watchful civil servants of the Home Office

---

104 TNA:PRO HO 144/201/A47465/127.

Lipski.

– which presents the mood in the room as one of sudden elation, and then the dawning realisation that the satisfaction of a confession was not enough.[105] All the energy which had been expended in revisiting the evidence, and examining new leads, vindicated; all the long hours spent in consultation, and in hostile sittings of the House of Commons, justified; the *Pall Mall Gazette*'s theory of Lipski's innocence, shattered – but these little victories could not be enjoyed. A woman was not coming back, and the law held that a man would still have to die.

Israel Lipski was hanged shortly after 8.00 am on the morning of Monday 22 August 1887. If Ernest Bowen-Rowlands is to be believed – and he is not – Lipski actually died of fright on the way to the scaffold ('I know that the sentence pronounced on him in court that "you shall be hanged by the neck until you are dead" was never executed. ... He was dead – before he left the cell.')[106] A jury of thirteen men, under the direction of the coroner Samuel Langham, signed and sealed the usual execution papers – in this case, with the dates amended in manuscript from the 'fifteenth day of August' to the 'twenty-second' – to show that Lipski had been executed in the correct manner, under the law.[107] He was buried, as the law commanded, at Newgate Prison, the place in which the prisoner had last been held; and these 'eight weeks in the summer of Queen Victoria's jubilee' – as a recent novel about the Lipski case puts it – came to their quiet end under shovelfuls of lime, and heavy flagstones.

The *Pall Mall Gazette*, however, was not quite done. Its edition of 22 August – it was not a morning paper, but still managed to get through numerous editions every day – declared, 'All's Well that Ends Well'. 'He has been hanged,' it wrote, 'and few criminals ever went to the gallows who better deserved their fate'. No apology was given for the shamelessness of the paper's tactics. 'We never sought in any way to interfere with the course of justice in Lipski's case until Lipski's solicitor assured us solemnly that the judge who tried Lipski had grave doubts as to the justice of the verdict. ... Of course, if Mr Hayward was mistaken, we were misled.' Rosenbloom and Schmuss, who had been the subjects of some of Stead's most damaging imputations, were declared to be 'freed from all blame ... and we heartily rejoice that a suspicion so widespread has been so conclusively dissipated'.[108]

And yet, questions remained. Lipski's confession failed to resolve a number of issues which, now, appeared to be rather more germane than they had been

---

105 *Star*, 18 November 1921.
106 Bowen-Rowlands, 208.
107 TNA:PRO HO 144/201/A47465/139.
108 *Pall Mall Gazette*, 22 August 1887.

Introduction.

before. Stead had saved the best for last.

Lipski had stated that he entered Miriam Angel's room with the object of stealing money from its occupant. Why would a thief lock the door behind him? Why, if he had not been rendered unconscious by the violence of Rosenbloom and Schmuss, would he lie down beside the bed and *pretend* to be unconscious? Had he no opportunity to flee the room? If so, he must have been disturbed when Dinah Angel knocked on the door, which, in turn, suggests that he must have killed Miriam shortly before 11.00 am. The time of death estimated by the doctor must, accordingly, have been erroneous. Lipski cannot have entered the room until after nine at the earliest, by which time Miriam Angel was routinely up, dressed, and at her mother-in-law's house, having breakfast. Why would Miriam still be there, asleep, so late in the morning? And why should Lipski have wished to commit suicide? He had started a business, and was spending money on supplies. Can he really have been intending to poison himself with nitric acid? If he was, why would he bother attempting to steal money from Miriam Angel – especially when he could see that she was in the room, simply by looking through the window on the staircase? Would it not have been easier to wait until she went out to breakfast, as she always did, and to attempt to steal from the room then? Perhaps the door – as the defence suggested – would have yielded to a little pressure, if he had found it locked at all.

As ever, Stead could not help himself. This (one might say) 'adulterated article' – by-lined to 'A Compatriot who Laboured on his [Lipski's] Behalf' – has Stead's fingerprints all over it. Mr Buchner makes a reappearance, long after his evidence had been deemed useless, and so do meaningless allusions to 'the movements of Schmuss, the obliviousness of Rosenbloom ... and the breaking open of Mrs Lipski's box'.[109] We have hardly had a moment to consider the purposelessness of the extensive explorations which were made into the abrasions on Lipski's elbows, but the evidence suggests that they must have occurred either as he slipped down the bedroom wall in a swoon as he was being propped up by two police officers (if indeed he did), or as PC Kean stumbled while going down the staircase at 16 Batty Street, or in the squabble with the mob in the street. Nobody can hope to resurrect this clue now, as if somehow it might point to the guilt of Rosenbloom and Schmuss. But Stead – failing to let go – ensured that it, too, crept into what was still his most insightful article about the case. For all of Stead's pomposity, stubbornness and carelessness, real doubts existed about the veracity of the detail which Lipski gave in his own confession, and Stead, of course, was the man to articulate them. The

---

[109] *Pall Mall Gazette*, 22 August 1887.

article is reproduced here as Appendix XVIII – it is devoid of the radical gonzo characteristics of the 'conversion of the judge' article of 12 August – indeed, its author hides rather demurely behind a pseudonymous by-line – but it gives one a sense of what Stead could achieve in his more perspicacious moments.

XI.

All that remains is to try to understand why these sad events occurred. Perhaps the only plank of the defence platform which remained intact throughout the case was that no concerns had previously been raised about Lipski's conduct or personality. Criminal behaviour – even stealing, let alone homicide – was not consonant with his known character. 'Mr Hayward,' Godfrey Lushington noted, 'lays stress on his [Lipski's] respectability' (and also on 'his physical incapacity to inflict injuries on Mrs Angel', although the *Pall Mall Gazette*'s description of Miriam Angel as a 'very tall and powerful woman' hardly suggests that she ought to have been able to resist Lipski's assault – Lipski was five feet and six inches tall, weighing nine stones, and had taken her by surprise; by the same token, Schmuss, whom Hayward thought had overwhelmed his client, and whom he described as 'a tall powerful man', was five feet and six inches tall, and Rosenbloom 'a smaller man').[110] For all Mr Hayward's complaints about the work of his barristers, Mr McIntyre had not omitted to impress upon the jury that Lipski was held to have 'an exemplary character'.[111] It is still difficult to know why someone like Lipski would abandon an apparently respectable existence to commit murder. The case was bereft of the usual ligatures binding a murderer to his victim – love, financial interest, jealousy, and so on. There was no evidence that Miriam Angel and Israel Lipski were even acquainted.

Elsewhere, I have argued that Lipski's offence was a proto-Modernist act, characterised by 'aspects of abstraction and futility which would be embraced by a generation whose outlook was eventually both shaped and epitomised by total war'.[112] By his own shaky account, he had 'long been tired' of his life, and, if so, perhaps it hardly mattered to him how he went out of it, eventually settling, almost by random allotment, on a gesture of meaninglessness to symbolise his *ennui* and his spiritual vacuity. In this sense, murder and suicide were much the same thing. Each route took him to the same destination, and each made the same dispiriting point about the purposelessness of life. Against this, it will be

---

110 TNA:PRO HO 144/201/A47465/139; *Pall Mall Gazette*, 17 August 1887; *Pall Mall Gazette*, 22 August 1887; TNA:PRO HO 144/201/A47465/14; TNA:PRO HO 144/201/A47465/22.
111 *Lloyd's Weekly Newspaper*, 31 July 1887.
112 Bell, Bond, Clarke & Oldridge, 177.

Introduction.

argued that a man who hoped to die would not have troubled himself to create a story exculpating himself from the crime of which he had been accused, and need not have denied his offence in court. There were, it is true, quicker and easier ways for a disaffected Lipski to obtain his desired ends.

But perhaps there is another explanation – one which was not offered at the time, with the defence team, and the *Pall Mall Gazette*, focusing on the flawed prospect of a reprieve, or even a pardon. We see, buried in the testimony, a clue which may lead us towards the very tentative view that Lipski was in an altered mental state, experiencing grandiose thoughts incompatible with the reality of his quotidian existence; for, on the day of his arrest, in his coat pocket, there was discovered a card reading, 'I. Lipski Limited Stick and Cane Dressers Protection Society'.

No other indication is available to suggest that Lipski was active in workers' rights or unionisation, though this was a familiar and well-documented aspect of the Jewish experience in the East End in the late nineteenth century. No witness testifies to Lipski's left-wing credentials, or even to his left-wing sympathies. Indeed, for the last few days before the murder, he had been an employer, not an employee. No doubt the 'stick and cane dressers' of the sweated industries operating in East London deserved representation – but nothing exists to show us that Lipski was capable of, or even interested in, organising it.

The 'I. Lipski Limited Stick and Cane Dressers Protection Society' was a delusion – it hardly merited a business card – it did not exist, and Lipski, as an employer, could scarcely have expected to manage a workers' co-operative. It may be thought that Lipski had the business card created because, before the murder interceded, he was hoping to launch a co-operative venture; maybe this was just another way of raising money, which was running terribly short, by subscription. It is equally possible that he had developed inflated beliefs about his own significance in the Jewish community in which he lived. By this reasoning, when these beliefs began to unravel on contact with reality, he undertook an insane act of unconsciously symbolic properties. Introducing a foreign substance into the body of Miriam Angel was an analogy for immigration, for pregnancy, for sexuality, for control – a contorted statement of outsider angst, or even a vicious expression of dominance directed – by proxy – at Kate Lyons, whose affections had, perhaps, slipped once, and might slip again. Most people reconcile themselves to the pain of existence without committing brutal exteriorisations of this variety. Someone in the grip of grandiose delusions, grating against a more mundane reality, may not subject himself quite so consistently to similar behavioural controls.

But this is the paradox of Lipski. I have suggested two distinctly polarised

Lipski.

explanations for his terrible crime: on the one hand, an inferiority complex marked by feelings of futility; and, on the other, a superiority complex mismatched to reality, with its dissonant effects leading to feelings of injustice and fury. All, or nothing at all. We will never know whether an insanity plea would have been successful, since the idea was never tested; but it must be possible to conjecture that he may have been in the grip of a mental disorder so severe that he was heedless to the nature and quality of his actions. We are some distance from the facts of the case, but this sort of speculative theory would seem to be all upon which those keen to exonerate Lipski can now rely.

Lipski's rabbi, Simeon Singer, who tended to the prisoner's spiritual welfare during his weeks in Newgate, came to wonder whether Lipski had martyred himself by his confession, believing that to do so would spare his community from anti-semitic reprisals for the murder.[113] Again, we will never know – although this last act of humanity, if that is what it was, may have originated in a mental space not so very far from the centres of grandiosity and hubris. Lipski slips the net – neither one thing nor the other, indefinable, ambiguous, even after his execution. His name was carried on the tongues of the residents of the East End for some time to come, but his formlessness demanded that he be reshaped in order to become useful. In January 1888, one Myer Jacoby of Umberston Street – parallel with Batty Street, and a little to the east – accused a tailor named Philip Solomons of having designs on one of his daughters. Jacoby went to Solomons's place of work. 'You Lipski!' he screamed. 'I'll murder you! What right have you to have my daughter?'[114] Jacoby did not murder Solomons, or even make any real attempt to do so, but the deployment of Lipski's name, and the character of Jacoby's anxieties, suggests that, for Jacoby at least, Lipski's offence had been a sex crime. The truth was that this was far from clear, but the idea that Lipski had sexually assaulted Miriam Angel must have been prevalent (and the known circumstances of her discovery, exposed from the chest down, must have contributed to this impression). Later the same year, Lipski's name attained infamy when it was apparently used by a man who was seen assaulting Elizabeth Stride (one of the women commonly thought to have been murdered by Jack the Ripper) in Berner Street, immediately to the west of Batty Street. Stride's body was discovered a quarter of an hour later, and the man who had witnessed the assault – Israel Schwartz, a resident of Ellen Street – was described by Inspector Abberline as being of 'strong Jewish appearance'. There was little doubt that Lipski had become an anti-semitic by-word, 'frequently used,' as Abberline wrote, 'as a mere ejaculation by way of endeavouring to

---

113 Friedland, 170-171.
114 *Lloyd's Weekly Newspaper*, 29 January 1887.

Introduction.

insult the Jew to whom it has been addressed'.[115] Similar 'ejaculations' had been registered in and around the same area since at least late July or early August 1887, and they did not depend on an accurate understanding of Lipski's crime, but on his availability as an unstructured, malleable allegory for sexual violence, or a hateful metonym for Jewishness.[116]

Of course, Lipski is as unfitting a representative of either of those concepts as he is of the Jewish social project in East London as a whole, or of the times and the social conditions in which he existed. His background and his circumstances disclose little to satisfactorily explain his actions. He is a man wrapped in a cruel mystery, and, despite the energy expended on his behalf, one justly convicted of a murder of particularly unpleasant properties.

But Miriam Angel's appalling sufferings ought not to be obscured by those once ascribed to him. She was laid to rest in West Ham Cemetery on 30 June 1887, and the hearse in which her body rested moved slowly away from St George in the East through 'narrow thoroughfares …thronged', as one newspaper put it, 'by an almost impassable crowd', lining the long route towards peace.[117]

****

In preparing this trial for publication, I have been grateful for the kindness, support and assistance of John Angel, Valerie Angel-Newstead, Kate Clarke, Nick Connell, David Green and Adam Wood.

---

115 TNA:PRO MEPO 3/140/221/A49301C.
116 Friedland, 118.
117 *Lloyd's Weekly Newspaper*, 3 July 1887.

Lipski.

SOURCES.

FROM THE COLLECTION OF THE PUBLIC RECORD OFFICE:
TNA:PRO CRIM 1/26/5
TNA:PRO HO 144/201/A47465
TNA: PRO HO 144/1540/A61535
TNA:PRO MEPO 3/140/221/A49301C

AVAILABLE ONLINE:
booth.lse.ac.uk
www.oldbaileyonline.org

SECONDARY SOURCES:
    Bell, N. R. A., Bond, T. N., Clarke, K., & Oldridge, M. W., *The A-Z of Victorian Crime* (Stroud: Amberley Publishing, 2016)

    Bowen-Rowlands, E., *Seventy-Two Years at the Bar* (London: Macmillan, 1924)

    Bresler, F., *Reprieve: A Study of a System* (London: George G. Harrap & Co. Ltd., 1965)

    Diamond, M., *Victorian Sensation* (London: Anthem Press, 2004)

    Fishman, W. J., *East End 1888* (originally published 1988; London: Hanbury, 2001)

    Friedland, M., *The Trials of Israel Lipski* (London: Macmillan, 1984)

    Gartner, L. P., *The Jewish Immigrant in England, 1870-1914* (London: George Allen & Unwin Ltd., 1960)

    Tennyson Jesse, F. (ed.), *Trial of Samuel Herbert Dougal* (Edinburgh: William Hodge & Company Ltd., 1928)

Leading Dates in the Israel Lipski Case.

1865		Birth of Israel Lobulsk in Warsaw.
Circa 1885		Israel Lobulsk emigrates to the United Kingdom and adopts the surname of Lipski.
1886	1 June	Isaac and Miriam Angel are married in Kolo
	Circa August	Isaac and Miriam emigrate to the United Kingdom.
1887	24 January	Lipski admitted to the London Hospital with a cut hand.
	Circa 20 June	Lipski leaves his employment at Mr Katz's factory.
	23 June	Richard Pittman begins to work for Lipski.
	25 June	Lipski persuades Simon Rosenbloom to leave Mr Katz's factory.
	27 June	Lipski hires Isaac Schmuss and Tartakowski.
	28 June	Murder of Miriam Angel.
		Arrest of Israel Lipski.
		Lipski admitted to hospital.
	29 June	Inquest on the body of Miriam Angel – first day.
	30 June	Funeral of Miriam Angel.
		Charles Moore identifies Lipski in hospital.
	1 July	Inquest on the body of Miriam Angel – second day.
	2 July	Lipski discharged from hospital and charged with the murder of Miriam Angel.
	9 July	Proceedings before magistrate – first day.
	16 July	Proceedings before magistrate – second day.
	22 July	Proceedings before magistrate – third day.
	29 July	Trial of Israel Lipski – first day.
	30 July	Trial of Israel Lipski – second day. Lipski convicted of the murder of Miriam Angel and sentenced to death.
	1 August	The *Pall Mall Gazette* writes that 'the trial of Israel Lipski leaves several points unsettled'.
	6 August	Home Secretary receives first petition from Mr Hayward, Lipski's solicitor.
	8 August	Mr Justice Stephen meets with Mr Hayward.
	10 August	Thomas Stevenson reports to the Home Office the discovery of nitric acid and sulphuric acid on Lipski's coat.
	11 August	Thomas Stevenson reports to the Home Office the discovery that Charles Moore's stock of 'nitric acid' is an 'adulterated article' consisting of sixty per cent sulphuric acid and forty per cent nitric acid.

Lipski.

	13 August	The *Pall Mall Gazette* reports the 'conversion of Mr Justice Stephen'.
		Home Secretary receives second petition from Mr Hayward.
	14 August	Death sentence respited for one week.
	15 August	Scheduled date of execution (respited).
	17 August	Emil Barsuch and Isaac Schmuss are interviewed at the Home Office.
		The *Pall Mall Gazette* reports that 'Rosenbloom has lost twenty-four pounds in weight'.
	18 August	Mr Buchner, chemist, of Houndsditch, makes a statement to Mr Hayward.
		Frederick Hopkins reports to the Home Office that no sulphuric acid can be found in Mr Buchner's stock of nitric acid.
	20 August	Isaac Schmuss is inveigled into a carriage and confronted by 'an old man' attempting to shore up Barsuch's discredited statement.
		Mr Hayward is notified that there are no grounds upon which the Home Secretary may interfere with Lipski's sentence.
	21 August	Lipski confesses to the murder of Miriam Angel.
	22 August	Execution of Israel Lipski at Newgate Prison.
		The *Pall Mall Gazette* publishes news of Lipski's confession under the headline, 'All's Well that Ends Well'.
1888	30 September	Israel Schwartz sees a man abusing Elizabeth Stride on Berner Street. He flees when the man shouts 'Lipski!' at him. Stride's body is later found and she is believed to be a victim of Jack the Ripper.

CENTRAL CRIMINAL COURT

Friday 29th and Saturday 30th July 1887

Before Mr Justice Stephen

The Queen
Against
Israel Lipski
For The
Wilful Murder
Of
Miriam Angel

Messrs Poland and Charles Mathews
conducted the prosecution.

Mr McIntyre QC with Mr Geoghegan
appeared for the defence.

Transcript of the notes of Messrs Barnett and Buckler,
shorthand writers to the court.
Rolls Chambers, 89 Chancery Lane.[118]

---

118   The transcript of the trial is found in TNA:PRO HO 144/201/A47465/16.

First Day – Friday 29 July 1887.

Opening Speech for the Prosecution.

Mr Poland, in opening the case said, the prisoner was indicted for the wilful murder of a young married woman named Miriam Angel.[1] The prisoner had lived at 16 Batty Street, Whitechapel, in which house there also resided the deceased and her husband. The prisoner was a stick maker, and he had engaged a boy named Pitman[2] and a man named Rosenbloom to assist him in that business. At 6 3[3] on the morning of Tuesday, June 28, the prisoner was seen in the yard of the house dressed. The husband of the deceased had gone to work at 6 o'clock. At 7 o'clock Rosenbloom came to work at the house, and the boy Pitman at 8 o'clock. The prisoner went to the shop of a general dealer in Backchurch-lane for the purpose of buying a vice and a sponge to be used in his business, and while there he asked what time an oil shop next door opened. Before the prisoner left the house a man named Schmusch[4] called and spoke to the prisoner about working for him. The prisoner told him to go up stairs and wait, which he did for some time, but finding the prisoner did not return he left. The prisoner went to the oil shop and purchased a pennyworth of nitric acid, which was used in his business. The prisoner returned to the house and asked the landlady to get him some coffee. The coffee was prepared, but as the prisoner was not present the landlady called out to him to come down and get it. The boy Pitman answered that the prisoner was not in his room. It was alleged that at that time the prisoner was in the deceased's room. Eventually, as nothing was heard of the deceased, some women lodgers in the house went up to her room on the first floor and called to her. Receiving no answer, and finding that the door was locked on the inside they burst the door open. The deceased was then found lying on the bed dead, with marks of nitric acid on her face and clothing. The alarm was given and a doctor was sent for. A medical man arrived and found that the deceased had been dead for about three hours, rigor mortis not having set in. As the death had been occasioned by nitric

Mr Poland

---

1   This account of Poland's opening statement is taken from *The Times*, 30 July 1887. The article was clipped by the governor of Holloway and Newgate prisons, Lieutenant-Colonel E. S. Milman, and retained by the Home Office in what is now TNA:PRO HO 144/201/A47465/5.
2   *Sic* in article. Should read: 'Pittman'.
3   *Sic* in article. Should read: '6.30'.
4   *Sic* in article. Should read: 'Schmuss'.

Lipski.

Mr Poland acid being poured down the throat of the deceased, search was made for the bottle which had contained the fluid. There was also a serious injury over the deceased's eyes. A man went under the bed for the purpose of looking for the bottle, and in doing so he touched a man's head. The prisoner was then found lying underneath the bed, and there were also marks about his mouth showing that he had taken some of the nitric acid. The bottle was discovered upon the bed. It was alleged on the part of the prosecution that the prisoner entered the deceased's room for some purpose, locked the door on the inside, and being discovered by the deceased it was suggested that he first battered her with his fist and then administered the nitric acid to her, when, finding that she was dead, he took a portion himself, but the quantity he took was not sufficient to occasion his death. A post mortem examination was made of the deceased, and it was found that she had died from suffocation caused by the nitric acid burning her throat. Mr Poland said it was clear that the prisoner could not have gone into the deceased's room with the door locked on the inside for any proper purpose. It was not suggested that the prisoner bought the nitric acid for the purpose of administering it to the deceased, but having it in his pocket at the time he used it. The prisoner was removed to the hospital, and through an interpreter he made a statement to the effect that on the morning in question a man spoke to him at the corner of Backchurch-lane about work; when he returned to the house he saw the man and another on the first floor, and they took him by the throat, opened his mouth, and poured some poison down, saying, 'That is the brandy you asked for'. They asked him whether he had any money, and he replied only the sovereign he had given for the brandy. They asked him where his gold chain was, and he said it was in pawn – they said, 'If you don't give us it you will be as dead as the woman'; they threw him down and put a piece of wood in his mouth – one of the men said, 'Don't you think he is quite dead', and the other answered, 'Yes, he does not want any more', and then they drew him under the bed and left him for dead. Mr Poland pointed out the improbable nature of this statement, and said that with reference to the sovereign spoken of by the prisoner he had asked the landlady to lend him 5s. that morning, but she refused. It was difficult to conceive a clearer case against the prisoner.

George Bitten GEORGE BITTEN, sworn and examined by Mr .[5]

You are a sergeant of the H division of police? — Yes. Number 23.
I believe you have experience in making plans, have you not? — Yes.
You have made three plans connected with the house in question,

---

5   Name omitted in transcript. Should read: Mr MATHEWS.

Mr. Harry Poland QC
Author's collection

First Day – Friday 29 July 1887.

which is the subject of this inquiry? — Yes.

The first of them shows the house on the outside, does it? — Yes, the illustration.

It is a house of three storeys, consisting of a ground floor, first floor, and second floor? — Yes.

The ground floor, I think, is composed of two rooms: one a bedroom, and behind it a kitchen? — Yes.

And there is a passage running along, through which you can get into the back yard without going into one or other of these rooms? — Yes.

Then there is a short staircase leading up to the first floor? — Yes.

Of seven or eight stairs only, I think? — About nine or ten.

And the first floor, again, is composed of two rooms: one front, and one back? — Yes.

Then there is another short staircase which leads to the top floor, and that is composed of one room? — One room only.

Can you tell the height of the first floor window from the pavement? — Twelve feet. That would be from the windowsill to the pavement.

You made a particular examination of that windowsill, did you not? — Yes.

Could you discover any marks on it? — None whatever.

As though it had been in any way roughly used? — No.

I pass now to the second of the plans you made, which is a plan of the interior of the first floor front bedroom, which was occupied by Mr and Mrs Angel. — Yes, that is the original plan.

That plan correctly shows the door by which you enter, does it? — Yes.

And the position of the bed? — Yes.

On 28 June? — Yes.

Can you tell me the height from the floor to the bed? — One foot, two inches and a half from the floor to the bedstead.

Fourteen and a half inches? — Yes.

Beneath that did you see a box which is called an egg box? — Yes.

What was the height of that? — Nine inches high.

So that there would be a distance between the top of that egg box and the bedstead of five inches and a half? — That is so.

Did you go up the staircase heading from the first floor to the second floor? — Yes.

It is a fact, is it not, that there is a small window through which you could look onto this bedstead from the staircase outside? — Yes, commanding a full view of the bed.

That window is correctly shown on the plan you have made? — Yes.

Are the coloured plans copies of the tracings? — Yes.

George Bitten

Lipski.

George Bitten

Mr Justice STEPHEN: The window is somewhat different. — It shows a muslin blind which was inside at the time of the occurrence. Since then it has been taken down.

Mr MATHEWS: Whatever there is against it, it looks out onto the staircase? — Yes, and being on the stairs you have a full view onto the bed.

That is as going up the stairs? — Yes, standing on the second step.

That muslin curtain was there? — Yes, but it is a very thin muslin, so you had just the same view.

Thin muslin, you say? — Very fine muslin.

Did you see in? — I saw through the muslin.

You could see through the muslin, and get, as you have said, a full view of the bed? — Yes.

And of anyone who was lying in it? — Yes.

Mr Justice STEPHEN [*referring to the plan*]: Is this a door at the foot of the bed? — No, merely an old panel.

I suppose this is a right angle, is it not? — Yes.

Mr MATHEWS: You have shown upon the plan how the head of the bed lay in the same direction as the front window? — Yes.

And it would seem to be very closely beside it? — Yes.

I do not know if your attention was particularly directed to the wall, as between the panelling on the one side and the head of the bed on the other? — I could not be positive on that point because the bed might have been moved.

Were there any nails on the wall? — There are some nails upon which some clothing was hanging.

Mr Justice STEPHEN: On the wall by which the bed stood? — Yes, at the foot of the bed the clothing was hanging. You may call it the partition, not the wall. The nails were in the partition.

Mr MATHEWS: Did you notice whether there were any nails on the wall running between the partition and the head of the bed? — No, I did not.

There is a third plan which you have prepared. That is a copy of the Ordnance sheet? — Yes.

Made to a scale of five feet to the mile? — Yes.

Showing Batty Street and the surrounding streets? — Yes.

Looking at that plan, tell me whether number 19 Batty Street is exactly opposite number 16? — Not exactly opposite – nearly to – more to than any other house in the street – within two or three feet.

From 19 you would be perfectly able to see 16, would you? — Yes.

What is the width of Batty Street? — Twenty-six feet, nine inches, from wall to wall.

First Day – Friday 29 July 1887.

George Bitten

I notice that one end of it runs to Commercial Road, and the other to a street called Fairclough Street. — Yes.

Going down Fairclough Street, you would come to Backchurch Lane? — Yes.

And at the corner of Backchurch Lane and Fairclough Street is Mr Lee's oil shop? — Yes.

How far distant is that from 16 Batty Street? — 229 yards.

Next door to Mr Lee's shop, on the same side of the way, is Mr Mark Schmidt's shop? — Yes, next door in Backchurch Lane.

That would be further off from 16? — Yes, adjoining.

I think, going to the Commercial Road end of Batty Street, you have shown on the plan Dr Kay's surgery? — Yes.

That would be almost at the corner of Commercial Street and Batty Street? — It is the corner of Batty Street, in Commercial Road.

You have shown Grove Street on the plan? — Yes.

About how far from Batty Street is that? — I have not measured the distance, I can tell you.

It is two streets off? — Yes.

Cross-examined by MR McINTYRE.

Let me have plan number 1. — This is the original plan [*handing it in*].

This is the outside elevation? — Yes.

When was that made? — At different times. I was on my holiday. I made it at different times.

When was it completed? — By the hearing at the police court.

You recollect the inquest. Was the plan made then? — No.

When was this made? — So as to be produced before the magistrate.

There were several hearings before the magistrate. Have you not got a date? — It was produced on the final hearing.

Completed? — It was completed, but Mr Sims objected to my putting a table in the room. He said he did not think it would be fair to put an article in the room, and that was taken out.

Were these plans complete at the time of the inquest? — No. The first one was: that has never been altered.

Do you mean the outside one? — No.

Then which? — The interior view.

Was this one completed before the inquest? — Yes.

And when was the last of the plans completed? — On the second hearing before the magistrate.

Is the partition in the bedroom in wood? — Yes.

I mean that which enclosed the bedroom, not the inner partition. — Yes.

Lipski.

George Bitten

Wood panelling? — Yes.

And is the panelling thin? — It is about a quarter of an inch panelling: it is inserted into it, about an inch and a quarter. Receptacle wood.

Isaac Angel

ISAAC ANGEL, sworn and examined (through an interpreter) by Mr MATHEWS.

Are you a boot riveter? — Yes.

Are you a native of Warsaw? — Some distance from Warsaw. From Poland.

Have you been about twelve months in England? — Ten months. Longer now: ten months at the time.

When you came to England were you accompanied by your wife, Miriam Angel? — Yes.

Who at that time was between twenty-one and twenty-two years of age? — Yes. Twenty-two.

About a week before Whitsuntide this year, did you go to live at 16 Batty Street, towards the end of May? — Yes.

And did you there occupy with your wife a room, which you furnished, in the first-floor front? — Yes.

Were you working at George Street, Spitalfields? — Yes.

And was it your custom to leave home to go to work about 6.30 every morning? — Sometimes 6.00, sometimes 6.30, sometimes 7.00. On that day, 6.15.

Up to this day – 28 June – had you known the prisoner to speak to? — I did not know him.

And to your knowledge did your wife know him? — Also not.

On the Monday night – 27 June – did you return home about 9.00? — Yes.

Did you see your wife? — She was waiting for me at the door.

Did she write a letter that night? — Yes.

About 12.30 or thereabouts, did she take it out in order to have it addressed? — After 11.00. 11.30.

Did you go to bed about twelve? — 11.30.

What did you drink with your supper that night? — She bought half a pint of beer.

Beer or stout? — Four ale.[6]

Did you drink it between you? — I alone.

Where was the glass put? — Left it on the table.

The table in the bedroom? — Yes, in my bedroom.

When your wife and you went to bed that night, was she in her usual spirits? — She was well.

---

6   Beer retailing at four pence a quart.

First Day – Friday 29 July 1887.

Isaac Angel

Next morning, about 6.15 was it that you got up? — At 6.00.

Did you speak to your wife whilst you were getting up? — Yes, I said, 'Here you are – here is your breakfast. What shall I prepare for your dinner?'

Well, there was some conversation between you. You left the house at what time? — 6.15.

Was your wife awake at the time you left the room? — Yes, she was awake when I went away.

Your wife was in bed when you left, was she? — Yes.

With her chemise or nightdress on? — Yes.

Did she seem perfectly cheerful and in her usual spirits? — She was well.

Did you notice the position of the table in the room at the time? — The table was at the window as usual. I said my prayers there. Her face was as splendid and red as that scarlet when I left her.[7]

Did you notice the condition of the blind at the window? — There was a curtain down, a curtain below, and the curtain was a little down.

The blind was not entirely drawn down? — No, not quite.

Was the window open or shut? — Closed.

Did you notice the top sash of the window as well as the bottom? — It was quite closed, the whole window.

Did you notice the egg box under the bed? — It is always under there. I did not observe it that morning, but it always did stand there.

Was there any top or cover to the egg box, or was it open? — Open.

Used you to use it to keep old clothes in? — Old washing and old clothes, dirty clothes, dirty linen.

Did you notice any coat lying on the floor by the bedstead? — All the coats hung on the wall and her clothes were on the chair.[8]

Then there was no coat lying on the floor? — No.

You say that you left some clothes, or a coat, hanging up on the wall? — My clothes and her clothes hung on the wall, and something covered the whole of the clothes to keep them clean.

That is, the wall running between the partition at the bottom of the bed and the head of the bed? — Yes. The bedstead is separated from the wall [*pointing to about nine to twelve inches*].

Mr Justice STEPHEN: The distance from the bed to the wall? — Yes, my lord.

Mr MATHEWS: Among the things of yours hanging on the wall, was there a coat which you produce here today? — Yes [*producing it*].

---

7   The witness gestured towards the judge's robe.
8   In his notes on the evidence, Mr Justice Stephen glossed this as 'her clothes on the floor'. It seems that he either misheard or overlooked the witness's answer.

Lipski.

Isaac Angel

That is it, is it? — Yes, and a pair of trousers.

Are they new or almost new? — No. I went to put on the best and I observed a stain or burns on the back of it this morning.

That is the coat and trousers? — Yes.

Were they almost new? — Yes. I have only been one Saturday in them myself. The vest is fellow to the trousers I have on: they match.

At the time you left them that morning were there any stains on them? — There were none. They were new, nearly.

You have since examined the coat and waistcoat and do you now find that there are some stains on them? — There is a stain or a burn on the waistcoat, on the back lining of the vest.

Mr MATHEWS: I think he is pointing out stains on the coat.

Mr Justice STEPHEN: On that coat, how many stains are there? — Two.

And on the waistcoat how many? — One.

And on the trousers? — Two.

Mr MATHEWS: All that time did you leave any bottle in the room? — I had no bottle except a little bottle in which I used to fetch brandy on the Sabbath.

Any such bottle as that did you leave behind you [*handing a bottle to the witness*]? — No, I have not got such a one in my room.

Mr Justice STEPHEN: I understand him to say that there was a stain on one of the clothes which he is now wearing and which he found out this morning? — No.

Mr MATHEWS: It was a vest which he discovered this morning? — The clothes I wear now are things I borrowed. They are not my own.

Did you shut the room door when you left the room this morning? — Yes, the same as usual.

Do you remember whether the key was in the door or anything about the key? — It was stuck in the lock inside.

Had you locked the door that night when you went to bed? — Yes.

Had you to unlock the door in order to get out? — Yes.

What kind of lock was it? A good lock? — I have lived there six weeks, and eight days after that they put the lock on, a new lock.

You said it was a good lock? — Yes.

And it worked properly, did it? — It locked well.

Was it your custom to come home to dinner about 2.00 in the day? — Yes.

When you were at your work, about 11.45 in the day, did one of the lodgers, Mrs Levy, come to you? — Nobody came to me.

How was it you were called home that day? — Mrs Levy came to me and said, 'Go home'.

Mr Charles Mathews QC
Author's collection

First Day – Friday 29 July 1887.

Isaac Angel

That would be 11.45, would it? — Yes.

In consequence of what she told you, did you go home? — Yes.

What time did you get there? — I ran there as quick as I could. I cannot tell the time.

Directly after? — Directly after. I left everything. I was eating lunch and ran there.

When you got home, did you find that your wife was dead? — Yes. They would not let me go into my own room.

Did you afterwards go into the room on that day? — No, not on the same day.

Your wife was six months gone in pregnancy was she? — Yes.

Cross-examined by Mr McINTYRE.

The lock was not put on by a locksmith, was it? — No, the landlord of the house.

He is a tailor, is he not? — I don't know.

Did I understand you to say that your clothes that were hanging up were covered over? — Yes, they were all covered.

When did you first discover the mark on your waistcoat? Do I understand you that it was this morning? — Today, before I came here.

When did you discover the marks that you say are on the coat? — On the same day that this matter happened.

Have the clothes been in your possession from that time to this? — When they took all the things out, they took them out too.

Who has had possession of them from that day to this? — At my father's, where I am living now.

Then did you take your clothes, on the same day, to your father's? — My sister and brother took the things.

And have you lived at your father's and away from that house from the day this happened to the present time? — Yes.

Philip Lipski

PHILIP LIPSKI, sworn and examined by Mr POLAND.

Do you understand English? — Yes.

Are you a tailor? — Yes.

Do you live at 16 Batty Street, Whitechapel? — Yes.

Do you occupy the ground floor? — Yes.

A parlour in front? — Yes.

And kitchen behind? — Yes.

Does your wife live with you? — Yes.

And seven children? — Yes.

About how old is the eldest child? — Fifteen.

On the first floor front, Mr and Mrs Angel lived? — Yes.

Lipski.

Philip Lipski

And in the back room, first floor, did Mrs Levy live, and Mrs Rubenstein? — Yes.

Mrs Rubenstein is related to you? — Yes, she is my mother.[9]

In the top room, the prisoner lived? — Yes.

He had lived with you before you came to Batty Street, in Batty's Gardens? — Eighteen months.

When did he come to live in Batty Street? — When I removed there.

Would that be 23 May? — I cannot tell the day.

Was it some time in May? — Yes.[10]

His room at the top was one room? — Yes.

Did he first of all pay you two shillings a week for it? — Yes.

Did he furnish it himself? — No, that is mine.

You let it furnished? — Yes.

Then when he wanted to use it as a workshop did he pay five shillings a week? — Yes.

Is he by trade a stick maker? — Yes.

Formerly he used to go out to work, and at this time was he establishing a workshop in that room upstairs? — Yes.

On Monday night before this happened you went to bed as usual? — Yes.

What time did you get up in the morning? — About 6.30.

Where did you go? — To the yard.

Did you see anything of the prisoner? — Yes, I saw the prisoner come down from upstairs, to the yard.

Is the closet in the yard? — Yes.

How was he then dressed? — In trousers and a shirt.

No shoes on? — No, no shoes on.

Or stockings? — No stockings.

Did he speak to you about anything? — No, he did not speak to me about anything, only I saw him looking onto the table.

Did he tell you what he was looking for? — Yes, a small piece of gas pipe.

A small piece of gas pipe. — Yes.

Did he say what he wanted it for? — I asked him, 'What are you looking for?' He said, 'For a piece of pipe'. I said I had seen a piece of pipe a couple of weeks ago, but I did not see it. I asked him what he

9   *Sic* in transcript. Mrs Rubenstein was, in fact, Mr Lipski's mother-in-law.

10 Note that in his evidence to the inquest into the deaths at the Hebrew Dramatic Theatre, given on 4 February 1887, Philip Lipski gave his address as '16 Batter Street', according to the mishearing of the court reporter for the *Evening Standard*. This indicates that he and his family (and Lipski) had lived at 16 Batty Street for more than a couple of months. There must have been some confusion in the questioning sequence. Isaac and Miriam Angel had moved into 16 Batty Street in late May 1887, not Lipski.

First Day – Friday 29 July 1887.

wanted it for. He said he wanted it to use for his sticks.

What became of him? Where did he go? — He went upstairs.

And did you go out to your work? — No, I went in the kitchen afterwards.

Shortly afterwards, did you go out to work? — No, I said my prayers and then went to work.

About what time was it when you went out? — About ten minutes or a quarter hour.

Was the street door unfastened? — I shut it after me when I went out.

About ten minutes or a quarter of an hour after you saw him looking for the pipe? — Yes.

Was your wife up at that time? — No.

She was in bed? — Yes.

And the children? Where were they? — Everyone was in bed, only myself, when I went out.

I think some time in the middle of the day – about 12.30 – you heard what had happened at the house and came home? — Yes.

Do you know at all, had the prisoner said anything to you about any person coming that Tuesday morning? — No.

You do not know at all? — No.

Cross-examined by Mr McINTYRE.

Had the prisoner fitted up his room for the purpose of this being a sort of workshop? — Yes.

He had put benches there? — Yes.

So that more than one person could work in the shop? — Yes.

You say he had lodged with you for about eighteen months altogether? — Altogether about two years.

Was he a well-behaved young man? — Oh, yes he was.

Steady and industrious? — Steady and honest so long as he was in my place.

Although he has the same name that you have, I believe he is not any relation of yours? — Oh, no, he is not.

No relation at all? — No.

Do you know that he was engaged to be married to a young woman? — Yes.

And had been engaged for some time? — Yes. I cannot tell you how long.

You know about the lock being put on, don't you, to this room? — Yes.

Was it put on by a man who was a retired tailor, Mr Peters? — That is my landlord.

Was it he who put the lock on? — Himself.

Philip Lipski

Lipski.

Philip Lipski Do you know he was not a locksmith but a retired tailor? — Yes, he told me some time that he was a tailor.

Simon Rosenbloom SIMON ROSENBLOOM, sworn and examined (through an interpreter) by Mr POLAND.

Do you live at 27 Philpot Street, Commercial Road? — 37.

Are you a native of Poland? — Yes.

And have been in England something over eighteen months? — Yes, not quite eighteen. Not a twelvemonth.

Do you work as a stick maker? — Yes.

At one time did you work for a Mr Marks Katz?[11] — Yes.

Of Watney Passage, Commercial Road? — Yes.

During the time you were working there, was the prisoner working in the same employment? — Yes.

Did the prisoner continue to work there up to Monday 20 June or thereabouts? — Till the jubilee week.

And was the boy Pittman also employed at Mr Marks Katz's? — Yes.

On Saturday 25 June, the Saturday in jubilee week, did you meet the prisoner? — The same Saturday of the jubilee week.

What conversation passed between you? — He said that he had made for himself a workshop and he said, 'You come to me to work'. He did not earn much at Mr Marks Katz's. He said he would give me regular wages and I went to work at his place on Tuesday morning at 7.00.

Had you been to Lipski's on the Sunday before the Tuesday? — Yes, and they were making samples.

It was then arranged, was it, that you should come on the following Tuesday at 7.00 to work? — Yes.

And at 7.00 on the Tuesday morning, the twenty-eighth, did you go to the front door of 16 Batty Street and knock at it? — Yes.

What time was it you got there? — 7.00.

Who opened the door to you? — He came down having been at work and he opened the door.

How was he dressed? — Trousers, shirt and bare-footed, as they go to work.

Did you go into the house and go with him up to the top floor? — Yes.

Was anybody else there then besides yourself and the prisoner? — Only he and myself.

Did he give you some work to do? — Yes, he gave me points to bend.[12]

Handles, or what? — They were not then made. They were in a new

---

11 The transcript gives 'Mr Macartz'.
12 The judge's notes, held in TNA:PRO HO 144/201/A47465/7, say, 'He gave me "Spitze" (for handles)'.

First Day – Friday 29 July 1887.

Simon Rosenbloom

state.

Were they to be put on the top of the sticks? — On the top, handle.

Had they to be filed? — Yes, I filed them.

And did the prisoner at that time commence to do some work himself? — He commenced to work, but only worked for a few minutes.

At that time was there one vice in the room? — Yes, there was one in the room.

Was there only one? — One: the second one he went to buy.

What did he say before he went out to buy the second vice? — He said, 'There will come another man, a filer, and he will require another vice'.

Anything more? — He would go and buy a sponge for the boy to varnish with.

Did he say anything more about the filer? — No.

Did he not say anything as to who had recommended him? The filer? — He only said that he would come to the work and that was all.

Then did the prisoner put on any clothes before he went out? — He put on his boots, a shirt, coat and a hat.[13]

Was it such a coat as that that he put on [*handing one to the witness*]? — Yes, such a one as that is the coat, and that is the same hat. There were no stains on the coat then.

Did you hear him shut the street door as he went out? — No, that I did not hear.

After a short time, did the prisoner return? — Yes, he came back and said, 'The shop is still closed'.

Did he say what shop was still closed? — That Mark's, where he went to buy the vice.[14]

About how long was he out? — I cannot tell because there was no clock.

Could you say about? — I cannot tell.

When he came back, did he begin to do any more work? — No, he went up and down the stairs till the boy returned.

And did no work? — No.

Until the boy came? — Until the boy came to work.

About what time was it that the boy came? — 8.00 by the clock.[15]

---

13   Lipski was said to be wearing a shirt when he opened the front door to Rosenbloom. Rosenbloom told the inquest that Lipski 'put on his boots and a black jacket and hat' (TNA:PRO CRIM 1/26/5).

14   It seems likely that the witness indicated Mark Schmidt.

15   A manuscript annotation on the transcript reads, 'There was no clock'. Rosenbloom's evidence at the inquest was that 'the boy told me it was 8.00 a.m.' (TNA:PRO CRIM 1/26/5).

Lipski.

Simon Rosenbloom

Was the prisoner upstairs in the room when the boy arrived? — No, he came up directly after the boy came, and he said, 'I am going to buy a sponge for the boy to varnish'.

Was that the boy Pittman? — I don't know his name.

[*The witness Pittman was here called into court.*]

Is that the boy you have been speaking of? — Yes, that is the boy.

Then where did the prisoner go? — He went to buy for the boy a sponge.

Was he dressed in the same way as he had been when he went out on the last occasion? — Yes.

After the prisoner had gone, do you remember a man coming up into the room? — After he had gone away the last time, a man came. The boy was there.

[*The witness Schmuss was here called into court.*]

Is that the man who came? — Yes.

Had you some conversation with that man? — He did not speak much, as he did not stay long.

But what he did speak, did he speak in your own language? — Yes, Yiddish.[16]

Did that last man wait there a little time? — He did not.

Did that man wait there a little time? — Yes.

About how long? — I could not say how long: either fifteen minutes or longer. I cannot tell.

During that time, did the prisoner return? — No.

The prisoner did not return, and the other man went away, did he?

[*Mr McINTYRE objected to this.*]

Did the prisoner return during that time or after that? — No: he did not return again.

And did Schmuss leave? — Yes, he went away.

Where was the boy when Schmuss went away? — With me in the room.

When did the boy leave? How long after the man left did the boy leave? — I cannot think. There was no clock.

Cannot you say about? — I cannot say whether it was an hour or an hour and a half.

When the boy left, how long did he remain away before he returned? — I cannot say.

Could you say about how long? — I cannot say. I won't tell any lies.

But the boy did go away for his breakfast? — Yes.

During the whole of that morning, did you leave that upstairs room at

---

16   Given as 'Yueddish' in the transcript.

First Day – Friday 29 July 1887.

all? — When I heard the disturbance downstairs I went down.

Up to then, had you left the room from the time you went there at 7.00 in the morning? — From seven till the time I heard the disturbance.

After the prisoner went out the second time, did he ever return to the room? — I did not see him any more.

You have spoken just now of the disturbance you heard. Could you tell me about what time it was that you heard the disturbance downstairs? — The mother-in-law said downstairs it was 11.00.

Well, some time afterwards. You don't know the hour yourself? — Yes.

What disturbance was it you heard downstairs? — Clapping, knocking and screaming, and the boy ran down the stairs.

Mr Justice STEPHEN: He has not told us yet when the boy came back. He went to his breakfast: did he return? When? — I cannot think.

Mr POLAND: Did he come back?[17] — Yes.

And when he came back did he come up into the room at the top of the house? — Yes.

And did he stay there with you until you heard the disturbance downstairs? — Yes. I was filing the handles.

When you heard the screaming and the knocking, did you and he go downstairs together? — Yes.

And did you go together or nearly together into the front room, first floor, and there see Mrs Angel lying dead on the bed? — Yes, and the women were inside, in the room.

Simon Rosenbloom

Cross-examined by Mr McINTYRE.

How long were you in Lipski's room on the Sunday? — Not half an hour. I was not there long.

When you came on the twenty-eighth, that was Tuesday, was it? — I cannot write … it was a Tuesday in the morning.

Could you tell me how long you were there before the boy came? — I cannot tell. There was no clock.

Were there these the sort of thing that you were working on [*produced*]? — Yes, those and other forms.

Was what you were doing fine filing? — Yes.

Does fine filing make much noise or not? — You hear a little, but not much.

What was the boy doing? — He did nothing. He was standing.

---

17 The transcript attributes this question, and all subsequent questions asked during Rosenbloom's examination by the prosecution, to Mathews. This must be an error, and 'Poland' has been preferred here.

Lipski.

Simon Rosenbloom

The boy did nothing at all while he was there? — No, he had gone for the sponge for the boy to varnish.

And you say the boy did nothing at all? — He was doing nothing. He was standing.

How much work did you do that morning? — I cannot remember whether it was two dozen or not … a two dozen.

How long does it take to fine file a thing like this? — I cannot say. I am not a filer. I could only file a little.

I thought you did file two dozen or about two dozen? — Yes, but I cannot do many. I am not active at the work.

You recollect the man coming? — Yes.

Did you speak to him in your own language – not in English, but in Yiddish? — Yes.

In English? — No, I cannot speak English.

Did you know him before? — No, I did not know him.

Did you ever see him before? — No, that was the first time I had seen him, when he came up.

Did you tell the boy that you had known him before? — I did not say that to the boy, because I cannot speak English.

Do you mean to say that you did not speak to the boy in English? — No. I could swear that I did not speak with him in English.

Not a word? — No.

Did you tell the boy that the prisoner had gone for a vice? — No, I did not say to the boy at all.

Just be careful about this. Did you not, in English, tell the boy that Lipski had gone to buy a vice? — No, I did not.

And did you tell the boy that you knew the strange man that came before? — No, I did not say that to the boy at all.

And that you had been in the man's company before? — I did not say that. I could swear it.

Did you see the man before he came into the room? — I only saw him in the room for the first time.

I think you have said – not today – that you heard no knock at the door when the man came? Before the magistrate? — No, I did not say.

Did you hear any knock when the strange man came, when the second man came? — No, I did not hear.

Mr Justice STEPHEN: Did you put it to him that he said he did hear?

Mr McINTYRE: No. You did not hear a knock when the boy came, did you? — No.

Were the windows and the door of the room in which were, open? — Yes, the window was a little pulled up, and the door a little open.

Did you have breakfast in the room belonging to Lipski? — Yes, I had

First Day – Friday 29 July 1887.

Simon Rosenbloom

bread and butter, and the boy saw me.

In this business of stick maker, is shellac used? — Shellac and varnish.

Is the shellac dissolved in spirits? — The shellac is put into the varnish.

But is it dissolved in spirits of wine? — No, they call it varnish.

They call it varnish, don't they, when the shellac is dissolved in the spirits? That makes it varnish, does it not? — In the varnishing.

Mr Justice STEPHEN: How do you make varnish for the sticks? — I do not know.

Do you know what they do with shellac? — I was told by my old master that they put the shellac into the varnish.

Do you know what the varnish is made of? — No.

Mr McINTYRE: Have you been engaged in this business of stick making any length of time? — Since I have been here.

How long? — About eight months.

Don't you know that brandy is also used for the purpose of dissolving shellac? — I do not know anything about the brandy.

Did not Lipski ask you to get some brandy? — No, he did not ask me.

Do you know whether Lipski used to take brandy in his coffee for breakfast? — I do not know that.

Did not Lipski give you a sovereign to buy a quartern of brandy for him?[18] — He did not give me a farthing. I could swear it.

And did not Lipski tell you, when he gave the sovereign to buy the small quantity of brandy, that he wanted change? — He never said anything to me. He did not send me for brandy. I went upstairs and I went to work.

You have been working with Lipski, I think, for some time. Do you know that he had a watch and chain? — He did not say so to me.

Do you know that he had? — No, I do not know.

Have you not seen him on the Sabbath wearing a watch and chain? — No.

What have you seen him with? — He had a sort of pin there [*putting his hand to his neck*].

Be careful and think how you answer this question. Were not you and the strange man standing at the door of Mrs Angel's when Lipski came back? — No, no, I did not know who lived down there.

Mr Justice STEPHEN: Ask him this again, that there may be no mistake.

A JUROR: Repeat the question, please.

Mr McINTYRE: Were you not, and the strange man, standing by Mrs Angel's door when Lipski returned? — No, I was not.

---

18 That is, a quarter of a pint.

Lipski.

Simon Rosenbloom

Were you there standing by Mrs Angel's door when Lipski returned? — No.

And was not the door of Mrs Angel's partly open at that time. — No. I did not see.

Will you swear that you were not there when the door was partly open? — Yes, I will swear. In the Temple I will swear it.

Mr Justice STEPHEN: Did you at any time that morning stand before Mrs Angel's door? — No, I was not before the alarm took place.

Mr McINTYRE: Were you not standing just outside the door and the strange man just inside the door of Mrs Angel's room? — No, I was not out, and I had not seen the man before he came up.

Did you have any small parcel in your hand when Lipski came up the stairs the last time? — No, I did not have any parcel. I can swear.

And did you not throw the parcel down and say to the strange man, 'He is here. Come on!' as Lipski was coming up? — I can swear I had no packet and I saw no packet.

Did you say, 'He is here. Come on!'? — That is all lies. I did not say that.

Did not the strange man catch hold of Lipski? — No.

And did you yourself catch hold of Lipski by his two hands or his wrists? — I did not catch hold of him at all. That is all lies.

And did not you and the other man throw him down?

Mr Justice STEPHEN: Is not this useless? I can always allow a prisoner to make a statement.

Mr McINTYRE: Did not you yourself force open Lipski's mouth? — No, I did not. I am not such a strong man as to do that.

Whilst the other man held him? — The other one was not there. All lies, all lies!

What part of Poland do you come from? — From Plotz.

Is that near Warsaw? — Seventeen or eighteen Polish miles.

Richard Pittman

RICHARD PITTMAN, sworn and examined by Mr MATHEWS.

You live at number 2 White's Gardens, Star Street, Commercial Road? — Yes.

How old are you? — Sixteen.

How long have you known the prisoner? — About a month. I was working at the place where he worked.

About a month before 28 June? — Yes.

Do I understand you to say that you had been at work with him at Mr Marks Katz's?[19] — Yes.

---

19   The transcript gives 'Mr Martz'.

Mr Justice James Fitzjames Stephen
Author's collection

First Day – Friday 29 July 1887.

And he was employed there? — Yes.
Do you remember seeing him on Wednesday night, 22 June? — Yes.
He spoke to you, did not he? — Yes.
Did he speak to you in English? — Yes.
What was it that he said? – He said, 'Dick, come along with me. I have got some work for you.' I said, 'What, to work for Mr Marks Katz?' He said, 'No, for myself, because I am going into business for myself'.
And did you not agree to go and work for him? — Yes, sir.
And did you go with him that night to number 16 Batty Street? — Yes.
And he showed you where you were to go to work when you came? — Yes.
I think you went to that same house next day, Thursday? — Yes.
Which day did you go to work for him first? — Thursday, the twenty-third.
You went home to your mother at night? — Yes.
You lived with your parents at White's Gardens? — Yes.
You came again, I think, on the Friday? — Yes.
Saturday would be the Jewish Sabbath; and on Monday you came again, did you? — Yes.
Now we come to the morning of Tuesday 28 June. Before we get to that date, and after you had come on the premises, do you remember having gone to Mr Lee's shop to make purchases for the prisoner? — Yes.
What for? Things for the workshop? — Yes.
How often did you go, should you say? — About nine times to both places.
Who told you to go there? — Lipski, and I went along with him.
Did you always go with him, or sometimes alone? — I always go with him.
And he would make the purchases in your presence? — Yes.
Now let us go to the Tuesday morning, the twenty-eighth. What time did you get to number 16 that morning? — 8.00.
That was your regular hour for coming, was it? — Yes.
Did you go upstairs to the room on the top floor? — Yes.
Was the prisoner there when you got there? — No.
Anybody else? — Simon Rosenbloom.
Had you seen Rosenbloom before that morning? — No.
After you had got up there, and were there with Rosenbloom, how long did you stay there before you left? — About an hour.
You arrived at 8.00 and stayed there till somewhere about 9.00? — Yes.
During that time, did the prisoner come into the room? — Yes, sir.

Richard Pittman

Lipski.

Richard Pittman

Did he say anything when he came into the room? — He said, 'I have been to buy a vice, and the shop was shut up'.

Anything more that you remember? — Yes: in a little while after that he went out again and said, 'I am going to have another try and see if I can buy the vice'.

And then did he go out? — Yes.

Can you tell how he was dressed at that time? — Yes, he had an old hat on and an old coat.

Look behind you and see if the coat and hat were such as those? — Yes, this is the coat. It looks something like it. It had a little white on it when he went out.

It was such a coat as that? — Yes.

Is the hat there? Was it such a hat as that that he wore? — Yes.

Can you tell me at all about what time it was he went out? — About 9.05.

When Lipski went out? — Yes.

After he had gone, do you remember any strange man or any third person coming up into the room? — Yes, sir.

[*The witness Schmuss was here called into court.*]

Look at that man. Is that the man who came up? — Yes.

Did he speak to Rosenbloom? — Yes.

They had some talk together, had they? — Yes.

Was it in a language that you understood? — No.

How long did Schmuss remain? — About five minutes, no longer.

And then what became of him? — He went out.

Did you go out after him? — No, before him.

You have just said that Schmuss remained about five minutes and then went out? — Yes.

Were you there when Schmuss left? — No.

You left him behind you? — Yes.

You left, going downstairs, leaving Rosenbloom and Schmuss upstairs? — Yes.

You went home to breakfast, did you? — Yes.

About how far off are White's Gardens from this house in Batty Street? — About a quarter of a mile.

You walked, of course? — Yes.

Can you tell me what time you got home? — No.

Your mother is here, I think? — Yes.

You saw your mother when you got home? — Yes.

Had your breakfast? — Yes.

And came back to Batty Street? — Yes.

Did you come back straight? — No. I had a little game in the street

First Day – Friday 29 July 1887.

and then went back.

How long were you playing in the street? — About a quarter of an hour.

And then you went back? — Yes.

When you went back, did you go up to the workshop? — Yes.

Who was there at that time? — Simon Rosenbloom.

Anyone else? — No, sir.

And did you stay there with Rosenbloom? — Yes.

How long? — About an hour.

And then what happened? Anything to call your attention downstairs? — In about half an hour, Lipski came in.

Half an hour after you got there, the prisoner came in, you say? — Yes.

Was Rosenbloom there still at that time? — Yes.

What did the prisoner say, if anything? — He did not say anything.

What did he do? — Nothing.

What became of him? — He stood still in the room.

How long did he remain? — About five minutes.

Standing still? — Yes.

Then what became of him? — He went out again.

As though to go downstairs? — Yes.

How was he dressed at that time? The same as you had seen him before? — Yes.

And was much the same as you had seen him before? — Yes.

Did you notice anything peculiar about him? — No, sir.

And after he left did you see him again that morning, up to hearing the disturbance? — No.

You remained in the room with Rosenbloom? — Yes.

And about what time was it you first heard any disturbance? — About eleven o'clock.

And you went down with Rosenbloom, did not you? — Yes.

What was the disturbance you heard? — The people were saying that a woman was dead.

Did you hear any knocking? — No.

Did you go down with Rosenbloom? — Yes.

And into the room on the first floor? — Rosenbloom went into the room and I went downstairs.

Did you go into the room on the first floor all that time? — No.

He went in? — Yes.

Cross-examined by Mr McINTYRE.

You were in the room with Rosenbloom for some time. Did you speak together? — Yes, sir.

Richard Pittman

Lipski.

Richard Pittman

Did he speak to you in English? — No, sir.

What did he speak to you in? — He kept on saying, 'Get on with your work, don't be knocking about like this'.

He said that in English, did he? — Yes.

What work were you doing? — Knocking with the hammer.

What were you doing with the hammer? What were you knocking? — Knocking at the place where all the tools were.

Were you knocking at the sticks, or just playing with the hammer? — Playing with it.

Was Rosenbloom talking to the strange man who came in while he was there? — Yes.

Did you ask him whether he knew the man? — No.

Did he say whether he knew the man? — Yes.

What did he say? — I did not understand if he knew the man. The reason why I *thought* he knew the man was speaking in his own language.

Mr Justice STEPHEN: But did he tell you that he knew the man? — No, sir.

Mr McINTYRE: Did Rosenbloom tell you that he knew the man? — No, sir.

Did not Rosenbloom say to you, 'I know that man. I have been in his company before'? — Yes, sir.

He did say that? — Yes.

Mr Justice STEPHEN: Just now you said that he did not tell you. Now you say he did tell you? — I forgot my words.

Do you now remember that Rosenbloom did say that? Did he? — Yes.

Mr McINTYRE: And did he tell you that speaking the same language you did, which we call English? — Yes [*crying*].

Did he also tell you a second time that he knew the man a little time? — Yes, sir.

Did he tell you that twice? — Yes.

Did Rosenbloom tell you that Lipski had gone for a vice? — Yes.

Were those the words that he said in English? — Yes.

'Lipski has gone for a vice'? — Yes.

When you went to breakfast, you say it was about 9.00? — Yes.

Did you leave the room door open when you left? — Yes.

The room where Rosenbloom was sitting and working? — Yes, because there was a bed there – a sofa.

Mr Justice STEPHEN: What, to keep the door open, do you mean? — Yes, sir.

Mr McINTYRE: Did the filing make much noise, or only a little noise? — Much noise.

Could you hear the people in the street speaking? — Sometimes.

First Day – Friday 29 July 1887.

When you are doing fine filing, does it make much noise? — No.

Now, recollect: was not Rosenbloom doing fine filing that morning? — Yes.

That did not make much noise, then? — No.

I suppose while you were hammering you did make more noise than the filing? — Yes.

Re-examined by Mr POLAND.

Do I understand you that the prisoner told you he was going to buy the vice? — Yes.

You have just told my friend that Rosenbloom told you. — Rosenbloom told me afterwards, when I came in at first at 8.00 – when I came in to work.

Told you what? — That he had gone to buy a vice and a sponge.

How did he speak to you? — In English.

What sort of English? — Half his own language and half our language. I just understood him.

Could you understand him always? — Not always, sir.

You said at first that you thought Rosenbloom knew this man that came because he spoke the same language. — Yes.

Is that right? — Yes.

Then you afterwards said that Rosenbloom told you he knew the man. Just say what he said to you. — He said, 'I know this man'.

As if he was speaking to you now, tell us what he said. — He said, 'I know that man because I have been in his company before, where he used to work'.

Did he say that all in English or part in the foreign language? — Half in English and half in his own language.

Mr Justice STEPHEN: Which part of it did he say in English? — He said as much English as his own language.

There are only a few words. Can you tell us which words he said in English, and which in his own language? — He had been in his own company before.

He said that in English, did he? — Yes.

Then in what language did he say, 'I know that man'? — He said it in half-English.

But you said that the half of all he said was in his own language? — Yes.

Do you mean that he talked like a foreigner, or a man who did not know English, or did not know much? — He did not know much of English. He just told me what I could understand.

You could make out what he meant? — Yes.

Richard Pittman

Lipski.

Richard Pittman

Mr POLAND: Could you make out all that he meant? — Yes.

The part that was in English, of course, you understood? — Yes.

But the part that was in the foreign language you could not understand, I suppose? — No.

Are you quite clear that they did speak together in a foreign language? — Yes.

Did you think they knew each other when they spoke in the foreign language? — Yes.

Before you were told anything? — Yes.

When the prisoner, you say, came in – on the occasion that he said nothing – did nothing, stood still, and went out of the room again --? — Yes.

The prisoner spoke English? — Yes.

Do you mean that he said nothing at all? Just think what you are saying. Do you mean that he just walked into the room when you were both there, said nothing, did nothing, stood still and then went out of the room again? — He stood thinking to himself about something.

Did you speak to him? — No.

Did Rosenbloom speak to him? — No.

Not a word? — No.

None of the three said a word? — No, sir.

That is, not a word said by either of the three? — No.

Just tell me what part of the disturbance about 11.00 you first heard. What kind of disturbance did you first hear? — People screaming downstairs.

You are sure that was the first of it? — Yes.

When you were before the magistrate, did that gentleman sitting there ask you a number of questions? — Yes.

Mr Geoghegan asked you a number of questions? — Yes.

After you had been examined first of all? — Yes.

And you answered him? — Yes.

Mr Justice STEPHEN: I want to read you a bit that is written down: what you said, you know. I want to read you what you said. 'The prisoner came in' – that is Lipski – 'about 9.00. He had his coat and hat on: black coat, and black hat. He said, "The shop is shut up and I have been to get the vice."' — Yes.

'He stayed about five minutes. He said, "I am going out to see if the shop is open."' Is that right? — Yes.

Was that the last time you saw him? — No.

He came in again afterwards? — Yes.

About what time was it that you saw him again? — About 10.00.

What you have been telling us now ... You say he came into the room

First Day – Friday 29 July 1887.

and said nothing and went out again. Do you say that that was about 10.00? — Yes.

I see that before the magistrate you said 10.30. Have you anything to enable you to tell the time? — I don't know the time exactly, but I thought it was about ten.

But you can't say to a little, one way or the other? — No.

Recross-examined by Mr McINTYRE: When you came at 8.00, was the door open? — On the jar. It was not bolted nor nothing. I just pushed it and it came open.

The house door? — Yes.

ANNIE PITTMAN, sworn and examined.

Do you live at 2 White's Gardens, Star Street, Commercial Road? — Yes.

And are you the wife of Richard Pittman? — Yes.

The last witness is your son? — Yes.

Is he fourteen years old? — Yes.

You know that he was working for the prisoner? — Yes.

Used he to come home to breakfast? — Yes.

On this Tuesday morning, 28 June, can you say at what time he came home to breakfast? — It was a little after 9.00.

Can you say how much after? — Well, about 9.15.

How long did he remain there with you? — He did not remain there another quarter of an hour or twenty minutes at the outside, and then he left to return to his work.

I suppose you have no means of fixing the exact time? — No.

You cannot say nearer than you have? — No.

MARK SCHMIDT, sworn and examined by Mr POLAND.

Do you keep a general store? — Yes.

At 94 Backchurch Lane? — Yes.

What countryman are you? — A Russian Pole.

How long have you kept that shop? — Eight years.

Do you know a great many of the foreign Jews who come over to this country to work? — I can't say a great many. I know some of them.

They come to your shop sometimes? — Yes, not very much.

On Monday 27 June, were you at your shop? — Yes.

What time was it? Did you see the prisoner that day? — Yes. It was in the afternoon.

Had you known him before? — I did know him.

For how long had you known him? — I suppose for a year before.

When he was in your shop, were there some other men there? — There

Lipski.

Mark Schmidt

was a couple of workmen there.

Was one of them a man named Schmuss? — Yes.

What did the prisoner say to you on that afternoon? — He asked me if I could send him a man to work.

Did he say to do what work? — I knew that.

What was it? — Stick maker.

You knew the prisoner was a stick maker? — Yes.

Did he say what part of the work this man was to do? — Filing.

What did you then say to him? — I said, 'There are four men here. You can have which you like.'

Who were the four men? Schmuss was one? — Yes.

Who were the other three? — I can't tell their names.

Have you seen them outside? — Yes.

Do you know their names now? — Yes, but not from memory.

Are they here? — Yes. [*Schmuss and Rosenbloom were here called into court.*[20]] Barsuch is not here.

[*Barsuch was here brought in custody from the gaol.*]

Are those three of them? — Yes, they always came to me. I can't tell exactly this time. Those are three of them.

Which is Schmuss? — The middle one.

Look at Barsuch. Is that one of them? — Yes, one. He did not work for me; only he was with them together.

When the prisoner asked you about this man who he wanted as a filer, what did you tell him? — I told him, 'You can have one of those four'.

Then what took place? Did you know what he said to them? — I did not send them. He went outside with them and talked with them. I don't know what they talked.

Did you see him afterwards, the same afternoon? Did he come into the shop again? — No, I saw no more of him.

Did you see anything of the four men? — Yes, they came tomorrow as well, and they were there all day Monday afternoon.

On the following day, Tuesday morning, did the prisoner come to your shop? — Yes.

What time did you open? — I was open by 7.00, and I think he came about 8.00.

Did you see him? — Yes.

What did he ask for? — To buy a vice.

Did you show him some? — I did: a few.

---

20   *Sic* in transcript, but Shmuel Robinski, rather than Rosenbloom, was called into court at this point, alongside Schmuss, Tartakowski and Barsuch. See also the evidence of Isaac Schmuss, below.

First Day – Friday 29 July 1887.

Mark Schmidt

What price did you mention? — I suppose it was the last for three shillings and sixpence.

Did he make an offer? — Three shillings and threepence.

Did you take that? — I did not want to take it. I left him outside the shop.

Before he left your shop … Is your shop next door to Mr Lee's, the oil shop? — Yes. He asked me when did the oil shop open. I told him 8.30.

Did you see where he went? — No.

Did you see him outside your shop? — Yes. He was talking about the vice.

But afterwards? — I did not see him after?

When did you last see him? — When he offered me for the vice. He was then outside the shop and there I left him.

About what time was that? — I suppose it only took about five minutes altogether.

About what time was it you last saw him? — About 8.00. I don't know exactly.

Later in the day, were you outside number 16 Batty Street. — I was passing.

What time was that? — I don't know.

Morning or afternoon? — In the morning: about 11.00, or 10.00. I don't know.

Did you see anything of Mrs Rubenstein at the door? — No.

On that Tuesday, did you see Schmuss again? — Yes.

What time? — About 12.00.

Where did you see him? — At my shop.

He came to your shop? — Yes.

You must not say what was said but, at that time, did you know that Mrs Angel had been killed? — I heard it.

You had heard the report that Mrs Angel was killed? — Yes.

Schmuss was in the shop about what time? — About 12.00.

Did you have some conversation with him? Talk to him? — Yes.

Was that talk about Mrs Angel's death? — Yes. I told him.

How often did you see him after that Tuesday? — I saw him about five or six days.

Every day? — Yes, he was there every day. He came to ask for a job.

Do you know that he left London? He came and said goodbye to you? — Yes, he told me that he should go to Birmingham.

Do you understand stick making? Have you been a stick maker? — Yes: seventeen years I was a stick maker.

Do you know what *aqua fortis* or nitric acid is used for? — Some use it for sticks. I do not know what sort it is – if it is *aqua fortis* or vitriol. I

Lipski.

Mark Schmidt

do not know what it is. I do not use it.

But is *aqua fortis* or nitric acid at all used in the stick trade?

Mr Justice STEPHEN: Do people make any use of *aqua fortis* in making sticks? — Yes, they do.

Cross-examined by Mr McINTYRE.

That depends upon the sort of stick, I suppose? — Yes. They use it – not everyone. It is used for staining or burning out sometimes.

You were examined, I think, before the coroner and before the magistrate. — Yes.

Did you tell anything about what you have been asked about Schmuss on those occasions? — I did not tell.

When you saw Lipski on the morning of the twenty-eighth, was anything said about the sponge? — No.

Just recollect. — No.

Are you sure? — Nothing at all.

Only about the vice? — Only about the vice.

You seem to know these four men. What are they? What is their business? — Lock makers. They make locks and do general jobs.

What we call locksmiths, are they not? — Yes.

All of them? — Yes. They told me that. I do not know.

Re-examined by Mr POLAND.

Did you know Schmuss by name? — No, I did not.

Isaac Schmuss

ISAAC SCHMUSS, sworn and examined by Mr MATHEWS, through the interpreter.

Do you come from Elizabethan Graff, near Odessa? — Yes, in Russia.

Up to recently, have you been working at 42 Gough Street, Birmingham? — Yes. I am lodging at that place in Birmingham.

And did you work in Ince Street, Birmingham?[21] — Yes.

Are you a locksmith by trade? — Yes.

But have you been recently employed as a slipper maker? — Yes.

Did you come to England about seven or eight months ago? — Yes.

Among other places, did you go to Mr Schmidt's in Backchurch Lane in the hope of finding employment? — Yes, and also to work at jobs.

Did you meet there with other Russian Jews? — Yes.

Was Tartakowski one? — Yes.

And also Robinski? — Yes.

Do you remember being at Mr Schmidt's shop on a Monday afternoon? — Yes.

---

21   *Sic* in transcript. Should read: 'Inge Street'.

First Day – Friday 29 July 1887.

Were you there with Tartakowski and other persons? — Yes.[22]

Whilst there, did the prisoner come in? — Yes.

Did he speak to you, or to you all, as you stood there? — Yes.

What did he say? — He asked where they came from, and what trade they were. He asked what they were, and whether they wanted work.

What trade did you say you were? — I said I was a locksmith.

What did the prisoner say to that? — 'Do you think you can file sticks?'

What did you say? — I said, 'I will see. I never filed them. I will try.' He said, 'Come with me and I will show you the door, and tomorrow you will come to me, and I will engage you.'

Upon that, did you go with him to the door of number 16 Batty Street? — Yes.

And there did the prisoner tell you to come the next morning? — Yes.

At what time? — About 8.00.

After you left the prisoner, did you go back to Schmidt's? — I can't say certain; it appears to me I did go back.

And there did you see Tartakowski, that same day, after going to number 16? — I do not remember for certain whether I went back.

Do you remember going next morning, Tuesday the twenty-eighth, to Schmidt's? — Yes.

At what time? — 8.00.

Was Tartakowski there? — No, he had not come.

Did you wait there a little time? — Yes.

And then did you go to number 16, where you had been shown the day before by the prisoner? — Yes. I waited fifteen minutes and then went to the door there.

About what time was it that you got to the door? — It must be about 8.15.

Was the door open or closed? — It was open.

Did you go into the passage? — As I came to the door, the man came to me.

Which man? — Lipski, the stick maker.

Is that the man [*the prisoner*]? — Yes.

You had some conversation with him. Tell us what. — He said to me,

Isaac Schmuss

---

22 These 'other persons' were Barsuch and Robinski (compare the mistake in the transcript of Marks Schmidt's evidence, which mistakenly places Rosenbloom at the scene). The judge's notes of Schmuss's evidence at this point make the situation clear: 'Met with Russian Jews there: –ouski, Basak & Robinski' (see TNA:PRO HO 144/201/A47465/7). In submitting his notes to the Home Office on 3 August 1887, Mr Justice STEPHEN wrote, 'I suggest that you should also refer to the Old Bailey Sessions Papers'. These give the following: 'I there met with other Russian Jews, Tottakoski, Barsuch, and Robenski.' *(Old Bailey Proceedings Online [www.oldbaileyonline.org, version 7.2, 29 January 2017], July 1887, trial of Israel Lipski [t18870725-817])*

Lipski.

Isaac Schmuss

'You shall go upstairs, wait a little, and I will come upstairs and then I will give you something to do.'

Where did he go then? — I don't know.

How was he dressed at that time? — I did not know how it was.

Well, where did you go? — I went upstairs.

When you go upstairs, did you go to the top of the house? — Yes.

And in the room upstairs did you find two persons, a man and a boy? — Yes.

[*Rosenbloom and Pittman were called in.*]

Were they the two? — Yes.

Did you speak to Rosenbloom? — I did not speak much to him.

What did you speak to him? In what language was it? — In Yiddish.

How long did you remain there? — Ten or fifteen minutes.

Did the prisoner come into the room while you were there? — No.

Which of the three first left the room: you, the boy, or Rosenbloom? — The boy.

How long did you stay after the boy left? — About a minute's time, not more.

And then did you leave? — I went to eat my breakfast.

That same day, did you return to Mr Schmidt's? — Yes.

What time was it that you went there? — About 12.00, midday.

While you were there, did Tartakowski come in? — Yes.

Did you return after that, at all, to 16 Batty Street? — No, I did not.

While you were at Schmidt's, did you first hear that the woman was dead? When was it that you first heard that the woman was dead? — Mr Schmidt told me.

When? — When I came there.

That was about 12.00? — Yes.

I think at this time you were lodging at 60 Oxford Street, Stepney? — Yes.

And you remained in London for the next eight or ten days, at that address? — Yes.

How many days? — Eight or ten days.

During that time, did you return from time to time to Mr Schmidt's? — Yes, I went to Mr Schmidt's every day.

At the end of that time, did you go to the country, in order to get some work there? — Yes.

I think you went to Birmingham? — Yes.

I think Robinski came to see you off by the train to Birmingham? — Yes, to the railway.

And, in Birmingham, you went to lodge at 42 Gough Street, and worked at Ince Street?[23] — Yes.

First Day – Friday 29 July 1887.

As a slipper maker? — Yes.

And from there did you write this letter [*handing one to the witness*] — Yes.

To who? Mr Antonine[24] Rabinowitz, 60 Oxford Street? — Yes.

He was your landlord, was he? — Yes, my lodging master, and my countryman.

Did Robinski lodge at 60 Oxford Street? — Yes.

Afterwards, an inspector of police came to Birmingham and brought you to London? — Yes.

Cross-examined by Mr McINTYRE.

Is slipper-making a new trade to you, or an old trade? — Only since I went to Birmingham.

Do you speak English? — No.

Not at all? — Not at all.

Not a word? — I can't say not one word.

Did not you see the prisoner at all after you left the shop on the morning of the twenty-eighth? — No, I had not seen him.

Did not you yourself go into the room that belonged to Mrs Angel? — What Mrs Angel? I did not go in.

The first floor in the house where you went to work? — I went in nowhere.

Were you not standing in the doorway of her room when Lipski was coming up the stairs? — No, I was not there. I was nowhere.

You were not with Rosenbloom? — No.

Did you know Rosenbloom? — I saw him once … then I saw him for the first time.

Do you mean that you never saw him till you saw him in Lipski's room? — I saw him never more. I saw him the first time there.

Mr McINTYRE: My lord, I do not propose to go through all the same cross-examination as with the last witness, as this man denies being there at all.

Mr Justice STEPHEN: No, there is no use in doing that.

Mr McINTYRE: Have you been brought up as a locksmith? — Yes, I learned it at home.

Before you went to Birmingham, did you hear that Lipski was taken up by the police? — Yes.

Did you hear of the inquiries before the magistrate? — Where is the magistrate?

Well, by the judge? — Yes, I heard it by the newspaper.

Isaac Schmuss

---

23   *Sic* in transcript. Should read: 'Inge Street'.
24   *Sic* in transcript.

Lipski.

Isaac Schmuss

You heard it from the paper, did you, before you went to Birmingham? — I can't read.

Did you have it read to you? — Mr Schmidt told me that they had locked him up.

Did you hear that he was to be taken before the magistrate? — I did not hear that.

Can you fix the day when you say you went to Birmingham? — Yes.

What day was it? — Sunday night.

But how long after you had been at Lipski's? — Eight days, or ten days.

Was it the Sabbath, or Sunday? — Sunday night.

Up to that time, were you seeing Mr Schmidt every day? — Yes.

Why did not you go back after you had had your breakfast? — I saw that I should not have a great chance of work there, so I did not come back.

Steva Tartakowski

STEVA[25] TARTAKOWSKI, sworn and examined by Mr POLAND, through the interpreter.

You come from Odessa? — Yes.

You came over to England in search of work? — Yes.

Among other places, did you go to Mr Schmidt's in Backchurch Lane? — Yes.

And there did you meet the last witness, Isaac Schmuss? — Yes.

Do you remember being at Mr Schmidt's on a Monday evening when Lipski came in and spoke to you and Schmuss? — Yes, Lipski came in.

Was work spoken of? Did he offer you work? — He said he could give work for two people.

And – in your hearing – did he tell Schmuss that he would show him where he lived? — I heard him say to Schmuss he would show him where he lived.

Did he tell Schmuss to go there next morning to work? — Yes.

Had you some appointment yourself with Schmuss that night, as to meeting him at Schmidt's next morning? — Yes.

And you went to Schmidt's next morning? — Yes.

What time was it you went there? — 9.00 or 10.00.

Schmuss was not there then? — No.

You waited there some little time, did you not? — About an hour, or more.

And then did Schmuss come back, and did you see him and have some conversation with him? — Schmuss afterwards came to Schmidt's.

---

25 Sic in transcript. TNA:PRO HO 144/201/A47465/90 gives *Favel*.

First Day – Friday 29 July 1887.

And you stayed there some little time together? — Till 5.00 in the evening.

After that time, did you upon several occasions see Schmuss during the time he was in London? — I saw him about four times.

Steva Tartakowski

LEAH LIPSKI, sworn and examined by Mr MATHEWS.

Are you the wife of Philip Lipski? — Yes.

And you live with him at 16 Batty Street? — Yes.

You there let out the two upper floors of the house, the first and second floors? — I live in the bottom.

And let the two upper floors out to other persons? — Yes.

And the prisoner was a lodger of yours at that house, living on the top floor? — Yes.

To your knowledge, in the same house there lived – on the first floor front – Mr and Mrs Angel? — Yes.

To your knowledge, was the prisoner acquainted with Mrs Angel? Did he know her to speak to? — No, he did not know her.

On the Tuesday morning, did your husband go out to his work somewhere about 6.30? — Yes.

Leaving you in bed in the front room, ground floor? — Yes.

What time did you get up that morning? — 8.30.

Did you go into the kitchen when you got up? — Yes.

Was anybody there when you got there? — No.

Directly after you got there, did anyone come in? — Yes.

Who? — Lipski. The prisoner.

Was he fully dressed at the time? — Yes.

Had he his coat and hat on? — Yes.

He spoke to you, did not he? — Yes.

What did he say to you? — To go out and get his coffee for him.

Had you been in the habit of doing that? Had you done that before? — Yes, every day.

And did you go and get some hot water? — Yes.

Taking a coffee pot with you, buying the hot water, and bringing the coffee back ready to drink? — Yes.

Before you left the house that morning, did he say anything more to you? — No.

Except about his coffee? — He told me he wanted breakfast coffee, that is all.

Did not he say something more to you at that time? — No.

Nothing about money? Did he not say something to you about money? — Yes.

What did he say? — He asked me for five shillings.

Leah Lipski

Lipski.

Leah Lipski

What more? — I said I had not got it.

What more? — I said, 'I have not got it. Go to your young girl's mother: she lends you so much, she will lend you the five shillings too.' And he said to me, 'I am ashamed to go to her. She only gave me last night twenty-five shillings.'

The young woman's mother you refer to ... was that Mrs Hannah Lyons? — Yes.

The mother of Kate Lyons, the young woman of whom you were speaking? — Yes.

When he spoke to you, in what language did he speak? — Hebrew.

Was it after that you went off to get the hot water for the coffee? — Yes.

Did he say anything to you before you left? — Nothing.

Anything as to where he could be when you came back? — He said he would be here in the kitchen. 'Go for coffee, and I shall be here when you come back with the coffee.'

You went out to Backchurch Lane, did not you? — Yes.

And there got the hot water? — Yes.

Leaving the house about what time? — Just about 8.30.

Was the door open or shut when you went out? — Open.

How was the water paid for? Did the prisoner give you the money for it, or did you pay for it yourself? — I paid for it.

You brought it back and got back to the house about what time? — About twenty minutes I was away.

That would bring you back somewhere about 8.50? — Yes.

When you got back did you go to the kitchen? — Yes.

Was the door still open? — Yes.

Was there anybody in the kitchen when you got back? — No.

The prisoner was not there? — No.

At this time was your lodger, Mrs Levy, downstairs? — Yes, she just met me in the passage with the coffee?

What did you do with the coffee? — I put the coffee pot on the table and went to call him down.

Who? — Israel Lipski, the prisoner. I called out, 'Come down and have your coffee!'

Was there any answer at all, the first time you called? — No.

You called a second time, did you? — Yes, and the boy answered, 'He ain't here'.

Then you had your breakfast? — Yes.

And sent your children off to school? — Yes.

And was it about 9.30 your mother, Mrs Rubenstein, came down? — Yes.

First Day – Friday 29 July 1887.

She lodged in the same room with Mrs Levy? — Yes.
The coffee was still on the table, was it? — Yes.
The coffee remained in the same place? — Yes.
About ten, did you go out with Mrs Levy to shop in Petticoat Lane? — Yes.
Had you seen the prisoner up to the time you left at 10.00? — No.
The coffee was in the same place? — Yes.
And you left with Mrs Levy about 10.00? — Just 10.00.
Between the time you returned and 10.00 that morning, had you seen anybody come in and leave the house? — I could not say. I was busy with my children for school. I did not see anybody.
When you left, did you leave your mother, Mrs Rubenstein, in charge of the house? — Yes.
And gave her certain directions about the coffee? — Yes.
You were away about an hour in Petticoat Lane? — Just an hour.
You came back with Mrs Levy, therefore, somewhere about 11.00? — Yes.
When you came back, did you see your mother? — I saw my mother sitting on a chair in the passage outside in the street.
At the time you came to the house and saw your mother, did the mother of the deceased woman come to the door? Mrs Dinah Angel? — Yes, the mother-in-law just met me in the passage.
She spoke to you? — Yes.
After she had spoken to you, she went into the house and went upstairs? — Yes.
Did you then hear her knock at the door upstairs? — Yes.
Did you then hear her try the door? — No.
What did she do? Did she call down to you? — Yes, she called down to me.
On that, did you tell Mrs Levy to go upstairs? — Yes.
And she went up, did she? — Yes.
And then Mrs Levy called out something to you? — Yes.
And in consequence of that you went upstairs? — I threw everything down and ran upstairs.
In what condition was the door of Mrs Angel's room? — I did not try the door. I only looked through the little window.
You went up beyond the first floor and looked through the little window? Could you see through from the staircase? — Yes.
Was there any curtain over it at that time? — A muslin curtain.
Could you see through the curtain? — I saw … a little like fainting, she was. She was lying like fainting, she looked to me.
Mrs Angel? — Yes.

Leah Lipski

Lipski.

Leah Lipski

Did you then come down to the first floor landing? — Yes.

What did you three do? — I burst open the door.

Was the door fastened or open? — I did not try much about the door because Mrs Levy said it was locked.

Did you burst the door open? — The three of us.

The three of you, all together? — Yes.

Was the door locked at that time, before you burst it open? — I did not try so much.

But having to burst it open … The three of you, did you do it together? — Yes.

Was it fastened? — Yes, shut.

And the three of you had to push hard? — I was so frightened, I could not say.

But the three of you did get the door open? — Yes.

How did you get it open? — Pushed with my leg, my knee.

Did all the three push with their knees, or how? — I cannot tell you that.

Had you fixed yourself against anything so as to be able to push harder? — No.

You just pushed your knee against the door? — Yes.

Was your back against anything? — No.

How long was you before you got it open?[26] – Only a second.

Had you difficulty in getting it open? — No. I pushed with my knee and it opened.

Were you the first to go into the room after the door was open? — Yes: all the three.

All together? — Yes.

Did you go round to the bed on which the woman was lying? — Yes.

Were you the first to get round there? — Yes.

You took hold of the deceased and shook her, did you? Yes, I took her by one arm and shook her, and called to her. She did not answer me.

Did you notice how her face was lying? Whether it was towards the wall or not? — Yes.

How? — Sideways.

Looking in what direction? — I cannot tell you that.

Was she lying on her back, or how? — Sideways.

Were the bedclothes over the whole of her, or was any portion of her person exposed? — Half over.

Was any portion of her body exposed? — I did not see.

Mr Justice STEPHEN: I thought you said part of her was exposed. —

---

26 *Sic* in transcript. Presumably a misrecording of 'How long were you …?' or 'How long was it …?'

First Day – Friday 29 July 1887.

Leah Lipski

Half covered.

Then was the other half uncovered? — Yes.

Mr MATHEWS: She was wearing a chemise? — Yes.

A nightdress? — No nightdress, only a day shirt.

Did you notice anything on the day shirt? — Yes.

What? — Like burnt in the front.

How was her hair? Did you notice that? — No.

There was some furniture in the room? — Yes.

Did you notice any sign of disturbance of the furniture? — I did not notice that.

When you found this, did you – all of you – begin to call out? — I began to run down and scream in the street.

Leaving the door open? — Yes.

And you went for Dr Kay, did not you? — Yes.

He was out? — Yes.

You returned to the house and to the room? — Yes.

And went a second time for Dr Kay? — Yes.

You saw his assistant, Mr Piper? — No, another assistant.

And then returned to the house? — Yes.

And, as you were returning, you saw the doctor in the carriage? — Yes.

He came to the house direct, and went up to the room where the deceased was? — Yes.

After going to Dr Kay, did you go back to your own house? — Yes. I found the same persons there. I then went to Dr Kay again. I saw nobody – only the assistant said he would come in in a minute.

And, as you were going home, you met the doctor? — Yes.

And immediately after, the doctor came? — Yes.

Cross-examined by Mr McINTYRE.

The prisoner has been lodging with you for nearly two years? — Yes.

Was he a steady, respectable young man? — Yes.

And always bore a good character with everyone? — Yes.

My friend has asked you about his wanting to borrow five shillings of you that morning. Did he tell you a particular amount he wanted? — He wanted it for his work.

He told you that he had borrowed from his intended mother-in-law twenty-five shillings before? — Last night.

And that was true, was it not? — Yes.

Was he then fitting up his room for the purpose of making a workshop? — Yes.

And was he purchasing about that time materials to some considerable

Lipski.

Leah Lipski

amount? — Yes.

Some pounds? — Yes.

And his rent was increased from two shillings to five shillings a week? — Yes.

Was Mrs Angel, the very day before, obliged to borrow money to pay her rent? — Yes.

Borrowed five shillings to pay you her rent? — Yes, from Mrs Levy.

About this lock to the door ... Was the box of that lock higher than where the lock turned? What was the state of the lock? Did it fit properly? — Yes.

Was one portion rather too high? — No, it just fitted.

After the twenty-eighth, did Mr Angel leave the house? — Yes.

And did you let the room to other people? — Yes.

And did the lock remain on the door while the other persons were using the room? — Yes.

And did it remain on that door three weeks before the policeman came and had it cut off? — Yes.

Was not the box of the lock higher than the lock itself? — No. It would just fit, the two of them.

Do you recollect the old lock being on before the present lock was put on? Is this correct: 'Where the old lock had been a hole was left, large enough for three fingers, and the box of the lock was higher than the lock itself'? — Yes.

Is that correct? — Yes.

Is this correct: 'With the key inside, I could catch the key from the outside through the hole left from the old lock'? — Yes, you could just touch it.

Mr Justice STEPHEN: Could you have locked it from the outside? — No.

When the key was inside, you could not – from putting your hand through the hole – lock it from the outside? — I could not.

All you mean is that when you were outside the door, you could put your hand through and touch it? — Yes.

But not enough to lock it? — Not by the fingers.

Mr McINTYRE: When was the lock taken off? — Two weeks after, just exactly.

It was sawn off, was it not? — Yes.

Who went out with you when you went to go a-shopping? — On that day, nobody ... I myself on that day, when the lock was taken off.

I mean on the day this happened, the twenty-eighth. — Mrs Levy.

And was your mother the only person left in charge of the house? — Yes.

First Day – Friday 29 July 1887.

Is your mother almost blind? — She can see a little light.[27]
But very little? — Very little.
Very little indeed? — Yes.
She is obliged to feel as she goes about, is she not? — Yes.
Is the street door sometimes left so that anyone pushing against it can come in? — Yes.
That is the ordinary way, is it not? — Yes.
Had you a pawn ticket belonging to the prisoner for a gold chain? — Yes.
Did you know that he had, until just at this time, a silver watch? — Yes.

Re-examined by Mr POLAND.

Do you mean a silver watch on this Tuesday morning, or that he had had one? — I don't know.
You know he had a watch? — Yes.
When did he have it? When did you see him with it last? — One Saturday … I cannot recollect.
Can you tell when it was? — I saw it some time when I took notice of him.
Did he pawn his watch? — I don't know. He did not tell me.
When did you see him with it last? [*The interpreter here interpreted to the witness.*] — Not for some time.
When? — I cannot think of it.
Did you see it within a week before? — I cannot recollect.
After this Tuesday, was anything done to the lock of this door before it was cut off? — He sawed off a lump.
Up to that time, had you had anything done to it? — No.
You had not had a locksmith in to do anything to it? — No.
And was it used to lock the room up? — Yes.
Then the police came with a man and cut off the piece? — Yes.
Mr McINTYRE: Before it was cut off, had you been shown the lock which was partly burst off? — Yes.
On this Tuesday, was the lock broken off at all? — Yes, a man upstairs broke it off the door.
When was that? — On the Tuesday.
How long after you broke the door open did it happen? — Two weeks.
Mr Justice STEPHEN: When did you see anything done to the lock? Did you, on the Tuesday when this happened, see anything done to the

Leah Lipski

---

27 The reading given in the judge's notes – 'She can see a little light …' – is preferred to the reading given in transcript – 'She can see a little like …'. (TNA:PRO HO 144/201/A47465/7.)

Lipski.

Leah Lipski

lock on the door?[28] — The lock was good.

Did anything happen to it on that Tuesday? — Nothing had happened to it. The lock was good.

When was anything done to the lock? — Two weeks after this happened.

Nothing happened to it for two weeks? — No.

I thought you said that someone broke it off the day that the thing happened? — No: two weeks exactly afterwards.

What happened to it then? — The man came and broke open the door.

A man belonging to the police? — Yes.

He broke open the door? — Yes.

What did he do with the lock? — He did not notice that the lock was broke. I was out at the time. I came back and the woman that lives in the place now was out. I came home before her. When I came in the passage, the woman told me a man had broken open Mrs Jacobs's door. I went upstairs and saw the door open.

Did you see the lock? — Yes.

What state was the lock in then? — Bad: broken, hanging down.

That was a fortnight after the death of the woman? — Yes.

But you did not see who did it? — I did see him. I know him. A detective.

[*The witness Bitten here came into court.*]

Is that the man? — Yes.

What did you see him do? — I did not see anything done to the lock. When I came to the room, I saw the lock hanging. I said, 'What have you done this for?' and he said, 'I will send a carpenter to put it on again'.

Did a carpenter come? — No.

When was it cut off? — The next few days after. A week after, he came with two men to saw off the lock altogether.

Then the only thing that happened to the lock after the twenty-eighth was that Bitten broke it so that it was hanging down? — Yes.

And, a week after that, it was cut off? — A few days.

Then, till it was broken by Bitten, did it continue as good as it used to be? — It was not like it used to be.

During the fortnight before Bitten broke it, was it as it used to be? — Yes, the woman used to lock it.

---

28   Mr Justice Stephen had experienced some frustration as Mrs Lipski's testimony threatened to become confusing. 'Long questions', he wrote, in parentheses, in his notes. However, it seems likely that he did not run the re-examination of the witness from this point on, as the attributions in the transcript would appear (albeit somewhat ambiguously) to suggest. 'Did anything happen to it on that Tuesday?' would seem to have been Mr Poland's question, as are those that follow, until Mr Justice Stephen's plenary intervention (TNA:PRO HO 144/201/A47465/7).

First Day – Friday 29 July 1887.

Mr Justice STEPHEN: Just listen to this: I want to be quite sure I have got it quite right. 'Nothing happened to the lock for a fortnight from the twenty-eighth'? — Yes.

Then Bitten broke it? — Yes.

And, a week after, it was sawn off. — Yes.

GEORGE BITTEN, re-examined by Mr POLAND.

When you went into the room for the purpose, how did you get in? — Merely opened the door: just turned the handle.

Did you ever find the door locked so that you could not get in? — No.

Did you force it in any way, or damage the lock. — Not in any way whatever.

Mr Angel had left the room? — Yes.

Was anybody occupying it? — Yes.

Who? — I don't know the name: they were foreigners. I went there on thirteen or fourteen occasions.[29] I never forced the lock. The lock is exactly in the same condition as it was on the night of the occurrence. There might be some little difficulty to explain about the locking of that particular lock. [*The lock was here produced.*] This is the inside of the door. This is the lock that has been spoken of. The landlord is here that put it on, and he could explain it.

On the night of the occurrence, these screws were drawn out? — On the day of the occurrence, the screws had been forced out so as to get the door open.[30] This is an actual piece of the door and door post.

Cross-examined by Mr McINTYRE.

Sometimes when you went, there was no person in the room. — No, there was no person in the room sometimes; sometimes Mrs Lipski would come up with me.

You said before the magistrate that – except twice – the occupier opened the door to you. Is it correct? — She did open the door on one or two occasions.

But you said *except* twice she always opened the door to you? — That was with reference to the time she had been there, but it takes a time to make the plan.[31] I was there a week before she went there. When the

---

29   The judge's notes say, 'I was there 14 or 15 times' (TNA:PRO HO 144/201/A47465/7), but the Old Bailey Sessions Papers agree with the transcript (*OBP*, July 1887, Israel Lipski [t18870725-817]).
30   The judge's notes say, 'The screws on the night of the occurrence were forced out about ¼ inch' (TNA:PRO HO 144/201/A47465/7).
31   A contemporary amendment to the transcript amends 'the plan' to 'it plain'. The original reading is preferred.

Lipski.

George Bitten

room was unoccupied, I used to open the door in the usual way. If you locked the door, it would not answer: only just to keep the wind off. If you just touched the door it came open.

Dinah Angel

DINAH ANGEL, sworn and examined (through an interpreter) by Mr MATHEWS.

Did your son live with his wife at 16 Batty Street? — Yes.

Did you see her on the Monday before this happened? — Yes, in the evening part.

Used she to come to you to breakfast? — Yes.

About what was her usual time for coming? — Sometimes at 8.30, sometimes at 9.00.

Ever later? — Not often later.

On Tuesday the twenty-eighth, she did not come home to breakfast? — No.

About what time did you go round to her house? — About 11.00.

Was anyone at the door when you got there? — There was no-one.

Did you see anything of Mrs Rubenstein? — No, no-one.

Did you see anything of Mrs Rubenstein after you got there? — Yes, afterwards.

Did you go upstairs to your son's room? — Yes.

Before you did that, had you seen Mrs Lipski and Mrs Levy? — Mrs Levy, but not Mrs Lipski.

Then did you go to the door of your son's room? — Yes.

Did you try the door? — I tried it, and it was closed.

Did you try the handle? Could you get in? — I saw Mrs Levy try, and she said, 'The key is inside'.

Then did you hear Mrs Levy go upstairs to look through this place in the partition? — Mrs Levy looked through it.

Then did you knock at the door at all? — Yes, I did – and before.

Could you get any answer? — No.

You were there and saw Mrs Levy … and did Mrs Lipski come up? — Yes. … Only Mrs Levy.

How many of you were there when the door was forced open? — Me and Mrs Levy.

How did you get the door open? — We knocked it, mostly with the hand.

What way? — With force, with the hand.

Was Mrs Lipski there at that time? — No, only Mrs Levy.

Who went into the room first? — Me and Mrs Levy, both together.

When you got into the room, did you see your daughter-in-law? — I and Mrs Levy ran to the bed and I thought she was fainting. She laid[32]

First Day – Friday 29 July 1887.

with her hands so, with her head aside, and we put her hands in front and moved her head, thinking she was fainting. I then saw she was dead, and went out and created an alarm.

Did you see how she was lying on the bed? — On her side, her hands behind. And uncovered.

What part of her was uncovered? — The whole.

How was her nightdress or chemise? — Up.

Did you see where the covering to the bed was? — I did not see that. I rushed out at once.

Before you rushed out, did you notice the furniture in the room? — I did not look.

Did you, at all, notice the window? — The window blind was pulled down.

Was the window shut, or not? — Closed.

Then, you say, you rushed out? — Yes, into the street.

Later on, did you see the policeman come, and the doctor? — No, I did not see that. I was in a fainting condition and they took me away.

When did you go to the room again? — They would not let me in.

Cross-examined by Mr McINTYRE.

You say the blind of the window was pulled down. Was it a fact that the window had no fastening? — That I did not try.

Dinah Angel

LEAH LEVY, sworn and examined (through an interpreter) by Mr POLAND.

Are you the wife of Abraham Levy? — Yes.

But you are living apart from him and have been lodging at 16 Batty Street? — Yes.

What time did you come down on the morning of 28 June? — Quarter to nine.

Did you look into the street shortly after you came down and see Mrs Lipski in the street coming to the house? — Yes.

She had a coffee pot in her hand? — Yes.

After Mrs Lipski came in, did you call up to the prisoner, telling him his coffee was ready? — Yes.

And the boy upstairs answered? — Yes.

What time was it you went out with Mrs Lipski that morning? — 10.00.

How long was[33] you away before you returned to the house? — At 11.00.

Leah Levy

---

32   *Sic* in transcript.
33   *Sic* in transcript.

Lipski.

Leah Levy

At that time, was Mrs Angel senior at the house, or coming to the house? — She came on there ... she was coming in then.

Did Mrs Angel go upstairs and knock at the door of her daughter's bedroom? — Yes.

And then did you go up and look into the bedroom through the little window? — Yes.

Did you see young Mrs Angel lying on the bed? — Yes.

How did she look? — Bad. She looked very bad.

Did you see Mrs Angel try the door and find it locked? — No.

Did you come down to the landing yourself? — Mrs Lipski also came up. They looked into the window and I said, 'She looks bad'. The mother-in-law then said, 'Perhaps she is fainting'.

Did the three of you come down from the landing to the bedroom door? — Yes, and the mistress said, 'We shall open the door'.

What was then done? — The whole three then pushed the door open.

Before they did that, did you look through the keyhole in any way? — Yes, and I saw the key inside.

In the lock? — Yes.

You pushed the door? — Yes.

And then you went into the room? — Yes.

And saw the woman as she lay in bed? — Yes.

Cross-examined by Mr McINTYRE.

Were you the person that, the day before this occurred, lent the five shillings to Mrs Angel? — Yes.

To pay her rent? — Yes.

After this occurrence, do you recollect the police, about a fortnight after, coming into the house? — Yes.

Sergeant Bitten? — Yes.

Was he alone, or anyone with him? — He was alone.

Did he get into the room? — He wanted me to go upstairs. I said, 'It is locked'. He said, 'I must go in, very particularly,' and I said, 'It is locked'. He said he would open it. He then pushed in the door and went in.

Who was the tenant of the room at that time? Was it Mrs Jacobs? — Yes.

She was out at the time, was she? — No, she was not at home.

Rachel Rubenstein

RACHEL RUBENSTEIN, sworn and examined by Mr MATHEWS.

You live at 16 Batty Street? — Yes.

You occupy the back room, first floor? — Yes.

With Mrs Levy? — Yes.

First Day – Friday 29 July 1887.

Rachel Rubenstein

You slept there with Mrs Levy on the Monday night? — Yes.

And, on the Tuesday morning, what time was it when you went downstairs? — Either 9.30 or 10.00.

Afterwards, did Mrs Lipski and Mrs Levy go out shopping? — Yes.

At that time, had you seen whether the prisoner's coffee had been prepared for him? — Yes, I heard him called.

While Mrs Lipski and Mrs Levy were out, were you downstairs, in charge of the premises? — Yes, and also took care of the children.

Whereabouts were you? — In the back room.

At any time were you by the front door? — Yes, I was at the street door. I took a chair out from the room and sat myself down because I cannot see well.

During the time they were out, did anyone enter the house? — Not direct. I first went into the yard. I was minding the children in the yard, and came back. I sat down in a chair there so that the children should not go to the water. Somebody came. I was still sitting there and he wanted to go upstairs. I said, 'Where are you going?' He said he was going upstairs. I said, 'Why?' and I would not let him go up.

Did you know the man? — I did not know him.

He wanted to go up to Angels' room? – Yes.

You would not let him go up? — No.

He enquired for some boots, did he? — Yes, he asked if the boots were done.

Cross-examined by Mr McINTYRE.

Did not one of the children run away to the back? — Yes, and went into the yard.

You had some trouble in catching the child, had you not? — Yes. I was afraid it had run away.

And were you in the back yard some time looking after the child and trying to catch it? — Only a few minutes. I did not take particular notice. I did not think I should be asked about it.

You cannot tell how long it was? — I do not know.

When you came from the back yard to the front, did you come and sit out in the street? — Yes.

On the pavement, outside the door? — Yes, on a chair.

Is that a little to the right-hand of the door? — To the left-hand.

You put the chair there for yourself, did not you? — Yes.

Samuel Spiers

SAMUEL SPIERS, sworn and examined (through an interpreter) by Mr POLAND.

Is your name Samuel Spiers? — Yes. He is also called Lamed the

Lipski.

Samuel Spiers

teacher.[34]

Do you live at 24 Brunswick Street, St George's[35] in the East? — Yes.
Are you a Hebrew teacher? — Yes.
The deceased woman, Mrs Angel: did she come to your house on Sunday 26 June? — Yes.
Did she take away with her two pairs of boots to be repaired? — Yes.
On the Tuesday morning – the twenty-eighth – did you go to Batty Street? — Yes.
What time in the morning did you get there? — At 9.30 or 10.00.
Was anybody seated outside the door when you got there? — The old one: he does not know her name.
The last witness, Mrs Rubenstein? [*Mrs Rubenstein was brought forward.*] — Yes.
You spoke to her? — Yes, said he wanted to go in.
How long did you remain outside the house that morning? — A quarter of an hour. He stood there with a man and spoke about his own affairs.
You went there to get your boots, did you? — Yes.
During the time you were outside, was your attention called to the window of the first floor, and the blind to it? — It was down.

Harris Dywein

HARRIS DYWEIN, sworn and examined by Mr MATHEWS.

Are you are general dealer? — Yes.
Living at 52 Fairclough Street, Commercial Road? — Yes.
You know Mr Angel and you knew his wife, did you not? — Yes.
Did you last see her alive on the night of Monday 27 June? — Yes.
About midnight, was that? — It was past 12.00.
She came to you to ask you the address of a letter? — Of a postcard.
When she left you on that night, did she seem cheerful in spirits and well in health? — Yes.
Did you know the prisoner at all up to 28 June? — No.
On the morning of 28 June, were you in Batty Street? — I was outside my shop.
About what time was it your attention was called to number 16? — About 11.00, or 11.15. I could not tell you exactly the time.
What was it called your attention? — I heard a noise and ran into Batty Street to see what was the matter.
Did you go into number 16? — Yes.
Up to the first floor, front room? — Yes.
There did you see old Mrs Angel, who spoke to you? — Dinah Angel.

---

34 The interpreter relayed several of Spiers's responses, this one included, in the third person.
35 *Sic* in transcript.

First Day – Friday 29 July 1887.

I met her on the stairs. **Harris Dywein**
   She spoke to you, did she? — Yes.
   Going into the room, did you see the deceased woman lying on the bed? — Yes.
   How was she lying? — On her back.
   How was her face? — Her face was towards the wall, looking on the wall.
   How were her hands? — One hand was just on her chest, and one hand was behind her back.
   How was her hair? — Disarranged all over the bed.
   Did you notice anything on the right side of her face? — Yes, there were several marks here. I could not tell you whether scratches or not.
   How was her chemise or nightdress? — It was right up, up to the breast: just here [*describing*].
   Was her person exposed? — Yes.
   A pillow on the ground: did you see one pillow? — I could not tell you. I did not notice that.
   Were there any signs of struggle in the room? — No, I could not see any signs of struggle.
   Did you cover her up in some way? — Yes.
   After you had done that, did Mr Piper, Dr Kay's assistant, come? — Yes.
   And did he say something to all of who were there, in consequence of which they all went out of the room? — Yes.
   Who was there at the time? Was Rosenbloom there at the time? — I could not say who was there.
   About how many were there? — I never counted the people there. There were several people in the room.
   Before you left the room, did Mr Piper speak to you in reference to the door key? — Yes, he wanted the door key.
   In consequence of what he said, did you go to the door? — Yes. Mr Piper said we had all got to clear out of the room, and he would lock the door; so Mr Piper took the key out from inside the door and he could not lock the door until he had unlocked the lock, and he could not take the key out to lock the door from the outside because the join was out.
   And was that done in your presence? Did you see him do it? — Yes.
   Saw him turn the bolt back and take the key out? — Yes.
   Then you left the room? — Yes. Mr Piper left the room – locking the door – and he took the key with him.
   I think about ten minutes after that, Dr Kay came? — Yes.
   Then did you, Dr Kay, Mr Piper and some others go back into the room? — Yes.

Lipski.

Harris Dywein

The door being unlocked to enable you to go back? — Mr Piper unlocked the door.

When you got back, was something said about a bottle? — Yes.

That was said by Dr Kay? — Yes.

In consequence of that, what did you do? — We were looking for a bottle.

Mr Justice STEPHEN: You looked for a bottle? — Yes, and Mr Piper and Dr Kay said we should take everything from underneath the bed. We took away from underneath the bed an old coat.

You did yourself? — Yes.

What did you do? — Took away from underneath the bed an old coat, and then pulled away an old egg box – several old clothes were in that – and Mr Piper and Dr Kay said, 'Is there anything underneath the bed?' I looked underneath the bed and said, 'There is something underneath the bedstead'. And Mr Piper or Dr Kay – one or the other – said, 'Go and see what it is'. I laid[36] down and felt like a hand. While I was coming back, Dr Kay jumped on the bed and took away the pillow which was towards the wall and said, 'Why, it is a man!' So he told me I should call for the police.

Mr MATHEWS: At that point, was anything done to the bedstead? — The bedstead was pulled away.

What did the doctor do to the prisoner in your presence? — Slapped his face. He felt his pulse and slapped his face.

Mr Justice STEPHEN: How was the prisoner got out from under the bed? — He was lifted up by two constables.

Afterwards --?

Mr MATHEWS: Was he still on the ground when the doctor had first seen him? When the doctor felt his pulse and slapped his face? — Yes, still on the ground.

Mr Justice STEPHEN: You felt a man's hand? — Yes.

Dr Kay jumped on the bed, threw off some of the bedclothes and said, 'Why, it is a man'? — Yes.

Tell us particularly how the man was found out after that: what was done, who it was who did it, and how he was brought out. — He was lying on his back and his short sleeves were tucked up. His Guernsey sleeve was down, his waistcoat was unbuttoned.

Mr MATHEWS: Had he any coat on? — No.

Had he any boots on? — Yes.

You say he was lying there … In what condition did he seem? In what state? — He was like unconscious.

Mr Justice STEPHEN: Did you see an egg box there? — Yes.

---

36   *Sic* in transcript.

First Day – Friday 29 July 1887.

Where was the egg box? — The egg box was underneath the bed.
You had pulled that from underneath the bed? — Yes.

Was the man behind the egg box, or in front of the egg box? — Behind.

He was lying there 'like unconscious'. Now what was the first thing done with him? — Dr Kay told me, 'Call down for the police'.

Mr MATHEWS: Before that, did not he feel his pulse? — Yes.

Mr Justice STEPHEN: You say he was 'like unconscious'. Was he brought out into the room? — Yes, my lord.

Who brought him out? — Two constables.

Dr Kay had sent for constables some time before? — No: Dr Kay told me I should call for constables. I jumped on the table – I wanted to open the bottom window, but it was impossible to open it. It was too tight. I opened the top window and called for constables, and two constables came up.

The man was not got out from under the bed before the two constables came up? — No.

He remained under the bed? — No, between the bedstead and the wall.

Mr McINTYRE: They pulled the bedstead out before that. I don't know if your lordship caught it?

Mr Justice STEPHEN: He was between the bedstead and the wall … Did you pull the bedstead away from the wall, or how did it come away? — I cannot remember now.

Then Dr Kay told you to call a constable, and you went to the window. You could not get it open because it was so tight? — The bottom window.

Then you called the constables over the top of the window, and they came in? — They came into the room.

What did they do when they came? — They lifted him up and --

And brought him where? — Dr Kay told him, 'Look what you have been doing to the poor body!'

Where did they put him? — Held him against the wall.

Leaving him still between the bed and wall? — No: just took him in the corner. They just lifted him into the corner.

They lifted him out from behind the bed? — Yes.

And put him up in a corner? — Yes.

Now go on.

Mr MATHEWS: Could he stand when they put him in the corner? — I could not tell that, because the two constables were still holding his hands.

They still held him? — Yes.

Then? — Then Dr Kay told the constables to take him to the station.

Mr Justice STEPHEN: What did Dr Kay do to the man? — He slapped his face when he was lying on the ground.

Mr MATHEWS: And felt his pulse? — Before he slapped his face.

Harris Dywein

Lipski.

_{Harris Dywein}

Mr Justice STEPHEN: Did the man speak? — No, he did not speak much.

Not after his face was slapped? — No, he opened his eyes. He never spoke.

Mr MATHEWS: Can you tell what distance the bedstead was from the wall? — I cannot tell because they have German feather beds. The bed covers were half on the wall and half on the bed. I could not tell how far away the bed was.

With regard to the bottle spoken of by Dr Kay … You were told to look for it under the bed in the first instance; you looked for it there. Did you find it there? — No.

Were you present when it was found? — Yes.

Who found it? — The bottle was seen by a constable. I pulled the bed off, prevented the bed from falling down from the bedstead. I put the feather bed on the bedstead, so I found the bottle as it was lying, and showed it to the constable.

Did you see it before the constable, or the constable before you? — I saw it before the constable.

Where was it when you first saw it? — On the bed.

Where on the bed? — Just the middle part of the bed.

Was it on the wall side, or on the room side? — On the wall side.

And about the middle of the bed, do you say? — Yes.

Mr Justice STEPHEN: I understood you to say it was under some part of the bedclothes? — When we pulled the bedstead away for Dr Kay to come in there to see the man, the feather bed fell away, and then I saw the bottle.

You lifted up the feather bed, and then you saw the bottle under the feather bed? — Yes, my lord.

Mr MATHEWS: Was that the bottle you found, or was it a bottle similar to that [*showing one to the witness*]? — I cannot say if it was the same bottle.

Like that, I mean? — Yes, like that. There was no cork.

It was a bottle without a cork? — Yes.

Did you take it up from where it was? — The constable took it up … I cannot exactly tell whether the constable or Dr Kay.

You left it in charge of Dr Kay? — I did not have anything to do with the bottle.

It was left with Dr Kay.

Cross-examined by Mr McINTYRE.

Before you went into the room, were other people in it? — Yes.

About how many? — I could not tell you, sir.

First Day – Friday 29 July 1887.

Was Rosenbloom there? — I cannot tell you.

Did you not see him there? — I did not see him in the room.

Can you tell me what people were in the room when you first went in? — I cannot tell you. It was not necessary for me to look over the people.

Was it four or six people? — I could not say. I don't know. It was not necessary for me to count at all.

Mr Justice STEPHEN: You could not tell? — No, I cannot tell.

Mr McINTYRE: Did you see, were there women there? — No women there.

No women when you first went in? — No.

You did not see the mother-in-law of the deceased there at all? — I met the mother-in-law on the stairs.

She had been there? — She had been there before me, but she was fainting in the back room.

Mrs Lipski was there, was she not? — I did not see Mrs Lipski.

Were there women and men there? — There was no woman in the room when I first went in.

Where were the women? — In the back room, because Mrs Dinah Angel was so bad that the women went in there.

Did not Dr Kay and Mr Piper tell you to look under the bed for the bottle? — Not to look for the bottle … To take the things out from under the bed.

Did Dr Kay say there must be a bottle somewhere? — Yes.

Then did Dr Kay and Mr Piper tell you to look under the bed? — Yes.

And then did you and Simon look under the bed? — Yes.

Then he was there? — Yes, afterwards.

At any rate, before the bottle was found, Simon was there? — Yes. The first time I entered into the room, I did not see Simon there.

At all events, he was there before the bottle was found. Did not Simon hand the bottle to the doctor? — No.

Did not you see Simon with the bottle at all? — No.

Could you say whether the clothes had been disarranged by the women? — What clothes?

The clothes of the bed. The bedclothes. — The bedclothes were lying against the wall.

Right up to the wall, the bedclothes were? — Half on the wall and half on the bed.

And was the bedstead itself about eight to ten inches from the wall before it was moved? — It must have been.

About that? — About that, yes.

Then how far did you move it out when you were told by the doctor to move it? — So far that the doctor could go down to see to the man.

Harris Dywein

Lipski.

Harris Dywein

Until you moved the bed, the doctor could not get down to see to the man? — I could not say.

He did not? — No, he did not go down until the bed was pulled over.

Did you pull it over two or three feet? — I could not tell you that.

When you saw the man, was he lying on his back? — Yes.

And were his eyes shut? — Yes.

In what position was he when the doctor slapped his face? Was he still on his back? — Yes.

Near to the wall? — Between the bedstead and wall.

When the policemen got him up, you say they put him against the wall. Did he fall down? — I could not tell that.

You were there? — Yes ... I never took particular notice whether he could stand or not, or whether he fell down. I took particular notice that the two constables were holding his hands.

Did you get out the bed from the wall before you found the bottle? — Yes.

After the doctor had gone down to the man? — Yes.

It was after the bed was moved that you found the bottle? — Yes.

William Piper

WILLIAM PIPER, sworn and examined by Mr POLAND.

You are assistant to Mr Kay, this surgeon in Commercial Road? — Yes.

On the Tuesday morning, did you go to number 16? — Yes.

Were you fetched, or did you hear something had happened there? — They stopped me in the street.

You were stopped in the street. You went there at once? What time did you get to the house? — About 11.30.

Did you go at once upstairs? — Yes.

Did you go into the front bedroom on the first floor? — Yes.

At that time, can you tell me, who were in the room? — Dywein – the last witness – and Rosenbloom, and two or three women, and perhaps another man.

Did you see the woman lying on the bed? — Yes.

Describe her position. — She was lying on her back with her head inclined to the right, with her right arm more or less over her breast.

Her parts exposed? — Yes.

The chemise? — Drawn up.

Rolled up so that you could see the lower parts exposed? — Yes.

Rolled up to whereabouts? — Rolled up to just underneath the breast.

And one leg? — The right leg drawn up.

Was she on her back? — Yes.

How was her head? — Inclining to the right.

First Day – Friday 29 July 1887.

William Piper

Towards the wall? — Yes.

Did you at once go to her to see? — Yes.

Did you move her? — I moved her head towards me.

Mr Justice STEPHEN: Her head was turned towards the wall, you say? — Yes, my lord.

Mr POLAND: Could you form any opinion at that time as to her state, as to whether she was dead? — Yes. I moved her arm; I found she was dead.

Did you alter her position at all? — I put her back in the same position as I found her.

Then what did you proceed to do? — I looked round, and I cleared the room.

You sent the people in it out? — I told them to go out.

The window and the blind: did you notice that? — Yes.

How were they? — There was a top blind down, and an ordinary curtain across the lower panes.

How was the sash of the window? — Shut.

Was the upper sash shut? — Slightly open.

A few inches? — I would say an inch and a half, or two inches.

Did you see any clothes about the room? — Yes.

Where were the clothes? — Female's clothes on a chair, as if undressed from the night before; and a pair of trousers lying on the floor.

On the floor? — Yes.

And a pillow? — There was a pillow on the floor, a square pillow.

And was the woman lying on the sacking of the bed? — Lying on the bare sacking.

Did you see where the ordinary covering of the bed was? — Pushed down to the foot.

Between the bed and the wall? — No, pushed down towards the foot the bedstead.

Now, the chair in the room, and table --

Mr Justice STEPHEN: Do you say there were some trousers on the floor? — Yes.

Mr POLAND: Could you say how far the bedstead was from the wall? — No, I did not notice at that time.

Did you see a table in the room? — Yes.

Where was that? — In front of the window.

Did you see anything of a glass on the table? — A glass on the table.

Did you look at it? — Yes, and smelled it.

What did it appear to be? — Beer or stout.

Is that all that you noticed at that time? — Except the acid on the woman's chemise and on the floor.

Lipski.

William Piper

You saw marks of acid on the floor and on the woman's chemise? — Yes, and on her face.

What colour? — Yellow.

What part of her face? — Mouth, and lips, and chin.

And on the chemise? — On the chemise.

At that time, did you notice her face at all? Whether that was injured? — Not at that time.

You had not noticed it at that time? — No.

Is that all you noticed before you proceeded to leave the room? — Yes.

When you went to the door to leave the room, did you see the lock and the key of the door? — Yes.

Where was the key? — On the inside, in the lock.

Did you take it out? — Yes.

Did you see whether the bolt of the lock had been shot? Whether it was fastened? — I did not find that out until I got outside the door.

You took the key out, and then went to shut the door? — Yes.

Then did you find the lock had been locked so that the bolt was shot? — Yes.

Did that prevent you from shutting the door completely to? — Yes.

Mr Justice STEPHEN: Did you unlock it? — It had a queer look, so I went back and unlocked it from inside.

Mr POLAND: Did you then notice in what state the catch was, into which the bolt shoots? — This [*pointing on the lock, which was handed to the witness*] was shot. It would not come to. The bolt came on the box, so I had to unlock it here, and unlocked it on this side. And the box was slightly loosed; when the bolt came on there, it got more forwards so that it would not shut.

You are quite sure that part into which the bolt shoots was loose? — Yes.

Mr Justice STEPHEN: It is a spring lock? — Yes.

Only one part is spring? — Yes.

Mr POLAND: It appeared to you by pushing against it, forcing[37] it away, it would loosen the thing into which the lock shoots? — Yes.

The box into which it shoots? — Yes.

Mr Justice STEPHEN: You found it was locked? You found this out? — Yes.

Then you went to the outside. You were able to unlock it? Did you lock it from the outside? — Yes, I locked it from outside. I put the key in on the outside.

At that time, were these little -- Is this exactly as it was? — Yes. It has been tightened since.

---

37   'Forced' in transcript.

First Day – Friday 29 July 1887.

One of the witnesses said the box was rather shorter than the lock.

Mr POLAND: Mrs Lipski, my lord.

Mr Justice STEPHEN: It is, if you look at it.

Mr POLAND: Did you touch the box at all to push it when it was locked? — The box of the lock?

Yes. — No, I did not do anything to it.

Afterwards, you went outside, pulled the door to … and did you lock the door from the outside? — Yes.

At that time, the room had been cleared and nobody went in? — Nobody went in.

Then did you take the key and keep it in your possession? — Yes.

Afterwards, who came too? — I went and fetched Dr Kay, my principal.

Did he return with you? — Yes.

How soon? — A very few minutes afterwards, perhaps ten minutes.

Had the police arrived then? — There was one constable on the outside of the door, keeping the crowd back.

Who unlocked the door again? — I did.

And who entered the room with you? — Dr Kay and I.

Who came in then? — Several others. I cannot tell … Dywein and Rosenbloom … people who were there.

And did the police come? — Not just then.

Shortly afterwards? — Yes, shortly afterwards.

Then Dr Kay examined the woman? — Yes.

Did you see this bottle – or a bottle like this – in the room? [*The bottle was shown to the witness.*] — I saw it, not then, but subsequently.

In the room? — Yes.

Did you see who actually found it? — Well, it was not exactly found. It was pointed out by Rosenbloom to the constable.

Where was it then lying? — In one of the folds of the feather bed.

We have heard it had no cork, and it was taken possession of? — Yes, I put a cork in.

Who took it? — Dr Kay took it.

Did you look at it at the time? — Yes, we both had a look at it and smelled it.

Was there any stuff in it? — Yes, just a little.

Did you form the opinion it was nitric acid, commonly called *aqua fortis*? — Yes.

You saw the prisoner there? — Yes.

How was he got from the place where he was on the floor? — In searching for the bottle, Dr Kay got on the bed to remove the pillow and discovered this man lying between the bed and the wall.

Did you see how he was got out? Was he pulled from out the bed, or

William Piper

William Piper

got from under? — I think I assisted someone in pulling the bed out.

The bed was pulled out? — Yes, and then we both got down on that side.

And then? — Dr Kay examined the man and found that he was not dead, so we woke him up.

Did you see whether he had a coat on? — Yes.

Shirt sleeves? — Shirt sleeves rolled up.

Did you see his coat found there? — No.

Or his hat? — No.

The police were there, and Dr Kay? — Yes.

Then the police took charge of the prisoner, and he was taken to the hospital? — To the station house.

And then to the hospital? — They took him to Dr Kay's surgery first.

Taken to the surgery? — And then to the police station.

Afterwards to the hospital.

Cross-examined by Mr McINTYRE.

When you first went into the room, were several women there? — Yes, three or four.

Were they in a very excited state? — Yes, very. They usually are.

Were they about the bed at the time you went in? — No, not very near the bed.

Not at the time you went in? — No.

Were the women behind you when you were coming away to leave the room? You had to make them come out? — I asked them to come out. Probably I might have put my hand on the shoulders of one or two of them and said, 'Go out. We want to clear the room.'

They struggled, did they not? — One wanted to catch a glimpse of the woman, and said, 'No, no,' and stood in front of her.

When you went in, the door was left open? — Yes.

And several people were behind you? — Yes, several.

Were they men, or women, or both? — Both men and women.

How long were you before you desired the people to go, and turned them out? — I should not say I was there ten minutes.

You say Rosenbloom pointed out where the bottle was? — Yes.

And was the bottle lying outside the bed when he pointed it out? — This 'bed' is the bed cover: they call it the feather bed. It was in one of the folds of the covering of the bed as this was being moved. We were searching for the bottle.

Arthur Sach

ARTHUR SACH (Policeman 389H), sworn and examined by Mr MATHEWS.

First Day – Friday 29 July 1887.

On Tuesday 28 June, about 12.00, were you on duty in Commercial Road? — Yes.

Arthur Sach

Were you called to 16 Batty Street? — Yes.

Did you go up to the room on the first floor and find Dr Kay, Mr Piper, and the witness Harris Dywein? — Yes.

At that time, the body of the woman laid[38] dead on the bed? — Yes.

Dr Kay spoke to you about the body of a man underneath the bed? — Yes.

Did you help pull the bed away, out of the recess? — Yes.

Was the bed, at that time, some little distance from the wall – at the time you began to pull it? — Yes.

You pulled it further away, did you? — Yes.

Immediately after you had pulled it away, can you tell me what distance you pulled it? How far? — I should think quite a yard.

Then was a man seen lying on the other side of the bed on the ground? — Yes.

That man was the prisoner? — Yes.

He was lying on his back, was he? — Yes.

And, as we have been told, in his shirt sleeves? — Yes.

His shirt sleeves being rolled up? — Yes.

Instructed by the doctor, did you assist to lift the man up from the ground? — Yes.

Did he seem to be conscious at this time? — He seemed to know a little.

How were his eyes? Opened or closed? — They were open when we lifted him up.

Did you notice any stains upon his shirt? — Yes.

What colour? — Yellow in colour.

Any upon his hands? — Yes.

Of the same colour? — Yes.

When you assisted him up, was he in a position that he could see the deceased woman as she laid[39]? — Yes.

After you assisted him up, what happened to him? — He fell down backwards again.

In consequence of what the doctor said, did you get a cab and take him first to Dr Kay's, and then to the police station? — Yes.[40]

And afterwards to the London Hospital? — Yes.

---

38 *Sic* in transcript.
39 *Sic* in transcript.
40 The judge's notes eliminate any ambiguity about whether Lipski was taken by cab from 16 Batty Street to the doctor's surgery at the top of the road (although they omit the detail about the police station): 'Took him first to Kay's and then to hospital in a cab'. (TNA:PRO HO 144/201/A47465/7)

Lipski.

Arthur Sach

And leave him there in charge of a police constable? — Yes.
Did he speak during the whole of this time? — No.
Did he seem to be in pain? — No, he did not seem to be in pain.
He was asked his name, was he not? — Yes, and he wrote it down.
He wrote the name of Lipski? — Yes.
When was that? — When he was in the hospital.
How long after you had left 16 Batty Street? — About three quarters of an hour.
Were you present when the bottle was found? — Yes.
Who actually picked it up from the bed? — Dr Kay.
Or was it Dywein? — Dr Kay.

Cross-examined by Mr McINTYRE.

You saw Dr Kay pick it up? — Yes.
Was he the first person who touched it? — I could not say.
Did Rosenbloom point it out? — Harris Dywein pointed it out.
You say the man seemed -- You have been on your oath before: be careful. You swore this: 'When he was on his back, he seemed to be unconscious'. That is what you have sworn. — I said that he did seem to be unconscious.
'He did not speak a single word. I do not think he could speak.' Is that right?
Mr Justice STEPHEN: You should read the whole of it. 'When he was on his back, he seemed to be unconscious. When he got up, he seemed as if he might know a little. He did not appear to be in pain. I asked his name at the hospital, three quarters of an hour after the arrest; he wrote it down. He looked at the woman for half a second and then slipped down by the wall. He did not speak a single word. I do not think he could speak.'
Mr McINTYRE: You could see, could you not, that the bedstead had been pulled out before you got there? — I did not notice that.
Who pointed the man out to you? The doctor? — Yes.
Dr Kay? — Yes.

Alfred Inwood

ALFRED INWOOD (Policeman 431H), sworn and examined by Mr POLAND.

On the Tuesday, were you passing through Batty Street? — Yes.
In consequence of what you heard, did you go there, and to the room upstairs? — Yes.
The first floor, front? — Yes.
There you found Dr Kay, Mr Piper, and the last witness, Sach? — Yes.
After the prisoner was taken away by Sach, did you search the room?

First Day – Friday 29 July 1887.

— Yes.

Did you find there the hat that has been produced? The prisoner's hat that has been spoken of? — Yes, this is the hat I found.

Whereabouts was that? — At the front of the bed, on the near side.

Do you mean by that the inside? — No, the near side as you approached the bed.

Where was it on the bed? — At the foot of the bed, covered over by a pillow.

And the old coat that has been identified as the prisoner's coat? Just look at that. [*It was handed to the witness.*] — Yes.

Where did you find that? — I found that at the foot of the bed, near the wall, underneath the bed on the floor.

Was anything over it? — There was another coat over it, a newer coat.

Look at the coat that was over it. [*This was handed to the witness.*] — That is the coat: the coat that was covered over.[41]

The newer coat was lying on the other coat, the other coat being on the floor? — Yes.

Did you notice whether, above that place, at all, there were any nails or pegs? — There were a row of nails. ... At least, I would not say whether nails or pegs, because there were some clothes still hanging there.

Clothes still hanging there? — Yes, a row of clothes.

That good coat you spoke of was underneath that? — Yes, on the other coat.[42]

Did you see anything the matter with the good coat at the time? — I did not notice anything particularly the matter. I noticed it was lying down as if it had been laid down, as if it had not fallen.

Did you see the marks on the old underneath coat? — Yes, I noticed stains, and also smelled a very strong smell coming from it, and it burned the skin off my fingers when I picked it up.

Was it wet or dry? — Very wet.

Mr Justice STEPHEN: What is that? — The old coat.

Mr POLAND: Did you see anything of a pair of trousers? — I saw an old pair of trousers lying on the floor against an old box, under the bedstead.

An old egg box? — Yes.

In the old egg box, were there some old clothes? — Yes.

Did you see where the waistcoat which has been spoken of was found? — No, I did not.

Alfred Inwood

---

41 The witness presumably meant to say something like, 'The coat which was covering the other coat'.

42 Another imprecise answer, or otherwise a mistake in the transcription: the preposition 'under' is surely to be preferred to 'on'.

Lipski.

Alfred Inwood

Did you notice what the things that were hanging on the walls were? — They were female clothing, such as dresses and petticoats, and I believe there was another coat.

Did you take charge of them? — I took charge of the two coats on the floor.

Did you take charge of the hat? — I simply took charge of the one coat and the hat.

Which coat was that? — The prisoner's coat.

The one stained: you took charge of that, and the hat. Did you leave the better coat, the other coat, there? — Yes.

Then, afterwards, you took the coat to the station ... The one you found with wet stuff on it, to the station? — Yes, and handed it to Inspector Final.

Cross-examined by Mr McINTYRE.

When you searched the room, had the prisoner been taken away in custody by the police? — Yes.

There was a crowd at that time on the stairs, and coming into the room? — No, I had removed them.

You had removed them, but there was a crowd coming in? — Yes.

On the near side of the bed, you say, you found the hat ... That was nearest the door? — Yes.

Can you tell me how long the prisoner had been taken away before you began your search? — He was in the room when I reached there.

When you began your search, had he been taken? — He had been taken a few minutes.

Charles Peters

CHARLES PETERS, sworn and examined by Mr MATHEWS.

You live at 222 Romford Road, Stratford? You own the house and manage it at number 16 Batty Street? — Yes, I am the leaseholder.

Have you been accustomed to fixing locks and doing repairs of that description yourself? — For about twenty years.

Do you remember fixing a lock on the door of the first floor, front room, of number 16 Batty Street? — Yes.

About how long was that before 28 June? — I have not particular note of that. It strikes me about a fortnight or three weeks before this sad affair.

Was it a new lock you fixed? — Brand new lock, and a very good lock, I believe.

After you had fixed it, did you try to work it in the presence of the deceased woman? — I tried it myself, previously, to satisfy myself it would lock and unlock and that. And after that I saw the deceased woman

First Day – Friday 29 July 1887.

sitting by the window. I tried to make her understand to come and try the lock herself, but I found I could make no effect on her, and I went then to the door, and tried it backwards and forwards, and beckoned to her, and she tried it, and bowed, and went away … Something that way.

It was then in perfectly good working order? — To my satisfaction.

Is that the lock which you fixed? [*The lock was handed to the witness.*] — This is the lock.

Is that the box that was there? — This is the box, but the wedge … I had cut a piece out and placed, there [*describing*], a solid piece of wedge, and that was not split in this way. I imagine that has got split in wrenching the door open.

You did place a wedge there to complete it, so that the box might be placed on it? — Yes, that it would be steady; so that it would unlock steady.

That done, the lock was – in your opinion – perfectly available to lock the door? — Yes, I thought so.

Cross-examined by Mr McINTYRE.

You were not brought up as a locksmith, I think? — No. I consider myself a practical man.

All round? — A little that way.

Were you brought up as a tailor? — I served seven years' apprenticeship to a tailor and worked at it ten years after.

Was the box a little higher up than the lock? — A little higher? I can't say that. I can't say whether a little higher or a little lower. It was, as it were, in the centre, a little below the top and a little higher than the bottom, so as to make it come in the centre of the lock. … I imagine so.

Mr Justice STEPHEN: You are landlord of this house. You may have other houses. Are you in the habit of using your tools as other people are? — I have got a set of carpenter's tools, all for my own use. I thought this case would not come on, and, to amuse myself today, I brought a little parcel with me with a hammer in it.

You amuse yourself with your tools? — Yes.

WILLIAM PIPER, recalled and further cross-examined by Mr McINTYRE.

Was the partition enclosing the room made of wood, or did it give? — Yes.[43]

And when the door was forced open, is it a fact it did not injure the lock? — It did not injure the lock in any way, but it interfered with

---

43 The judge's notes say, 'The partition was of wood and gave'. (TNA:PRO HO 144/201/A47465/7)

Lipski.

William Piper

the box of the lock. It shifted the box slightly from one of these things underneath.

The evidence you gave before was it did not injure the lock. — It did not injure the lock; it interfered with the box.

Thomas Warwick

THOMAS WARWICK, sworn and examined by Mr MATHEWS.

You live at 19 Batty Street? — Yes.

Is that almost opposite to number 16? — As near as possible.

Do you work in the front parlour of number 19? — Yes.

Is that on the ground floor? — Yes.

On the morning of Tuesday 28 June, were you at work in that room? — Yes.

Between what hours? — From 6.00, up to the time I heard of the sad affair opposite.

From where you sat in your room, could you see without effort across the street? — Yes, quite clear.

And up to your hearing of 'the sad affair opposite', as you call it, did you hear any noise or disturbance from over the way? — No, nothing whatever.

If any person had got out of the first floor window opposite on that morning, do you think you would have seen him? — Must have seen him.

As a matter of fact, did you see anyone get out of a window in that house that morning? — None whatever.

Did you know the prisoner, before this day, by sight. — Oh, yes.

Did you see him go in or out of the house that morning? — Once that morning.

About what time was that? — I should think about 8.45, sir.

Did he then go into the house? — He had his hat and coat on.

Was he going in or coming out? — Going in.

Hat and coat on? — Yes.

Was he carrying anything at the time? — He had a little small parcel, very small.

After that hour, you did not see him come out? — Never saw him after.

Did you notice the blind of the room on the first floor opposite to you on this morning? — Down, a long blind; and a short blind, as well, covered the lower part of the window.

The window itself: was it open or shut? — A little bit open at the top.

Did you see the witness Dywein pull it a little way further down? Did you see Dywein that morning? — That was the first I see: Dywein and Dr Kay put their heads out of the window.

Where was Dywein when you saw him? — When the top part of the

First Day – Friday 29 July 1887.

window was pulled down.

Did he pull it further down in order to call out? — He had to pull it down five inches or six inches, more than that.

Cross-examined by Mr McINTYRE.

Were you examined before the coroner? — No.

Were you examined before the magistrate? There were several examinations there. — No.

When did you first give your evidence to anybody? — About three weeks ago.

Were you at the police court? — Yes.

Was this occasion, when you say you saw Lipski, the only time you saw him that morning? Yes, go in.

Did you see him come out? — No.

You never saw him come out at all that morning? — No, go in.

Can you tell me the time, exactly? — About 8.45.

You say you work in the front room. What at? — Boot and shoe making.

I suppose, between 6.00 and the time the sad affair happened, you went to get your breakfast, did you not? — Yes.

You were not looking out of the window[44] all the time? — No, I was downstairs getting my breakfast.

What time did you get your breakfast? — About 7.00 or 8.00.

While at work, I suppose you are not always watching the opposite house? — I must have been blind if I did not see a man come out of the window opposite.

Re-examined by Mr POLAND.

What time did you get back from breakfast? — A little after 9.00.

You breakfast in the same house? — Yes.

You were at the police court? — Yes.

The court adjourned.

****

---

44 'Out of window' in transcript.

Lipski.

Second Day – Saturday 30 July 1887.

David Final

DAVID FINAL (Inspector of Police, H[45]), sworn and examined by Mr MATHEWS.

On 28 June this year, about 12.45, was the prisoner brought to Leman Street police station? — Yes.

In what condition was he at the time? — He appeared to be partially insensible.

Was he seen by Mr Phillips, the divisional surgeon? — Yes.

And after that, was some mustard and warm water given? — Yes. I gave him some, and Dr Phillips ordered him some afterwards.

It had not the effect of making him sick? — No.

After that, was it, you searched him? — Yes.

What did you find on him? — Two or three shillings in silver, and some copper, and a pawn ticket.

What became of that pawn ticket? — I put it back in his pocket, and the money.

And he was then sent on to the London Hospital? — Yes.

And did you yourself go to 16 Batty Street? — I did.

About what time did you arrive there? — It would be about 1.30, I think.

Did you go up to the room on the first floor, front? — Yes.

Of which, I think, at that time, a constable was in charge? — Yes.

Was the door locked when you arrived there? — Yes.

Was it opened by the constable in charge? — Yes.

Did you go into the room and examine the lock? — Yes, I did.

Did you notice anything about the box of the lock? — Yes. The screws were about a quarter of an inch drawn from the wood, as if the door had been forced.

How was the wood at that time? — Split.

As it now is? — Yes.[46]

What was the condition of the lock? — In perfect order, except that the bolt was shot.

Was it after this you went upstairs to see if you could see through the little window or partition? — Yes.

Could you do so? — Yes.

Was the deceased woman still lying on the bed at this time? — Yes.

---

45   *i.e.*, H Division.
46   The judge's notes say, 'Wedge of wood split as now' (TNA:PRO HO 144/201/A47465/7). Photographs of the lock show the split wedge of wood, with its thinner end positioned behind the uppermost screw of the lock's box.

Second Day – Saturday 30 July 1887.

Could you see her as she lay there? — Yes.

Later on, did Police Constable Inwood bring you this coat and hat? — Yes.

You searched the coat pockets? — Yes.

In one of them, did you find anything? — Yes.

What? — 'I. Lipski Limited Stick and Cane Dressers Protection Society', and a pawn ticket for a silver Geneva watch, pawned in the name of John Lipski on 23 June and the amount of six shillings, Myrdle Street.[47]

Was that all the search you made at that time? — Yes.

After that, was it, you received this bottle from Dr Kay? — Yes.

Had it a cork in it when given to you? — Yes.

On the evening of that same day, 28 June, about 7.30, did you go with Police Sergeant Thick to the London Hospital? — Yes.

Were you accompanied by an interpreter? — Yes.

His name? — Mr Smaje.

And in the hospital, accompanied by the interpreter, did you go into a ward where you saw the prisoner in bed? — Yes.

What was the prisoner's condition at that time? — He was insensible.

You speaking to the interpreter, the interpreter spoke to him? — Yes.

In a language you did not understand? — No.

Did the prisoner reply to the interpreter? — Yes, he did.

And did the interpreter translate the replies of the prisoner as they were given? — Yes.

And did you write down the replies as the interpreter translated them? — I did.

And at that time? — Yes.

Tell us, was it a statement made by the prisoner in answer to questions, or did he make a statement first of all without questions being put to him? — Voluntary.

Mr Justice STEPHEN: But do you mean without questions being put? — Yes, my lord.

Mr MATHEWS: At the conclusion of the statement the prisoner made, did you, in the course of your duty, put some questions to him? — I did, sir.

Through the interpreter? — Yes, sir.

Did the interpreter translate the answers given to those questions? — Yes.

And, at that time, did you write them down in the form of question and

---

47 The judge's notes say, 'Found card & pawn ticket produced' (TNA:PRO HO 144/201/A47465/7). The strange properties of the card – what exactly was the 'I. Lipski Limited Stick and Cane Dressers Protection Society'? – were not explored at the trial.

Lipski.

David Final

answer? — I did, sir.

Do you produce the book in which you wrote that statement down? — Yes.

As well as the questions and the answers? — Yes, sir; the whole of it.

After you had written it down in that book, did you read it to the interpreter? — Yes, sir.

What did the interpreter do? — He interpreted to the prisoner … through me to the prisoner.

Was anything said – through the interpreter, by the prisoner – after it had been read? — He said, 'I have nothing more to say'.

Mr Justice STEPHEN: In English? — No, through the interpreter.

Mr MATHEWS: Were you in uniform at this time? — I was.

On 2 July, did you charge the prisoner with this crime? — Yes.

Where was he then? — In the London Hospital.

Was the same interpreter with you? — Yes, sir.

Did he interpret the charge to the prisoner? — Yes.

And did the prisoner make some reply? — At the police station he did.

Was it on that day he was brought to the police station? — Yes, sir. Arbour Square.

As I understand, in the first instance he made no reply when he was charged at the hospital. — No.

He was brought to the police station? — Yes.

Was the interpreter still present? — Yes.

Once more was the prisoner charged? — Yes.

There did he make a reply? — Yes.

Which the interpreter translated? — Yes.

Did you make any note of that reply? — Yes.

At the time? — Yes.

You have it before you? — Yes.

On 20 July, were you present at 16 Batty Street? — I was.

When the lock and the box of the lock were sawn from the door of the first floor room? — Yes.

Did you see the condition of the lock and box at that time? — Yes, I did.

How was it, having reference to your examination on 28 June? — Exactly as it was when I first saw it.

Cross-examined by Mr McINTYRE.

Was the prisoner in custody of the police during the time he was at the hospital? — The police were watching him.

In the ward? — Yes.

Was there a detective officer there, in plain clothes? — Yes.

Second Day – Saturday 30 July 1887.

And sitting by his bedside? — Yes.

Is it not a fact you had him in charge on suspicion of having committed this murder? — He had not been charged.

No, but you had him in charge on suspicion of having committed this murder? — Yes.

When you first saw the prisoner on 28 June, was he insensible? — Partially so.

When he was brought to your station, did he not appear to be insensible? — Partially so. I will explain it. I slapped his face and he acknowledged it, and then I gave him an emetic – mustard and water – and he was not sick. And I also opened his eye and touched the pupil, and he acknowledged it.

That was all done before you were examined before the magistrate? — Yes.

On your oath, before the magistrate, did you swear he appeared insensible? — Partially so.

You did not say 'partially'. — The word 'partially' was not put in.

It was in examination-in-chief to the gentleman conducting the prosecution you swore that he appeared insensible? — I say so now.

No, you qualify it now: 'partially'. — Yes, partially.

Mr Justice STEPHEN: He qualifies it. He says about opening the eye and slapping the face.

Mr McINTYRE: You went and took the interpreter. Did you tell him then you intended to charge him with being a murderer? — The prisoner? Yes. — No.

Did you take the interpreter there for the purpose of getting a statement from the prisoner, whom you were then watching? — Yes, from what I had been told.

Were you doing this on your own responsibility? — Yes.

You are the man getting up this prosecution? — I am.

You took the interpreter with the intention of getting a statement from the prisoner? — Yes. I had been told he wished to make one.

Who told you that? — Miss Lyons, his young lady. She came to the police station.

You did not understand what the interpreter said to him? — Certainly not.

The interpreter spoke to him and said something before he made any statement? — I directed the interpreter to caution him: if he wished to make any statement to me, I should take it down in writing and it might be produced afterwards.

I did not ask that. — No, sir.

If you will be kind enough to confine yourself to answering questions

David
Final

Lipski.

David Final

... What the interpreter said to him, of course, you don't know. — No.

Is the interpreter here? — He is.

About how many questions did you direct the interpreter to put to the prisoner? — Shall I read them?

No, they will be read in due course. — Five, sir.

Were you before the coroner, at the inquest? — I was.

Did you say to the coroner that Lipski would not be produced if the inquest were adjourned? Was he in custody at that time? — No, rather being watched.

Had he been charged? — No, he had not.

Still, he would not have been allowed to go? — He would if the coroner had wished it.

And policemen with him? — Decidedly.

I don't mean the coroner ... He would not have been set at liberty from the hospital? — No.

At that time, although he would not be allowed to go, you had not charged him? — He was not charged then.

You were there before the coroner on 1 July? — Yes, I was.

And you charged him on the second? — I did.

Henry Smaje

HENRY DAVID SMAJE, sworn and examined by Mr POLAND.

You live at Leman Street, Whitechapel, and you are an interpreter? — Yes.

I believe you have acted as interpreter at Thames Police Court many years? — Yes.

On Tuesday 28 June, were you sent for to the London Hospital? — I was.

Did you see the inspector there in uniform? — I did.

Then did you sit on the prisoner's bed? — I did.

And did the inspector speak to you; and, in consequence of what he said, what did you say to the prisoner? — I told him that he was not bound --

As if you were speaking to him now. — I told him, 'You are not bound to say anything, but what you do say will be taken down in writing by the inspector and may be used as evidence against you at your trial'.

Then did the prisoner say anything to that? — The prisoner commenced to make a statement.

As he made that statement, did you interpret it to the inspector? — I did.

The inspector in his pocket book ... Did you see him writing it down? — I did, sir.

When he had made the statement, did the inspector ask you to put

Second Day – Saturday 30 July 1887.

some questions to the prisoner? — He did, sir.

Did you translate those questions to the prisoner? — I did.

And did you translate the answers to the inspector? — I did, also.

Did you see him writing down the questions and answers? — I did, sir.

When this had been done, did the inspector read out what he had taken down in his pocket book? — From the pocket book.

And as he read it, did you translate it to the prisoner? — I did.

When that was done and you had finished, did the prisoner say anything to that? — When he was finished, he said, 'I have nothing more to say'.

Afterwards, then, you left the bedside, did you? — Yes, I did.

Later on – I think 2 July – you, at the station, translated the charge to the prisoner? — Yes.

When he was formally charged with the murder of Miriam Angel? — Yes.

You read that to him and he made a reply? — I cautioned him first.

He made a reply? — He did.

You translated that reply to the inspector, and he wrote it down? — Yes.

Henry Smaje

Cross-examined by Mr McINTYRE.

This was at the police office, was it? — Police station.

Have you not made a slight mistake in saying that you cautioned the prisoner at the hospital that what he said might be used against him? — I did say something about trial.

You know at that time he was not charged? — It possibly arose from my custom, by being so used to it.

When before the magistrate, was not your memory rather better than it is now in respect of what actually took place? It was nearer the time. There is not a word before the magistrate of you having stated it would be used in evidence against him at his trial. Is not this what you said? 'I sat on the prisoner's bed. Mr Inwood spoke to me, and I said to him, "You are not bound to say anything. What you say will be put down."' — Possibly that is what I said at the police court.

You told the truth at the police court? — Yes.

Bearing that in mind, is not that exactly what did take place at that time? He was not charged till 25 July; your conversation was on 28 June. He was not charged for some days after that. — That is very true.

Don't you think you are confusing what you said to him when he was in the hospital with what you said to him when he was at the police office? — I don't admit that. I don't say 'confusing' it.

If you told him it would be used on his trial, why did you not tell the magistrate so? — I have been engaged in other matters, and the word

Lipski.

Henry Smaje

'trial' seemed to be so used to me that, possibly, I might have used it.

Mr Justice STEPHEN: What is your impression now? That you did mention the word 'trial', or not? — My impression is that I did, in Hebrew.

Mr McINTYRE: Your recollection was better immediately after the occurrence?

Mr Justice STEPHEN: It is not in the depositions. You can make an observation upon it.

Mr McINTYRE: You made a statement to him at the hospital on a second occasion? — I was not there on a second occasion. I was only there once.

At the police station, he was formally charged, in your presence? — Yes.

At the police station, when you charged him, did the prisoner make a reply? — Yes.

Mr Justice STEPHEN: I understood your evidence about the police station to be that you cautioned him, you charged him, he made a reply to you, you translated that reply? — That is so, my lord.

Mr McINTYRE: Were those the only two occasions on which you did see him and make a charge to him. — As far as the police are concerned, those are.

David Final

DAVID FINAL, recalled and further examined by Mr POLAND.

Mr Justice STEPHEN: Is this a copy of what you are going to read? Is it? — Yes.

Of what was taken at the bedside in the hospital? Will you read it, what you took down at the bedside, translated to you as the prisoner having said?

[*The following statement, as read by the witness, was translated to the prisoner sentence by sentence.*]

'At seven a.m., a man working for me came. He asked me for work. I told him to wait. I would buy a vice for him so as he could work. I went to purchase a vice. I went to the shop but it was too soon. As I was going along, I met another workman whom I knew at the corner of Backchurch Lane. I went back; the shopkeeper wanted four shillings. I offered him three shillings. He would not take it. I returned and came into the passage and I saw the man that I met in Backchurch Lane. He asked me, "Will you give me work, or not?" I said, "Go to the workshop. I am going to get my breakfast. Then I will give you work." I then told my landlady to make some coffee. I then told a man (meaning the first man) that called at seven a.m. to fetch some brandy. I then went to the yard. I went upstairs to the first floor. I then saw both these men. I saw

Second Day – Saturday 30 July 1887.

them open a box. They took hold of me by the throat and threw me to the ground, there – on the ground – opened my mouth, and put in some poison, and said, "That is the brandy". They got my hands behind me and asked me if I had any money. "I have got no more than the sovereign that I gave you to get the brandy with." He then asked, "Where is your gold chain?" I said, "It is in pawn". They said, "If you don't give it to us, you will be as dead as the woman". They put a piece of wood in my mouth. I struggled; they put their knees against my throat. One said to the other, "Don't you think he is quite dead?" The reply was, "He don't want any more". They then threw me under the bed and there I lay for dead.

David Final

'Question: Do you know who those two men are? Answer: I know one who formerly worked with me.

'Question: Do you know his name and where he lives? Answer: His name is Simon. I don't know where he lives.

'Question: Do you know anything of the other man? Answer: I don't know him. He is a stranger to me.

'Question: Is his name Simon Rosenbloom? Answer: I can't say.

'Question: Do you know if Simon lives in Philpot Street? Answer: I think so. I have nothing further to say.'

Mr POLAND: At the police station, the answer he made on 2 July?

Mr Justice STEPHEN: What question did Mr Smaje ask him at the police station? Will you say what question Mr Smaje asked him at the police station? You read over the charge to him at the police station? — Yes.

And cautioned him? — Yes.

What did he say in reply to that? — He said, 'I have not murdered her, and I have not done it'.

Did he speak in Hebrew or English? — He said, 'Ich habe nicht gehalhret, ich habe nicht getahren'.[48] 'I have not murdered her, I have not done it.'

---

48 *Sic* in transcript. Some difficulty was encountered in transliterating Yiddish words, particularly in the pacy environment of the court. For 'getahren', compare modern German *getan: done*. The judge's in camera notes, at this point, read 'Interpreter recalled', and give the impression that Lipski's account of what had supposedly happened in the Angels' room was read out by Henry Smaje, but this must be erroneous (TNA:PRO HO 144/201/A47465/7). Smaje was probably recalled after Mr Justice Stephen asked Inspector Final, 'Will you say what question Mr Smaje asked him at the police station?' Final had already admitted that Smaje spoke to Lipski in a language which he – Final – could not understand. He is an unlikely candidate to recount to the court Lipski's response to the charge in its original Yiddish.

Lipski.

John Kay

JOHN WILLIAM KAY, sworn and examined by Mr POLAND.

Are you a doctor of medicine and a member of the Royal College of Surgeons? — Yes.

You practise at 100 Commercial Road – that is, at the corner of Batty Street? — Yes.

On Tuesday 28 June, were you called to 16 Batty Street? — Yes.

Did you go up into a room on the first floor? — Yes.

What time did you get into the room? — At 10.45.

11.45? — 11.45.

Were there other persons in the room then? — I went in with my assistant and others followed us.

Your assistant was outside? — He went with me from the surgery.

On the bed, did you see the woman lying there? — Yes.

Just describe what position she was in. — She was lying on her back, dead, with her hair dishevelled.

Her mouth? — Her mouth had a stream of yellow coming from the corner on the left-hand side.

Her neck? — Her neck had two or three splashes; her breast had a splash.

Her hands? — Her hands were covered with the stains of nitric acid.

What were they, those yellow stains? What were they? — Nitric acid.

Commonly called *aqua fortis*? — Yes.

Mr Justice STEPHEN: Her hands were covered with it, you say? — Yes, covered with it.

Mr POLAND: How was she covered? — She was covered up to her breast with one of the German feather beds.

Did you remove that? — I turned it down to see if any violence had been offered to her.

How was the body? Exposed? How was the chemise? — The chemise was pulled up to the breast and the body was exposed.

Besides the marks of the acid in the places you have mentioned, did you notice any marks of blood anywhere? — I noticed blood on the feather bed ... splashes of blood and acid, mixed.

Would the effect of the administration of this stuff cause a person to cough? — Yes.

Violently? — Very violently.

There were no marks of violence on the body, the lower parts? — No marks of violence ...

... On the person at all. Did you form an opinion at that time as to how long she had been dead? — I formed an opinion: about three hours.

Was the body cold? — Not quite cold.

Had what is termed *rigor mortis* set in? — It was absent: no *rigor*

Second Day – Saturday 30 July 1887.

mortis.

Supposing about three hours, were you able to say with any degree of certainty as to the time? — It must be pretty near it.

What sort of habit was she? Stout woman or thin woman? — Stout woman.

You have taken into condition[49] the state of the room – and the weather, and her condition of body – in forming your opinion as to the three hours? — Yes.

Did you notice on her face at all, at that time, any marks? — No, not at that time, except the mark on it of the acid.

Did you look about the room? — Yes, to see what she had drunk it out of.

Did you see anything? — Saw a glass. It contained some beer, but no acid.

And then did you further look about? — Looked about for a bottle; said there must be a bottle.

Was a man – Dywein – there? — Yes.

What did Dywein do? — I pulled the bed away from the wall, and stooped over the corpse, and looked down between the bed and the wall.

About how near was the bed to the wall when you pulled it out? — It was near the wall, or I should not have pulled it out. I could not say exactly how near.

About that? — Yes, about that.

When you pulled it out, you said, you stooped over the corpse? — Yes, and looked down to see if there was a bottle there; and I saw there a man, lying on his back.

The prisoner? — The prisoner, lying on his back.

Could you see him without moving anything? — Yes.

In what state did he appear to be? — He was in his shirt sleeves. He looked pale, and his eyes were partially open. You could see the white of his eye and part of the pupil.

What did you do to him? — I felt his pulse, and then I said, 'He is alive'. Then I put my finger on the cornea to see if he was unconscious, and he was unconscious.

And then? — Then I slapped him on the face, and he opened his eyes wide.

At that time, did he say anything to you? — No, sir.

What took place then? — I called for police to help me out with him – out of the corner, near the window.

How was he got out? Was he lifted out? — On each side of him …

John Kay

---

49   *Sic* in transcript. Probably 'consideration'.

Lipski.

John Kay

took hold of his arm and pulled him out. The bed was pulled round and he was taken round the end.

Pulled round on the floor? — Yes.

Bare floor boards? — Yes, boards.

Pulled him near the window? — Yes.

What was next done? — I looked in his mouth, and saw he had taken some of the nitric acid: not so much as the woman.

Mr Justice STEPHEN: What position did the police put him in after getting him round the bed? — They held him up, standing.

Did he fall down again? — No, the police had hold of him.

Mr POLAND: Did you notice anything more about him then? — I asked him some questions, and shook him, but he did not answer anything.

Did you ask him in English or German? — Both.

Can you tell whether he could understand what you said to him then? — I don't think he could.

Then did the police take charge of him? — The police took him.

He was taken away? — Yes.

Taken away by the police. ... Had you examined him, at all, carefully? — Yes, I examined his arms to see if there were any scratches.

You said he was in his shirt sleeves? — Yes. His forearms were bare.

Did you notice the condition of his hands? — I examined his hands for scratches, and saw there was a little stain of acid on his hands. Not much.

Then he was taken away. When did you first see this bottle? — When I was examining the man on the floor, and my back was turned to the bed, Mr Piper called to me, 'Here is the bottle'.

Who had it then in his hand? — Mr Piper.

No cork in it? — No cork in it.

Was there very little of the stuff left? — Yes.

How much? — A few drops.

It is what is termed a two-ounce phial? — Yes.

From those drops, were you able to say it was nitric acid? — Yes. I tested it with copper.

The ordinary nitric acid of commerce? — Yes.

Did it smell of nitric acid? — Yes.

Afterwards, did you make a post mortem examination? — Yes.

A well-developed young woman? — Yes, a well-developed young woman.

About six months gone in the family way? — Yes.

On the lower part of the body, you saw no signs of violence? — Yes.

No signs of recent connection? — No.

You saw some discharge. That was the natural ... What was the date of

Second Day – Saturday 30 July 1887.

the post mortem? — Next day, Wednesday the twenty-ninth.

What did you notice about the right eye? — That it was discoloured, black and swelled.

What else? — I noticed the yellow stain at the corner of the mouth.

As to external injuries? — No other external injuries.

Did you examine the scalp? — Then I reflected back the scalp and saw, over the right temple, extravasated blood.

You cut the scalp and turned it back? — Yes.

In what state was the muscle? — The muscle was lacerated and bloody, and in a pulp from violent blows.

Could you tell whether the violence … Do you say whether more than one blow? — Must have been more than one blow.

And were they such that they might have been given with a man's fist? — Yes.

How many blows? Could you judge, at all? — I should think at least four blows.

What sort of blows? — Very violent blows.

Was the brain congested? —No, sir.

Does that come on at once from violent blows? — Not immediately. It must have time.

Could you tell from the appearance of those blows whether she would be rendered unconscious? — She would be rendered unconscious by such blows.

How would you describe it? — She would be stunned.

You examined her mouth. It was injured by poison? — Yes.

Then did you examine carefully the back of the throat? —Yes, it was all charred with the acid.

Charred? — Yes. Charred, we call it.

Did you find a portion of this stuff had gone into the stomach? — Yes.

And a portion …? — Had gone down the larynx, and trachea, and bronchial tubes.

Down the windpipe? — Yes.

What would that indicate? — That would indicate that it had been poured down her throat while she was insensible.

Is the glottis the covering to the windpipe? — Yes.

How was that? — Open.

In the ordinary course of swallowing, that closes? — Yes.

To protect liquid and food from going the wrong way? — Yes.

Where would the greater portion of the acid appear to have gone? — The greater portion appeared to have gone down the windpipe.

Could you, at all, estimate the amount of stuff – acid – at all? — Approximate estimate: about half an ounce.

John Kay

Lipski.

John Kay

And her hands? They were stained with the acid.

Whereabouts? — All over the back and front. All over.

Now, what was the cause of death? — Suffocation.

Was that produced by the acid acting on the --? — Acting on the windpipe.

Would that be acid acting on the windpipe and closing the passage for the air? — Yes.

How would it act? Would it produce convulsion of those parts? — Great convulsion.

And how soon after the administration would it close the windpipe? — About three minutes.

Now look at that coat – the prisoner's coat. [*It was handed to the witness.*] Now, the front part of it has a quantity of the acid there – burned away – every part of the coat … Is it all marked with the acid? — Yes.

It has the effect, has it, of burning away woollen --? Yes.

The outside and inside of the sleeve, coming against that part … and the inside as well as the outside?

Mr Justice STEPHEN: The coat is almost destroyed by it.

Mr POLAND: Then Mr Angel's coat. It is the coat that was on the other one. You looked at the other coat? — I have not looked at it. [*It was produced.*]

You see five or six stains on that coat? Are there some slight stains there on the lining, inside? — I don't see any … There is a slight stain.

Might that come from that coat? — Resting on the other coat? Yes.

Mr Justice STEPHEN: Is there only one stain? — I could not swear to the other.

Mr POLAND: And the waistcoat? — Yes, that is the stain of nitric acid.

Might that come from resting on the other coat? — Yes, it might.

Did you find any trace – besides nitric acid on the coat – any trace of blood, any spluttering?[50] — Not on the coat. On the bed.

Cross-examined by Mr McINTYRE.

Might the blood on the bed be caused by the woman coughing to get rid of poison put into her throat? — Yes, I attributed it to that at the time.

I believe the post mortem examination you made completely convinced you that there had been no recent connection? — That, and putting the discharge under a microscope.

You came to the conclusion there had been no recent connection? — No evidence of it.

---

50   *Sic* in transcript. Perhaps 'splattering'?

Second Day – Saturday 30 July 1887.

You say the man did not understand you, was unconscious. Was that from the effect of poison also? — No, not from the poison. I attributed it to mental perturbation.

Surely a man who does not flinch when you put your finger in his eye must have been unconscious? — He was not *very* unconscious. A slap roused him.

Mr Justice STEPHEN: Do you say a man, from mental causes, could be thrown into such a state that you could put your finger in his eye without his flinching? — I have seen a woman that I could put my finger on the cornea. … I don't remember a man.

I suppose, if a man was both in a state of mental perturbation and had drunk a certain quantity of nitric acid, one would help the other to make him unconscious? — Yes, but the nitric acid was not sufficient, in my opinion, to cause unconsciousness.

You saw this man about 12.00, I understand. Between that and 1.00?
Mr McINTYRE: About 11.45.
Mr Justice STEPHEN: There had been a quantity of people in the room and a good deal of noise. For how long would a mere fainting fit … What is the longest period that you have ever known a man remaining unconscious from mental causes? Or a woman? — I frequently have known a woman remain unconscious from mental causes for two hours, in spite of all restoratives – mustard plasters, and ammonia.

That is a long time. — Yes, but I have known them.

What about men? — I have not seen a man unconscious from mental causes.

Mr McINTYRE: Suppose this man had been seized, and men had knelt on his chest. Would that have produced, with the poison that was taken, such unconsciousness as you saw him under? — Violence would tend to produce unconsciousness.

WILLIAM DOBREE CALVERT, sworn and examined by Mr MATHEWS.

Are you house surgeon at the London Hospital? — House physician.
And you were there when the prisoner was brought there on 28 June? — I was.
Did you put some questions to him in English? — I did; or rather, I made some remarks to him in English.
Did he seem to understand them? — He did.
Did you see his fingers and his fingernails? — Yes.
What did you find on them, if anything? — On the fingers of his left hand, I saw some yellow stains … also on the nails of the left hand. On the second joint of the --

Lipski.

William Calvert

Mr Justice STEPHEN: Which fingers? — Nearly all his fingers. I think also on the nails of the same left hand, and a slight stain on the second joint of the third finger of the right hand.

Mr MATHEWS: Were they such stains as would be produced by nitric acid? — Yes.

Did you notice anything more on the hands? — I noticed some trivial scratches on the back of both of his hands.

Anything on one of the wrists? — A scratch larger than the rest.

On which wrist? — On the back of the right wrist.

Anything on the forearms? — There were some slight scratches on the forearms.

The elbows? — The skin was rubbed off both elbows – partially rubbed off, abraded.

The forehead? — There were one or two slight scratches on the forehead, and notably one on the right temple.

Were the appearances you saw indicative of any serious violence of any kind? — I think not.

Did you examine the mouth? — Yes.

From your examination of the mouth, what opinion did you form? — I thought the injuries were produced by the application of some corrosive fluid.

What were the injuries to the mouth? — There were some white patches at the back of the tongue and on the left tonsil.

The pharynx? — Little white patches on the pharynx.

Anything more did you notice about the mouth? — No.

With reference to these appearances, what opinion did you form as to their cause? — I thought they were produced by the action of a corrosive fluid.

Such as nitric acid? — Yes.

Were those injuries serious in their character? — No.

Did you examine the throat upon the outside? — I did.

No marks of violence upon it? — I found none.

Were there any marks of violence or of injury on the body, beyond those you have given us? — None.

You have spoken about injuries on the person. Were they such, in your opinion, as would prevent a man crying out? — They were not of such a nature, I should think, as to prevent a man crying out.

Cross-examined by Mr McINTYRE.

Now, was there not an abrasion in the inside of the mouth? — Yes, there was.

Did that indicate, to your mind, that some foreign substance had been

Second Day – Saturday 30 July 1887.

thrust into the mouth? — Yes.

When was it you made your examination of him? The day he came in, or next day? — I examined him when he came in, and I examined him every day.

Was it on the day he came in you examined him at 3.00, or a little after 3.00? ... 2.00, was it, or 3.00? — About 2.30, I imagine. I could not be sure.

Re-examined by Mr POLAND.

Do you know, to your knowledge, whether anything was used to the prisoner, from what you saw? Anything done to him? — I saw nothing done to him.

What was the abrasion you saw? Was it recent? — Yes, it was.

Whereabouts was it? — At the back part of the palate. Back part of the mouth.

Was it in such a position that if a stomach pump had been used, it would have made a mark? — Yes. I should think, in the condition of palate and condition of mouth, a stomach pump would have produced this injury, because it was in the locality of one of the white patches. The mucous membrane was there softened.

THOMAS REDMAYNE, sworn and examined by Mr POLAND.

What are you? — I am house physician at the London Hospital.

Did you see the prisoner there? — Yes. I saw him when he first came in.

What time? — 11.45 or 11.40, I should think.[51]

Did you use anything to him? — Used the stomach pump, yes.

Cross-examined by Mr McINTYRE.

Were you examined before the coroner? — No.

Or before the magistrate? — No, this is the first time I have had anything to do with it.

When were you asked to come here? — I got a notice I should probably be wanted yesterday, and a policeman came this morning.

I suppose you used the stomach pump successfully? — To the best of my ability. ... Got something into him.

Mr Justice STEPHEN: Do you think it likely that you could have produced such an abrasion as was spoken of by the last witness? — Very probably, yes. We had to use a gag to get his mouth open, and he broke that.

William Calvert

Thomas Redmayne

---

51   *Sic* in transcript. The judge's notes – correctly – read, 'Saw prisoner when he first came in at 1.45 – 50'.

Lipski.

Charles Moore

CHARLES MOORE, sworn and examined by Mr POLAND.

You are, I think, manager to Mr Lee. — Yes.
It is not your business, Mr Lee's business? — Yes.
196 Backchurch Lane? — Yes.[52]
What is the business? — Oilman's shop.
Oil and colour man? — Yes.
Is it an ordinary shop? — Yes.
Do you know the boy Pittman as coming to the shop to buy things? — Yes.
How long before the twenty-eighth, Tuesday? — The day previous, on the Monday.
What were the things he bought? — A quart of methylated spirit.
Mr Justice STEPHEN: What day was this? — On the twenty-seventh, the day before.
Then what? — Two pounds of shellac, and half a pound of drop black.
What is that? — Black that is used in drops for staining wood, previous to varnishing.
Mr POLAND: Are those things used by stick makers? — Yes.
Did you know where he was employed? — I did not know at that time.
On Tuesday 28 June, do you remember a man coming to your shop with a bottle? — Yes.
What sized bottle? — Two-ounce phial.
A bottle similar to this? [*Showing one to the witness.*] — Yes, similar one to that.
You have seen the prisoner before the magistrate. To the best of your belief, who is the man who came with the bottle? — Yes: the prisoner is the man, to the best of my belief, that I served the nitric acid to, and that I saw before the magistrate.
About what time was it? — About 9.00 in the morning.
What did he ask you for? — A pennyworth of *aqua fortis*.
What language did he speak in? — English.
He produced the bottle … and did you supply him with the pennyworth of *aqua fortis*? — Yes.
About how much would that be? — About one ounce. I weighed it to him.
Did you say anything to him about what it was wanted for? — I asked him for what purpose he wanted it.
What did he say? — He said he was a stick maker. He wanted it for staining sticks.
And then did you say anything to him about it? — I cautioned him that it was poisonous.

52   An error in the transcript: the shop was at 96 Backchurch Lane.

Second Day – Saturday 30 July 1887.

Do you remember what you said to him? — That is what I said to him.
Did you wrap it up in anything? — The bottle?
Yes. — No.
He took it away? — Yes, just as it was.
You corked it and he took it away with him? — Yes.
Your shop is next door to Mr Schmidt? — Yes.
Did you hear what had happened at 16 that day? — Yes, on the same day.
The same day, did the police come to you? — No, the day after.
That would be the twenty-ninth. I suppose you gave them information on the subject? — Yes.
Were you afterwards taken to the hospital? — Yes.
What day was that? — Friday morning.
Were you taken into wards where there were a number of patients in the beds there? ... That was the Friday? — Yes.
You went from bed to bed? — Yes.
Did you come to a bed where the prisoner was? — Yes.
What did you do when you came to that bed? — I pointed him out to the inspector.
And had you, previous to that, given a description of the person who had made the purchases at your shop? — Yes.

Cross-examined by Mr McINTYRE.

Do I understand you? You did not know the prisoner before? — Previous to the purchases?
Yes. — No, I did not know him.
Was the description as to the face – 'A little hair on the face' ... Was that what attracted your attention to the man who bought the nitric acid? — The hair on his face? No, that did not attract my attention particularly.
When you went to the hospital and into this ward, was there a police constable in plain clothes sitting at the head of this bed? — There was a man in plain clothes sitting by the side of the bed. I could not say whether he was a constable or not.
Was that the only bed in the room where a man was sitting by the side of the bed? — I believe so.
Were you in the ward about ten minutes? — Yes, about ten minutes.
Were you walking up and down the ward during that time? — I walked down once, and back again.
You walked from one end to the other? — No, I walked as far as the prisoner's bed and back again.
Was his the end bed? — No, I think it was near the fireplace.
Did not you walk to the end of the ward? — No.

Charles Moore

Lipski.

Charles Moore

Was the inspector with you when you went? — Yes.

He was in uniform? — Yes.

What did the man sitting at the head of the bed do when the inspector came up to the bed with you? — Did he get up?

Yes. — I did not take any notice of that. I could not say positively whether he did or not.

You were taken there to identify the man who had bought the *aqua fortis*, were you? — Yes.

Were you told you would most likely see him there? — Yes.

Mr Justice STEPHEN: Who told you that? — I could not say whether it was the inspector or the detective.

Mr McINTYRE: But either the inspector or the detective told you that? — Yes.

And you expected, of course, did you not, to find the man there when you went? — Yes.

At the time you sold this *aqua fortis*, were there many people in your shop? — About six people, I should say.

Were you busy at the time? — Yes.

Serving these people with different things? — Yes.

Do you sell all the things that are requisite for these stick makers? — Yes.

Everything? — Yes.

Hannah Lyons

HANNAH LYONS, sworn and examined by Mr MATHEWS.

You live at 2 Watney Passage? — Yes.

You are the wife of Moses Lyons? — Yes.

Have you a daughter named Kate? — Yes.

Was your daughter engaged to be married to the prisoner? — Yes: six months.

Do you remember the prisoner coming to your house on the Monday 27 June? — Yes.

What time in the day did he come? — About 1.00, to eat his dinner.

Did he say anything to you about money? — Yes, he said I shall be so kind enough as to lend him money. How much he did not say.

What did you say? — I said I got no money to lend him: I take, borrow money.

What did you take and where did you go? I went in Church Street and took a brush[53] and ring and pawned them.

For how much? — Twenty-five shillings.

---

53   The judge's notes are probably to be preferred, except for the question of spelling: 'I pawned a broach [sic] and ring for 25/-' (TNA:PRO HO 144/201/A47465/7).

Second Day – Saturday 30 July 1887.

To whom did you give that money? — I took it there.

Where? — To his house.

To whom did you give it? — To Mr Lipski.

Did he say anything as to repaying you? — I gave him the money ... Yes, he said, 'Saturday, please God, I will take in the work --' or, 'finish the work'. 'I shall pay you all I owe you.'[54]

Had you lent him any money in the week before this? — Yes: there is the ticket.

How much? — £1.

Has he ever paid you any portion of that £2 5s back? — No.

Cross-examined by Mr McINTYRE.

Had you known him some time? — Known him when he was working at my son's. I have known him two years.

Was he a man of good character? — So far, I cannot give him a bad character. He always behaved himself.

Did you know, when you lent him this money, that he was fitting up his room for the purpose of turning it into a workshop? — I think so.

Did you know he was having the money for the purpose of fitting up a workshop? — Yes.

And did you know he was working at home, and employing that boy that has been called Pittman? — Yes.

And did you know he was going to employ other men as well? — I don't know that. I was not there.

Did you know he was doing work for people in the city that he had to take home and get his money for it? — No.

You don't know what work he was doing? — Horn work.

Stick work? — Yes, stick and horn work.

Do you know whether he was working for a Mr Lewis in Aldermanbury? — I don't know.

These are the names on the things handed by him, your lordship. [*Handing papers to his lordship.*]

Mr Justice STEPHEN: These are the names of the people for whom he worked. No doubt he was a stick maker.

Mr McINTYRE: And those are the persons for whom these sticks would be made.

GEORGE BITTEN, recalled and further examined by Mr MATHEWS.

What is the distance between Batty Street and White's Gardens, where the boy Pittman lived? — 837 yards.

---

54 The judge's notes say, 'He said, "Saturday, please God, I will take in the work and finish the work and pay you all I owe' (TNA:PRO HO 144/201/A47465/7).

Lipski.

George Bitten — Is that the nearest way? — There is another way, just a little under 800 yards.

Closing Speech for the Prosecution.

Mr Poland — Mr POLAND accordingly proceeded to sum up the case for the Crown.[55] He said it appeared to him that the facts were simple and clear, and that upon the evidence that had been given the jury could only come to one conclusion. He said it was clear that at the time the deceased lost her life, she and the prisoner were the only persons in the room, and that on the very day on which the occurrence took place the prisoner had purchased the acid which was, undoubtedly, the cause of death. He remarked that, as to the question of motive, it was perfectly immaterial; but upon the facts it was reasonable to suppose that the prisoner might have intended to commit an outrage upon this young woman, or to commit a robbery; but the jury were not called upon to consider the question of motive, and the only point they had to direct their attention to was whether the evidence made out to their satisfaction that the prisoner was guilty of the crime that was laid to his charge.

Speech for the Defence.

Mr McIntyre — Mr McINTYRE then addressed the jury for the defence.[56] He said no doubt it was always a very responsible and a very painful duty on the part of a counsel to have to put forwards a defence which implicated others while it cleared the prisoner, but he had to point out to them that the prosecution had failed to make out such a case against the prisoner as should induce a jury to find him 'Guilty' of this fearful crime with which he was charged. There could not, of course, be adequate excuse for such a crime as this, but there might be circumstances which would make a man, if reckless in character, commit such a crime. The prosecution had failed to point out any such circumstances in this case. He at first thought the imputation was that the prisoner had entered this young married woman's room for an immoral purpose. But the medical evidence had, he believed they would hold, entirely destroyed that contention. That being so, absolutely no motive was adduced for the commission of so awful a crime. There might perhaps seem to be an alternative motive suggested of robbery, but they would remember that the prisoner had an

---

55   This account of Poland's closing statement is taken from *Lloyd's Weekly Newspaper*, 31 July 1887.

56   This account of McIntyre's statement is taken from *Lloyd's Weekly Newspaper*, 31 July 1887.

Speech for the Defence.

exemplary character, that he did not conceal his movements at all that morning, and that he must have been aware of the poor prospect Mrs Angell's[57] room presented to one in search of plunder. The motive of immorality then having been given up –

The JUDGE (interrupting) pointed out that Mr Poland had not given up the motive of immorality. What he had not attempted to prove was successful immorality – viz., adultery.

Mr McINTYRE then proceeded to argue on the improbability of an attempted outrage by the prisoner. While she was struggling with the man the woman might have screamed, and could not have been overmastered at all easily; but had there been two men, as the prisoner suggested, one could have been engaged in gagging the woman while the other administered to her those violent blows which the prisoner would have been unable to give, he should think, while his strength was employed in overmastering the woman and in preventing her outcry. All the circumstances seemed to him to indicate that this was the act of two men, and not of one. It was asserted that the door was locked on the inside when the prisoner was found lying in the room with the murdered woman. But, if they remembered, the door was pushed open by women shoving with their hands; and was it not, therefore, more likely that the lock had stuck?

Mr McIntyre

Charge to the Jury.

Mr Justice STEPHEN, in summing up, said whoever caused the death of the deceased the act was one of wilful murder.[58] There was no doubt that between the hours of 6 and 11 on the morning in question the deceased woman was murdered by some person or persons. There were only two motives which could be put forward for the commission of the crime – passion and avarice. There was nothing taken from the deceased's room, because there was nothing to take, and the circumstances did not seem to support the motive of avarice. His Lordship pointed out that it was more probable that passion was the motive for the crime, and that if that were so it would rather be the act of one man than two. It was shown that the prisoner had not been acquainted with the deceased and her husband, and consequently if it was the prisoner who committed the act it must have been under the influence of a sudden temptation, there being a window from which a view of the deceased's room could

Justice Stephen

---

57   *Sic* in article. Should read: 'Angel's'.
58   This account of the judge's charge to the jury is taken from *The Times*, 1 August 1887. The article was clipped by the governor of Holloway and Newgate prisons, Lieutenant-Colonel E. S. Milman, and retained by the Home Office in what is now TNA:PRO HO 144/201/A47465/5.

Lipski.

Justice Stephen

be obtained from the stairs. The prisoner was a man of good character and was engaged to be married, and these were circumstances which the jury should take into consideration in favour of the prisoner. The man Schmusch[59] remained in London for several days after June 28, and then went to Birmingham for work, writing from there to London, and his conduct certainly did not look like that of a man who had committed a horrible murder. There was evidence that the prisoner had nitric acid, but that no one else had. His Lordship read the evidence in detail and the prisoner's statement, referring also to the denials given by the men Schmusch and Rosenbloom to the questions put them in cross-examination. The prisoner's statement was a highly important part of the case, and the witnesses Schmusch and Rosenbloom had been cross-examined as to its truth. One could hardly imagine that two men who were strangers to each other should walk down from the workshop and go into the deceased's room for the purpose of committing an assault upon her, and it was almost as difficult to imagine that they should go into the room of a woman as poor as themselves for the purpose of taking a few clothes, which after all they did not take, and why should they rob the prisoner? How could they reconcile the prisoner's statement with the fact that the door was locked on the inside? The locking of the door was a circumstance of very great importance supposing the jury were of opinion that it was locked. The observations made on the part of the defence as to the improbability of the prisoner having committed the crime were of very great importance, and should be carefully considered by the jury. If the jury came to the conclusion that the prisoner was the person who committed the offence, then the natural inference was that he attempted to commit suicide afterwards.

The Verdict.

The jury retired at 4.43 and returned at 4.51.

Verdict: Guilty.

On being asked through the interpreter if he had anything to say why sentence should not be passed, the prisoner replied (as translated by the interpreter), 'He says he did not do it'.

Sentence of death was then passed.

---

59 *Sic* in article. Should read: 'Schmuss'.

Appendices.

APPENDIX I.

Pall Mall Gazette, 1 August 1887.

Occasional Notes.

The result of the trial of Lipski leaves several points unsettled. Was the door of the murdered woman's room locked or not? The whole matter hinges on that. The landlady is not sure that it was. And the solicitor for the defence raises a good point this morning by the inquiry where the second ounce of nitric acid came from, as two were apparently employed and Lipski only bought one. The case is one which calls for consideration at the hands of the authorities before the death sentence is enforced.

APPENDIX II.

The First Petition and Mr Hayward's Pamphlet, 6 August 1887.[60]

Home Office, No. A47465/14.

Date: 6 Augt 87.

Israel Lipski.

References, &c.: Mr A. McArthur M.P.[61] forwards petition & pamphlet on behalf of this man, & vouches for the respectability of the petitioning solicitor, who assures him he has thoroughly investigated the case & conscientiously believes prisoner to be innocent. Pressing.

Minutes: ?Ackn.[62] and refer to learned judge for his observations. CM, August 6, 87.[63]

GL, 6 Aug 1887.[64]

Done. 8/8/87.

To the Right Honourable Henry Matthews,
Her Majesty's Secretary of State,
Home Department.

The humble petition of John Hayward, the solicitor for Israel Lipski, now a prisoner confined in Her Majesty's Prison Newgate and sentenced to death for the murder of Miriam Angell[65] sheweth as follows:

1. Your petitioner is a solicitor carrying on business at 27 King Street in the City of London and was instructed to conduct the defence of the prisoner Israel Lipski now lying under sentence of death in Her Majesty's Prison of Newgate.

---

60 TNA:PRO HO 144/201/A47465/14.
61 Mr Alexander McArthur (Member of Parliament for Leicester).
62 Acknowledge receipt.
63 Initials of Charles Murdoch, clerk (third class) to the Home Office.
64 Initials of Godfrey Lushington, permanent under-secretary to the Home Office.
65 *Sic* in petition.

Lipski.

2. That in pursuance of such instructions your petitioner visited the said Israel Lipski several times in the prison; that he took down the statement of the prisoner very carefully and cross-examined him as to the truth of such statement in every possible way.
3. That he has since had the opportunity of comparing such statement with the evidence given at the trial and has found it confirmed in every particular and he is thoroughly convinced that the prisoner did not commit the offence of which he is convicted.
4. Your petitioner craves leave to point out two or three facts which were not sufficiently brought out at the trial and which are more fully set forth in the printed statement and to which your petitioner respectfully craves attention:

1. At least double the quantity of acid must have been used to that which was stated to have been purchased by Lipski and the identification of Lipski as the purchaser of any acid is most unsatisfactory and incomplete.
2. The marks of acid on the bed clothes were mingled with blood coughed up by the dying woman. There were no marks of blood on the prisoner's coat. The whole of one skirt of the coat was destroyed by acid, the back part of each sleeve was badly stained and in such a way as to indicate that the man must have been lying on his back when these burns and stains were made. Both elbows were abraded or rubbed seeming to shew conclusively that they were rubbed against the floor while the man was lying on his back. The prisoner was discovered lying insensible under the bed in his shirt sleeves and the inside of his mouth burned with acid. His damaged coat was found lying on the floor and another coat which had been hanging upon the wall was found on the top of it. The insensibility of the prisoner could not have been caused by the acid but mental excitement and violence would produce such insensibility.

    If the prisoner's statement be true – that he was assaulted by two men who first nearly suffocated him then poured acid into his mouth and pushed him under the bed – all these appearances could be easily accounted for. Otherwise it seems almost impossible to account for them.
3. The door was at first stated to have been locked on the inside but the lock was imperfectly put on and Mrs Lipski, the landlady of the house, who first pushed the door open, states that the door was apt to hang and that she only tried it for a second and she is not at all sure whether the door was locked or only latched. The lock was very little injured by the door being pushed open and this seems to show that the bolt was not shot.

For these and for other reasons your petitioner humbly prays that the life of the prisoner Lipski may be spared until further enquiries and investigations have been made.

Appendix II.

Your petitioner will ever pray.

Jno. Hayward,
Solicitor,
27 King Street, EC.
August 4th 1887.

We strongly recommend this petition to your consideration.

A. McArthur.
Lewis H. Isaacs.[66]
Geo. E. Banes.[67]
Morgan Howard.[68]
Arthur A. Baumann.[69]
W.A. McArthur.[70]
Wilfrid Lawson.[71]
T.W. Russell.[72]
Thomas Lea.[73]

The Case

of

ISRAEL LIPSKI

now lying under

SENTENCE OF DEATH

for the murder of

MIRIAM ANGEL.

Jno. Hayward,
King Street, E.C.
Solicitor for the Defence.

---

66 Member of Parliament for Walworth.
67 Member of Parliament for West Ham South.
68 Member of Parliament for Dulwich.
69 Member of Parliament for Peckham.
70 Member of Parliament for St Austell.
71 Member of Parliament for Cockermouth.
72 Member of Parliament for Tyrone South.
73 Member of Parliament for Londonderry South.

Lipski.

Sir,

I visited the prisoner Israel Lipski several times in prison before his trial. I took down his statement most carefully and tested the truth of it in every possible way. I am fully persuaded from the straightforward answers he gave me, borne out as they were by certain facts, that he told me the truth, and that he is wholly innocent of the dreadful crime for which he has been condemned, and that if he could have been cross-examined on his statement in Court his innocence would have been most manifest. He is a young man only 22, slightly built, most modest and retiring in his demeanour, and bears an excellent character for industry and good conduct. It does seem shocking thing that such a man should die for a crime of which it is to say the least possible, that he is not guilty. I do hope, therefore, that you will use the influence that you possess to have his life spared, at all events until further investigations have been made.

I send for your perusal an account of the transaction as it appeared in the evidence, and as detailed to me by the prisoner.

I have endeavoured to set out everything of importance whether it told for or against him, and I earnestly commend the statement to your notice.

I am,
Yours obediently,
Jno. Hayward,
Solicitor for the Defence.
27, King Street, E.C.,

August 3, 1887.

The Case of Israel Lipski, now lying under Sentence of Death for the Murder of Miriam Angel.

On the 28th of June, at 11 o'clock in the morning, Miriam Angel, a young married woman, was found brutally murdered in the front room on the first floor at 16, Batty Street, Whitechapel, her husband having left her in good health, to go to his daily work, about 6.15 o'clock that morning; marks of four or five severe blows, as if from a fist, sufficient to have produced insensibility, were found on her temple; her mouth, windpipe, and gullet were burnt with nitric acid, which had produced suffocation; the bed clothes were marked with the acid, *mixed with blood*, probably (as the doctor said) coughed up by the dying woman; about an ounce of the acid had been used, and the murder was supposed to have taken place between 9 and 10 that morning. (Mrs Angel usually got up to go to her mother's[74] to breakfast between 7.30 and 8.30 am.) The bed stood 8 or 9 inches from the wall, against which the bed clothes were piled; underneath the bed, and

---

74 *Sic* in pamphlet.

Appendix II.

close to the wall, Israel Lipski, the condemned prisoner, a slightly-built young man 22 years old, a lodger in the same house, was discovered lying insensible, in his shirt sleeves, with a large egg box in front of him, the inside of his mouth burnt with the same acid. The acid would have given him great agony, but was not sufficient to have caused insensibility; a few scratches, described as very slight, on his hands and forehead, but the *skin of both his elbows was abraded or rubbed off.*

Lipski's coat was found under the bed, one skirt was completely destroyed by the acid, the underneath part of both the sleeves was also badly burnt; splashes of acid, *not mixed with blood*, were also found on the front of the coat; altogether *a full ounce of acid* must have been used *upon and about the coat alone*; this coat was covered up by another coat belonging to Mrs Angel's husband, which had been taken down from the wall where it had been hanging, and placed upon the damaged coat.

A two-ounce phial which had contained nitric acid was found in the bed clothes, the key of the bedroom door was found on the inside, but as hereinafter appears, it is uncertain whether the door had been locked, or only latched. Very little damage was done in pushing it open, and it was easily locked again. The doctor's assistant, who took the key out of the door, found the bolt shot, but several people (among whom was a man named Simon), had previously been in the room, and the lock may have been shot by accident or design.

Lipski had fitted up a workshop in a room above the Angel's.[75] The partitions dividing the rooms from the staircase were of wood a quarter of an inch thick, and a person conversing in Angel's room could be easily heard in Lipski's room above.

On the morning of the murder, Lipski, who had just commenced business for himself as a stick-maker, had engaged two men, Simon Rosenbloom, formerly a fellow workman of Lipski, Schmuss, a stranger to Lipski, and a boy to work for him. The boy said Simon told him he knew Schmuss, but this Simon denied. The boy went to his breakfast about 9 o'clock, and returned about 10 or half-past 10 o'clock, leaving the two workmen upstairs.

Simon says that the other man went out after the boy, he could not say how soon after, whether it was a few minutes, an hour, or an hour and a half, but when the boy returned the man was gone to his breakfast and never returned, because, as he stated at the trial, it was a poor place and he did not think that there would be work for him to do. The fact is there were plenty of raw sticks lying about and he was a man apparently in abject need. He stated he heard of the murder about 12 o'clock the same day, and he knew Lipski was suspected; he remained about London for a few days and then went to Birmingham.

---

75 *Sic* in pamphlet.

Lipski.

The ground floor of the house was occupied by Mrs Lipski the landlady, no relative of the prisoner, the first floor back room next to Mrs Angel's was occupied by two women, Mrs Levy and the blind mother (Mrs Rubenstien[76]) of Mrs Lipski, but during the absence of the boy Mrs Levy and Mrs Lipski had gone out, and the only persons known to be in the house were Simon and, perhaps, the workman Schmuss. Schmuss stated at the trial that he only stayed a few minutes, but no one saw him leave; but if his story be true, there would have been no one known to be in the house but Simon, and he did not hear the slightest noise of any kind; Lipski had been out at different times in the morning purchasing materials for his business; some person of about Lipski's age had been to a shop that morning and purchased one ounce of nitric acid of a Mr Moore, who was afterwards taken to the hospital to see if Lipski were the man, but as, according to the statement of the hospital nurse, he was taken straight up to the bed where the prisoner lay and on which a detective was sitting, and as there was no other person of the same age or similar appearance in the ward, the expression that, to the best of his belief, he was the man, is not of great value, especially as he quite failed to identify the phial with the rather unusual label upon it, and which Lipski denies ever belonged to him.

The Suggested Motive for the Crime.

No outrage had been committed on the woman, and the prosecution quite declined to suggest any motive for the commission of the crime. A motive, however, was suggested by the Judge in his summing-up. He said that the prisoner might have seen the woman in bed through a window on the staircase; that he suddenly determined to enter the room for an immoral purpose; that being foiled by the resistance offered he became furious, and then beat the woman insensible with his fists, and afterwards poured down her throat the acid which he had purchased for his business. He then might have taken the remainder of the acid with the view of destroying his own life, and crawled or fell under the bed, where he was found. How his coat came off and became covered with the other coat, or how it became burnt, how his elbows became rubbed, and at what period he became insensible, the Judge did not explain. This theory, which no doubt led to the conviction of the prisoner, came upon the defence by surprise, and when there was no opportunity of commenting on it to the Jury.

It does seem wonderful that if all this happened while the man Simon was in a room upstairs all the time, he never heard the slightest noise or a single scream or cry, although a conversation in the ordinary way in Mrs Angel's room can be distinctly heard in the room in which Simon was at work, and it is to be remembered that according to the evidence he was the only person in the house at the time excepting the blind old mother of Mrs Lipski who was sitting in the

---

76   *Sic* in pamphlet.

Appendix II.

street *outside* the door.

Note also, Lipski had been going up and down the staircase for six weeks prior to that morning, and no sudden impulse to commit robbery or rape had ever come upon him before.

The Prisoner's Statement.

According to the statement made by Lipski to his solicitor, he had been out to buy a vice and returned, and had gone down to the yard to have a wash, and afterwards proceeded to Petticoat Lane to buy some sponges from the hawkers for varnishing.[77]

On his way he met a hawker at the Whitechapel end of the Commercial Road. He bought a shillingsworth of sponge of him and returned. He described the sponge hawker as an old man of about 60, with a beard. A man answering this description has been seen selling sponges, but he is a foreigner, speaking English most imperfectly, and says he recollects nothing of the matter; he refused to give his address.

He then returned home, and on his way upstairs to his workshop he saw the man Simon standing half way in the doorway of Mrs Angel's room. The other workman, Schmuss, who is a tall powerful man, was standing behind him. Schmuss immediately seized him by the throat and put his hand over his mouth; Simon laid hold of his hands and held them behind him, then they pushed him backwards; in the struggle and fall, his coat was pulled off his left arm by the man Simon, who had hold of him from behind. Schmuss then knelt on his chest or stomach until he became nearly insensible.

He was just able to tell them in answer to their questions that he had no money, but was not strong enough to cry out and if he had cried out there was no one at that time in the house.

Simon then forced his mouth open with a piece of steel used for scraping sticks, and poured some stuff into his mouth. He says the stuff gave him very little pain at first. He saw them drag his coat off his other arm and feel in the pockets. He remembers them pushing him under the bed. He then became insensible, and must have lain in that condition for about three hours when he was discovered. Dr Kay stated that he could not account for the insensibility. The acid would not have produced it. He had never known *a man* to become insensible under such circumstances, but he considered that mental excitement and violence would have produced it.

---

77 A handwritten annotation is made on the Home Office's copy of the pamphlet: 'He had enquired when Marks' shop would open, but afterwards thought he could buy cheaper in Petticoat Lane.'

Lipski.

Confirmatory Evidence.

The evidence which appears to confirm Lipski's statement is that, according to Dr Kay, one ounce of acid at least was found down the murdered woman's throat, and another full ounce, according to Mr Calvert, the House Physician at the Hospital, must have been spilt over the coat, and if that statement be correct, then the single ounce of acid, to whomever it was sold by Moore, could not have been the acid with which the deed was done.[78]

The coat was burnt on the inside, one skirt was almost destroyed, the back parts of both arms were much stained with the acid.

If he had been lying on his back when this was done his arms would have come in contact with the part of the coat already soaked with the acid, and the appearance would be accounted for; but if he had been standing up, and no one interrupting him, it was almost impossible that the coat could have been burnt in the manner described.

Moreover, the damaged coat was found lying on the floor covered up by another coat belonging to Mr Angel, and which he had left hanging on the wall. How Lipski could have first taken off his own coat, then taken this coat down and covered up his own coat himself, then crawled under the bed, dragging the eggbox after him, before becoming insensible, is most difficult to conceive. He could not have slipped off the bed on the inside as the bedclothes were found piled against the wall and filling up the few inches between it and the bedstead.

Again, the skin was abraded or rubbed on both elbows. Mr Calvert stated to Lipski's solicitor that these abrasions could be accounted for by the struggles of a man on his back endeavouring to get up, but that it would be difficult to account for them in any other way.

The door was stated to have been locked inside, but the prisoner's solicitor's clerk took with him a Mr Cameron, of the Commercial Road, a locksmith, who examined the lock in the presence of Mrs Lipski. He found that the lock was very badly put on; that unless the handle was carefully turned, or if there were any pressure on the door, the latch would not be moved, and Mrs Lipski, in his presence, tried the door, and declared that it was locked, when in fact it was held by the handle latch alone and not by the bolt of the lock, and she thereupon stated that she could not say whether it was locked or not, as she was much excited and had only tried it for a second before pushing it open. If held by the latch alone it would account for the door being so easily pushed open and so little damage being done.

Supposing that the door were locked, there was a large piece of wood broken

---

78 Another handwritten annotation: 'The coat was so saturated that it burnt the policeman's fingers who removed it three hours later.'

Appendix II.

away exposing the key-hole of the lock; and in answer to questions Mr Cameron said he did not think anyone could lock that door from outside by grasping the end of the key with pinchers, but that if the key had been left in, anyone knowing how to do it would easily turn the key from outside.

It turns out that the man Schmuss was a locksmith, and therefore skilled in such matters. Moreover, the partition was only a quarter of an inch thick, and almost any amount of spring could be got upon it.

It is much to be regretted that the prisoner's full detailed statement made to his solicitor, and which, with the facts above stated, were fully set out in his counsel's brief, could not have been read in court, or otherwise brought out, and he himself rigidly cross-examined upon it. Could this have been done, the solicitor for the defence is convinced that the jury, and everyone who heard him, would have been fully assured that he was not guilty of the crime for which he is now condemned.

He was engaged to be married to a very respectable young woman. His intended mother-in-law, and all the witnesses for the prosecution who had known him ever since he had been in England – being more than two years – gave him an excellent character as a well-behaved, quiet, inoffensive and industrious young man; and, taking all the circumstances of the case into consideration, it is earnestly hoped that his life may be spared, at all events until further enquiries and investigations have been made.

A paragraph having appeared in an evening paper of this date to the effect that the wealthy Jews have subscribed liberally towards the efforts now being made by me to save Lipski, I beg to say that this is entirely a mis-statement. The money subscribed for the defence was barely sufficient to cover counsel's fees, and since the prisoner's conviction no contributions have been asked for or received.

I am working for this man with all my might and energy, and at my own expense, simply because from the facts before me, and my intercourse with the unfortunate prisoner, I am thoroughly convinced he is not guilty of the crime for which he is condemned.

August 4th, 1887.

John Hayward.

Lipski.

August 5 1887.

The Right Honourable Henry Matthews.[79]

Dear Sir,

I know nothing of the case of the unhappy man Lipski, except what is stated in the petition which I have been requested to forward to you, and in the pamphlet which accompanies it. But I have known Mr Hayward, the solicitor in the case, for many years past as a highly respectable man, and I am perfectly certain he would not state anything he did not believe to be strictly true and accurate.

He tells me that he has thoroughly investigated the case, and that he most conscientiously believes Lipski to be innocent of the crime for which he is now under sentence of death. Mr Hayward therefore feels it to be his bounden duty to use all possible means in his power to prevent what he cannot regard otherwise than legal murder, if the extreme penalty of the law be inflicted. I am quite certain you will give the case your most careful and painstaking attention, and it is only necessary for me to add that I believe Mr Hayward to be incapable [of] telling a falsehood and thus he is actuated by the purest and best motives.

Yours faithfully,

A.W. McArthur.

---

79 Addressee.

APPENDIX III.

Special Report of Inspector David Final, 10 August 1887.[80]

H Division, Leman Street.

10 August 1887.

With reference to the attached, I beg to report that Lipski's coat was found under the bed of the deceased and another coat belonging to the husband of the deceased was found there, but did not appear to have been placed there purposely.[81] It (Angel's coat) had been hanging on a nail in the partition and had fallen down on the coat of the prisoner. Lipski had fixed a vice in his room where he had his food, worked and slept.

A person in Angel's room could not be heard speaking when anyone was at work in Lipski's room filing horn handles for sticks, which Simon Rosenbloom was doing on the morning of the murder. No doubt the boy made a mistake by saying that Rosenbloom said he knew Schmuss because he (Rosenbloom) cannot speak English and the manner in which he (the boy) gave his evidence at the trial no doubt he did not speak the truth. As the judge remarked that the boy had made some mistakes in giving his evidence.

Schmush has not the appearance of a person living in abject need. He (Schmuss) informed me through an interpreter that Lipski's place being so small and very little business being done he thought it was no good for him to waste his time by waiting for Lipski. He remained in the neighbourhood for several days and then went to Birmingham for work. He wrote a letter to a friend of his from there – Mr Nathan[82], 60 Oxford Street, Stepney – who gave me the letter in which Schmuss' address was written. I went to Birmingham, found Schmuss, who at once volunteered to accompany me to London for the purpose of giving evidence at the trial.

I, P.S. Thick and Mr Moore went to the London Hospital where the prisoner was, there being about twenty beds in the ward. Moore was not taken to the bed of the prisoner but after looking at the patients in the ward, he said, 'To the best of my

---

80   TNA:PRO HO 144/201/A47465/22.
81   Inspector Final had been asked to comment on Mr Hayward's pamphlet. His report is reproduced with the minimum of editorial interference – the errors of spelling (including 'Schmush' and 'Stevenson') and the erratic sentence construction are Final's own.
82   Referring to Nathan Rabinowitz.

Lipski.

belief, that is the man who bought the nitric acid,' pointing to the prisoner. A P.C. was employed in plain clothes to watch the prisoner. He (the P.C.) was there at the time of our visit but was not sitting on the bed. He is a very young looking person and being in a ward at an hospital no person would have an idea that he was a constable.

The room adjoining that of the Angels was occupied by Mr Levy and Mrs Rubenstein and if such a thing had happened as suggested by the prisoner they must have heard some kind of noise which they state they did not hear although they were in their room at the time the prisoner came in.[83]

Schmuss is not a tall powerful man as stated, he being about 5ft 6 and about 23 years of age.

Rosenbloom is a small man and does not appear to be a strong person. If the prisoner has been seized by the throat there would have been marks there, but the doctor at the hospital stated there were none. According to the prisoner's statement his mouth was forced open by a piece of wood and not steel as now stated. The doctor at the hospital stated that there were no marks inside the mouth that would be caused by forcing the mouth open with a piece of wood, except that there was a slight abrasion on the lower part of the mouth which he said no doubt was caused by the stomach pump.

I and Sergt. Thick minutely searched Angel's room shortly after the murder but did not find a piece of wood (broom handle) or steel of any description.

Lipski was not insensible when arriving at the hospital about one hour and thirty minutes after he was found in Angel's room. He was asked his name but would not speak and wrote it on a piece of paper.

D. Final, Insp.

T. Arnold, Supdt.[84]

The coat belonging to the prisoner is now in possession of Dr Stevension, Guys Hospital. I am now on way to enquire if he has completed his inspection of it. If so I will bring it to the Home Office at once.

D. Final, Insp.

---

83 The words 'in their room at the time the prisoner came in' were underlined at the Home Office, and a large question mark placed alongside them in the margin.
84 Superintendent Thomas Arnold, H Division, Metropolitan Police.

APPENDIX IV.

Report of Dr Gover, 10 August 1887.[85]

Home Office, No. A47465/24.

Date: 10 Augt 87.

Israel Lipski.

References, &c.: Dr Gover forwards report on the special points submitted to him. See /15. Pressing.

Minutes:

Dr Gover thinks that the causes of the prisoner's condition were probably complex, sudden fear or shock acting in conjunction with physical violence. No other explanation appears to him reasonable. CM, Aug 10.

I am not sure what Dr Gover intends to be inferred from this opinion. But I cannot attach importance to it if it is intended to point to Lipski's innocence. There were no marks of violence upon him. Are we to infer that a blow was given on the epigastrium, & that altho' this blow left no marks, altho' it had been delivered say one hour previously, yet the effect of it & the terror which it produced caused insensibility which lasted an hour or more? But that terror alone, physical or moral, could not have produced this effect?

I cannot help thinking that the proof of *actual insensibility* in this case is far from satisfactory. Do you think anything more can be learnt from Dr Kay? GL, 10 Aug 1887.

Mr Matthews.[86]

I don't understand what reason the supposed assailants had for hiding Lipski behind the bed – they left unhidden in the same room the woman they are supposed to have murdered.

---

85 TNA:PRO HO 144/201/A47465/24.
86 *i.e.*, recommending the report and minutes to be seen by Mr Matthews, the secretary of state for the Home Office. The minute, however, continues in Lushington's hand.

Lipski.

Home Office,
Whitehall, S.W.
August 10 1887.

Sir,

In pursuance of the request contained in your letter of yesterday, I have carefully read the evidence that you have forwarded to me, taken at the trial of Israel Lipski, who was convicted of murder on the 30th of last month, and I here report my decision upon the special points to which you directed my attention as follows:—

A healthy young man could not be thrown into a state of syncope (fainting) or unconsciousness for more than two hours entirely by mental excitement or emotion. There is nothing in the evidence that you have forwarded to me, or in the newspaper reports that I read, tending to shew that Lipski is of feminine sensitiveness, or that he is hysterical, or hypochondriacal, or that he inherits any epileptic taint.

The drinking of nitric acid would not render a condition of unconsciousness, whatever may be its cause, more probable, unless great force were employed in forcing it into the mouth. It is a remarkable and well established fact that in poisoning, both by sulphuric & nitric acid, the intellect remains clear to the last. The quantity of nitric acid taken by Lipski appears to have been small.

The functional activity of the brain may be suspended, through its nervous connections, by physical violence inflicted upon comparatively remote parts of the body, or a blow or pressure upon the epigastrium; and the violence need not be great to produce such a result, if complicated with the operation of other causes, as sudden fear, or shock.

The causes of the unconscious condition (not necessarily fainting) in which Lipski was found were in all probability complex – sudden fear or shock acting in conjunction with physical violence. No other explanation, under all the circumstances of the case, appears to me to be reasonable.

I am, Sir, your obedient serv^t,
R.M. Gover.

Godfrey Lushington Esqr.[87]

---

[87] Addressee.

APPENDIX V.

Report of Dr Stevenson, 10 August 1887.[88]

Home Office, No. A47465/26.

Date: Aug 10th 1887.

Israel Lipski.

References, &c.: Dr Stevenson reports on articles left by Insp^r Final which he has examined and analysed. See /71, /78, /101. Pressing.

Minutes:

This is a very curious result. It appears that the stuff in the bottle by which the woman was killed & which was spilt over Lipski's coat is not nitric acid pure, but a liquid consisting mainly of sulphuric acid, but with a certain quantity of nitric acid. Dr Stevenson says that sulphuric acid is the cheaper of the two, & tho' not useful is so used to stickmakers.[89]

I have sent instructions to Mr Monro[90] to purchase at Moore's some of the same nitric acid as was sold to the man with the 2 oz phial and also some sulphuric acid & to take these both to Dr Stevenson, who will analyze them before you[91] see the judge tomorrow at 5.30. I have also asked Dr Stevenson to attend at the same time. GL, 10 Aug 1887.

---

88 TNA:PRO HO 144/201/A47465/26.
89 Lushington, reframing his sentence as he goes, alights on the wrong preposition – 'to stickmakers' should presumably read 'by stickmakers'. A similarly spontaneous marginal note in Lushington's hand reads, 'Might have been sold as an adulterant'.
90 Referring to James Monro, Assistant Commissioner of the Metropolitan Police.
91 Addressing the Secretary of State.

Lipski.

Chemical Laboratory,
Guy's Hospital,
London, S.E.

August 10, 1887.

Re: Lipski.

Sir,

I yesterday received from the hands of David Final, Insp. of Police a coat stated to belong to Lipski, a 2 oz phial, a coat & waiscoat[92] stated to belong to a man, Angel. These I have examined & analysed.

Lipski's coat was extensively burnt by a corrosive acid, in splashes and smears. Most of the burning was outside, but some of the splashes were inside on the lining over the region of the back, and could not have been produced whilst the coat was in wear.

Although the burning was extensive, on fitting the burnt patches together I found that no very large quantity of the fabric had actually disappeared. I have produced an equal effect by applying half an ounce of nitric acid to a similar coat. I am of opinion that half an ounce of a strong corrosive acid might amply suffice to produce all the results met with on Lipski's coat.

The stains were not of uniform character, for whilst some had the character of nitric acid, the great portion had the character of sulphuric acid. Traces only of nitric acid, which is a volatile acid, were found in some of the stains; whilst sulphuric acid was abundant in nearly all the stains examined, and in marked contrast with the unstained portions of the coat.

The 2 ounce phial was empty. The cork had been acted on by nitric acid. On washing out the phial with pure water I obtained a liquid which contained an indubitable quantity of sulphuric acid, and traces of nitric acid. This phial was probably one that had contained nitric acid, and had subsequently been used for sulphuric acid. Of the minute quantity of acid adhering to the bottle the larger proportion was sulphuric acid.

Angel's coat was free from acid stains. On the nape of the neck of his waiscoat was a hole which might have been produced by a corrosive acid, the corroded piece having dropped out.

With respect to the taste or sensation on the tongue of nitric acid and sulphuric acid respectively, it is known that it is the immediate or almost immediate inflammation set up that causes pain; and it is possible that the absolutely immediate effect may be to dull acute sensation. Of strong nitric acid I can speak from personal experience, that it does not produce the expected acid (sour)

---

92   *Sic* in report.

Appendix V.

sensation but rather one of powerful astringency.

As for sulphuric acid patients usually describe its taste as immediate I know of one instance, however, of a girl of about thirteen who swallowed an ounce in mistake for her medicine (Epsom salts). She became at once very ill; but it was only whilst going to the hospital in a cab that he mentioned that she thought she had made a mistake in her medicine, & that it did not taste right.

I am, Sir, your obedient servant,
Thos. Stevenson.

To Godfrey Lushington Esq. C.B.
Home Office.

Appendix V

APPENDIX VI.

Report of Dr Stevenson, 11 August 1887.[93]

Home Office, No. A47465/33.

Date: 11 Augt 1887.

Israel Lipski.

References, &c.: Dr Stevenson reports on acid brought to him by Inspr. Final. Very Pressing. See memo /33 & directions. Mr Hayward to be informed within.

Minutes:

The nitric acid bought by the officer as the same acid purchased by Lipski is not ordinary nitric acid, but a mixture of nitric acid and sulphuric acid in the proportion of two parts nitric acid to three parts sulphuric acid.

A mixture of the two acids was found by Dr S. on the coat of Lipski, on the bed clothes, and in the acid bottle produced at the trial.

The mixed acids are used for manufacture of explosives, but do not form an ordinary article of retail commerce. CM, 12/8.

This has been considered by judge & S of S[94] & see my memo. GL, 12 Aug 1887.

Nil. HM,[95] 12 Aug 1887.

Wrote Judge, Under Sheriff & Govr. Also Mr McArthur M.P., Mr Bristowe M.P., Dr Stevenson, Mr Hayward, Dr Kay & Mr Calvert. 12.8.87.[96]

---

93 TNA:PRO HO 144/201/A47465/33.
94 Secretary of State.
95 Initials of Henry Matthews.
96 Apart from those recipients with whom the reader is already familiar, the list includes Mr George Rose-Innes (under-sheriff of London and Middlesex) and Mr Thomas Lynn Bristowe (Member of Parliament for Norwood).

Lipski.

Secretary of State, Home Department.

To inform Hayward that upon analysis it appeared that the acid which was found on prisoner's coat was found to be more sulphuric than nitric acid and that a similar result was obtained from analysis of the so-called nitric acid at Messrs Moore.

By Mr Lushington's desire. CM, Aug 16.

Wrote 16/8.

Chemical Laboratory,
Guy's Hospital,
London, S.E.

August 11, 1887.

Re: Lipski.

Sir,

I beg to report that I received today from David Final, Inspr of Police, two bottles, labelled 'Nitric Acid' and 'Sulphuric Acid' respectively. Final told me that he had purchased the acids at the shop at which Lipski is stated to have purchased nitric acid, & that he (Final) had requested to be supplied with the same kind of acid as was supplied to Lipski.

The nitric acid now purchased is not ordinary commercial nitric acid, but an adulterated article, containing sulphuric and nitric acids in the proportion of two parts nitric acid to three parts sulphuric acid.

A mixture of the two acids was found by me on the coat of Lipski, on the bed clothes of Miriam Angel, and on the acid bottle produced at the trial.

The mixed acids – sulphuric and nitric – are used for the manufacture of explosives, but do not form an ordinary article of retail commerce.

The sulphuric acid brought to me was the ordinary brown article.

I am, Sir, your obedient servant,

Thos. Stevenson.

To Godfrey Lushington Esq. C.B.
Home Office.

APPENDIX VII.

The Second Petition, 13 August 1887.[97]

The Right Honorable[98] Henry Matthews, M.P.,

Her Majesty's Secretary of State,

Home Department.

1. The humble petition of the undersigned[99] for a reprieve of the convict Israel Lipski sentenced to death for the murder of Miriam Angell[100] sheweth as follows:

2. The evidence at the trial of the prisoner was rendered judish deitch[101] & was not understood by the Judge, the Jury or by Counsel.

3. That very grave doubts exist as to whether the witnesses clearly understood the exact questions put to them although they may have gathered the general purport of the question.

4. That there was no evidence tendered by the prosecution of the probable motive for the crime although it was suggested that lust was the motive and by their verdict the Jury evidently thought that this was a correct conclusion. It now appears however that a circumstance known to the police and of the utmost importance to the prisoner was not brought forward by them at the trial namely that there are evidences of an attempted robbery in the murdered woman's house, trunks had been forced open and the contents thereof disarranged by someone making a hasty search therein. It is therefore highly probable and in fact there cannot be a doubt but that the motive of the crime was robbery & not lust and this being so the prisoner's unstained character will at once demonstrate that he did not commit the attempted theft and consequently did not commit the murder.

1. That the prisoner's statement that he gave Schmuss[102] a sovereign out of which he was to purchase some brandy for him is borne out by the fact that only a few shillings were found upon the prisoner whereas it is clear from

---

97   TNA:PRO HO 144/201/A47465/117.
98   *Sic* in petition.
99   As an annotation on the petition shows, it arrived covering '35 sheets petitions back and front'.
100 *Sic* in petition.
101 *Sic* in petition.
102 *Sic* in petition. Should read: 'Rosenbloom'.

Lipski.

the evidence of Mrs Lyons that she lent the prisoner 25/- the previous day to the murder.

2. That we now understood evidence is forthcoming that the nitric acid was sold to a man not at all corresponding with the description of the prisoner and that 2ozs were sold & not 1 oz as alleged. This would account for the large amount of acid found in and about the murdered woman and upon the clothes of the prisoner whereas it is difficult to conceive and really impossible [th]at 1 oz of acid could have first killed the woman, burnt her clothes, and the bedclothes, partially poisoned & burnt to a cinder a greater portion of the prisoner's coat.

3. That the jury no doubt were much impressed by the alleged fact the prisoner was found in the murdered woman's room with the door locked on the inside. Several locksmiths have now shewn that it is with the greatest ease able to open or lock a door from the outside notwithstanding that the key is inside, either by means of a button hook or strong piece of wire thrust through the keyhole, attaching it to the bow of the key & then twisting it. And there are many other ways at arriving at the same result.

For these & other reasons your petitioners believe that the prisoner is absolutely innocent of the crime for which he is condemned to death & pray that he may be reprieved.

And your petitioners will ever pray, &c.

APPENDIX VIII.

Pall Mall Gazette, 13 August 1887.

HANGING AN INNOCENT MAN.
CONVERSION OF MR JUSTICE STEPHEN.
BUT A REPRIEVE IS REFUSED.

Last night the Governor of Newgate received a communication from the Home Office with regard to the convict Israel Lipski, lying under sentence of death for the murder of Miriam Angel, in Whitechapel. It was to the effect that no reason existed for interfering with the sentence, and that the law must take its course. Consequently the prisoner will be executed on Monday morning. The decision of the Home Secretary is, therefore, that there is no new evidence or material fact to set aside the verdict at which the jury arrived.

The *Daily Chronicle* says:— 'The condemned man spends his time in reading – principally the Bible – and is very attentive to the ministrations of the rev. gentleman from the synagogue, who visits him from time to time. The Home Office inquiry has been a very exhaustive and searching one – a retrial, in fact, of the whole case. Mr Matthews has not only dealt with the details of the evidence given at the Central Criminal Court, but has called in the scientific aid of Dr Stevenson, the analyst, in reference to the allegations of the prisoner that the condition of his coat was such as to show that more nitric acid than he was proved to have purchased – one ounce – had been used upon the garment. The whole of one side of the coat and the sleeves were burned, not in spots, but in large patches, showing considerable saturation. The prisoner does not seem to have any relatives in this country. His only visitors have been Mrs Lipski – no relative – the landlady of the house in which the convict lodged, and Miss Lyons, the young woman to whom he was engaged to be married. In reference to the prisoner's meals, it may be stated that at his request he has been supplied with kosher food – *i.e.*, food prepared according to Jewish custom.'

The following appeared in our later editions last night:—

Lipski must not be hanged. Why not? – For a very simple but very sufficient reason. Mr Justice Stephen, who tried Lipski, and whose summing-up contributed not a little to his conviction, has since been converted, and is aghast at the prospect of hanging a possibly innocent man.

The extent and the circumstances of this conversion are of a remarkable and startling nature. The solicitor for Lipski's defence, Mr John Hayward, has

Lipski.

throughout been convinced of his client's innocence – a conviction which was rooted, he says, in the facts of the case, but which has been confirmed by the whole bearing of his client from first to last. This morning Mr Hayward called at our office and gave us the following information. At the conclusion of the case Mr Hayward wrote a pamphlet setting forth various facts, and building up a theory upon them, which for some unaccountable reason were not produced at the trial. A copy of this pamphlet was shown to the Solicitor-General, Sir Edward Clarke. This gentleman – an expert, as every one knows, in murder trials – was much impressed by Mr Hayward's case, and strongly urged him to send a copy of the pamphlet to Mr Justice Stephen. Mr Hayward demurred. 'It is altogether against legal etiquette,' he said, 'for a solicitor to communicate with the judge.' 'Never mind that,' replied the Solicitor-General: 'you had better do it.' Fortified by this opinion, Mr Hayward forwarded his pamphlet to Mr Justice Stephen, 'at the Solicitor-General's suggestion.'

At first it did not seem as if much had been taken by the move. Mr Hayward merely received a polite note from the judge, demurring to certain observations made in the pamphlet about his summing-up, but promising to give it his attention. The process of conversion seems to have soon begun. For the very next day Mr Hayward received a note from Mr Justice Stephen requesting him to call upon him in his private room at the Law Courts. Mr Hayward, of course, went – gladly, but not a little surprised, for 'never,' he says, 'in the whole course of my experience had I heard of a judge sending for a solicitor in this way before.' The surprise, however, did not stop there. It was on Monday that Mr Hayward saw Mr Justice Stephen at the Law Courts, and set before him in more fulness[103] and detail than had been done in the pamphlet the facts, so strangely neglected at the trial, which made for his client's innocence. The judge heard Mr Hayward, and pondered, and two days later sent for him again. This second interview took place yesterday evening; Mr Poland, who conducted the case for the prosecution, being also present. The matter was thoroughly threshed out, with the result that two out of three persons present were in Lipski's favour. Mr Justice Stephen had been converted.

It was in this way. Many small facts which came out in evidence were yet not commented on by Lipski's counsel, and still less were they strung into any consistent theory. This was what Mr Hayward did to Mr Justice Stephen – making out what to himself seemed an 'irresistible' case on Lipski's behalf.

'Well, hardly irresistible,' replied Mr Justice Stephen; 'I should rather call it very strong.' Mr Hayward, as may be imagined, was well satisfied with the words. 'But how was it,' naturally asked the judge, 'that all this was not brought before me at the trial?'

---

103   *Sic* in article.

Appendix VIII.

'It was not my fault,' replied Mr Hayward – adding, however, that it was not an afterthought, nor a case of straws clutched at to save a hanging man, as the judge would see by looking through the leading counsel's brief, which the judge had specially instructed Mr Hayward to bring with him. Every fact stated in the pamphlet was, Mr Hayward says, contained in the brief, except one very important circumstance, to which we need not here allude, and which came out in the evidence in court. 'I do not complain,' Mr Hayward added, 'either of the summing-up or the verdict. On the case as presented nothing else was possible. But I do ask you to give weight to the new facts and theories now adduced.' And Mr Justice Stephen did; he admitted, as we have seen, that the case was 'very strong.'

What makes this conversion all the more remarkable was the whole bearing of the judge. Sir James Fitzjames Stephen has not the reputation of being a very impressionable or softhearted man. But 'his anxiety, his agony of mind almost,' says Mr Hayward in describing his interviews, 'were obvious. "It would be a terrible thing," he said, "to hang this man, when in reality he may have been half killed by the real murderers, who by that means endeavoured to hide their guilt. Why was not all this," he asked again, "submitted to me before? I cannot tell you what I think. But I can tell you this, that if I were not I, I should heartily wish you success."'

With these words Mr Hayward's interview came to an end – Mr Poland remaining behind. Mr Poland was, of course, not converted; Mr Hayward's theory, he had said, would seem ridiculous to a jury. 'No, Poland,' Mr Justice Stephen had replied; 'there I don't agree with you.'

On leaving, Mr Hayward happened to speak with Mr Justice Stephen's clerk. What the clerk said entirely corroborated the impression which Mr Hayward had formed from his interview. 'The governor is terribly worried about it,' the clerk said. 'I've never known him so bothered about a case all the forty years I've been with him.' Mr Justice Stephen has, Mr Hayward believes, been down to the scene of the murder, to make observations and inspections for himself.

Mr Hayward, we should add, tells us that his personal conviction in Lipski's innocence is shared by every one who has come in contact with him. 'There is a halo of innocence about him,' Mr Hayward says, 'which seems to touch all his surroundings. Even the gaolers do not believe in his guilt. The man is so gentle and has such natural refinement that he has won their hearts. "That young man's delicate fist," said the gaoler to me yesterday, "never broke a woman's skull." The young fellow's resignation, too, is to me remarkable. I saw him last just before seeing the judge who tried and sentenced him. The judge was far more agitated than the prisoner.'

The above statements, communicated, as they were, by Mr Hayward in a manner

Lipski.

that could leave no doubt as to the intensity of his conviction of the innocence of the convict Lipski, made a deep impression on the editor of this journal. That which weighed most with him was the account which Mr Hayward gave of his conversation with the judge. If the judge who tried the case was thus moved – and that a judge of the severe and unbending rigour of Mr Justice Stephen – then assuredly no stone should be left unturned to prevent the consummation of a legal murder. But what could be done? The time was so short. The only chance of making any impression on the inert, apathetic opinion of the public was by bringing forcibly before them some striking fact before unknown, which would rouse public attention, and compel the executioner to stay his hand. Where was this fact to be found? Obviously the only fact which would convince the public was the conversion of the judge, especially when that judge was so notable for the severity of his logic and his superiority to all the emotions that perturb the mind and deflect the judgment as Mr Justice Stephen. Could that fact be brought out, no Government in the world would dare to hang Lipski. Nor would any Home Secretary dare even to consign to the living tomb of penal servitude for life an innocent man. But Mr Hayward protested. The interviews with Mr Justice Stephen were confidential. He could not and would not permit one word that passed at those interviews to be published. He had only mentioned them to induce us to call attention to the case of the doomed victim. The conversation was private, and must remain so.

When Mr Hayward left, the editor of this journal was placed in one of those difficult positions in which all the commonplaces of ethics seem to point one way and paramount and imperious duty in another. To save Lipski – to prevent a judicial murder of the most aggravated kind, one way lay open, and only one way. Publish the fact that Mr Justice Stephen is, to say the least, haunted by a terrible doubt as to whether Lipski is not as innocent as the poor woman for whose murder he is to be hanged, and his execution becomes morally impossible.

But then the conversation was private, the interview confidential. We were in precise terms interdicted from using it. If we published it, Mr Justice Stephen might be very angry. Mr Hayward would fall into disgrace, and we should have to face the odium of a breach of confidence. 'You have no right to use a private conversation.' 'If you don't, an innocent man will be hanged.' 'You may ruin Mr Hayward.' 'But save Mr Hayward's client.' 'And no one will trust you any more.' 'Well, when a life is at stake they had better not tell me anything that would save that life and expect me to keep it secret.'

And so, after many arguments pro and con, we decided that our first instinctive conclusion was the true one, and we publish the above statement just as we received it.

When going to press a boy brought up a letter from Mr Hayward, couched as follows:—

Appendix VIII.

Dear Sir. — I do most sincerely trust you will not report my private conversation with the judge; it would ruin my professional standing, and, what is of more consequence, it would be adverse to the interest of my poor client. — Yours very truly, John Hayward.

Once more a pause. Should we blast Mr Hayward's professional reputation to save an innocent man from the gallows? Certainly, if necessary; but Mr Hayward is not to blame. He had no idea that we would violate his confidence. But what about injuring his poor client? How can it injure him to convince the public that the judge who tried him is no longer certain of his guilt? In any case, we take the responsibility of our decision, and publish the statement as we received it.

APPENDIX IX.

Respite, 14 August 1887.[104]

Secretary of State, Home Department.

14th August 1887.

Sir,

In communicating the enclosed respite to Israel Lipski, be good enough to inform him distinctly that it is granted not from any doubt existing in my mind as to the verdict or sentence but merely to enable his solicitor to make certain enquiries which he has asked to be allowed to make. The convict must clearly understand that unless these enquiries put a new aspect upon the case, the sentence will be carried into effect.

I am, Sir, your obedient servant,
Henry Matthews.

To the governor of H.M. Prison Newgate.

---

[104] TNA:PRO HO 144/201/A47465/38.

APPENDIX X.

Evening News (London), 17 August 1887.

HOW THE LIPSKI RESPITE WAS WORKED.
SAVED BY HIS OWN HANDWRITING

There is no good in mincing matters. Lipski's life has been saved for a week by 'trial by journalism'. But how is 'trial by journalism' worked? That is what the public does not know. The story of how the Lipski respite was worked is a singular one, and is now published for the first time. The editor of *Society*, an enterprising little penny society paper, which may be recognised by its yellow cover, was anxious to obtain Lipski's autograph so as to reproduce it in *Society*. In order to do this he went to Mr Hayward, Lipski's solicitor, and asked him to obtain Lipski's autograph next time he visited the condemned cell. This Mr Hayward promised to do, and actually did do. 'Now,' said Mr Hayward, as he handed the editor of *Society* the autograph —

'WILL YOU SAVE LIPSKI'S LIFE?'

'Why, how can I?' said the editor of *Society*.

'Why, by devoting your paper to that purpose, of course.'

'But my paper does not come out till two days after the man will be hanged, and even if it did, I feel nothing but a powerful agitation in a daily paper could manage it. Besides,

'WHY SHOULD I SAVE HIS LIFE?'

'Because,' said Mr Hayward, 'he is innocent. I know it! I have proof.'

'What is your proof?'

Then the solicitor and the editor of *Society* went through the whole case, and Mr Hayward succeeded in pursuading[105] his listener that

THERE WAS SOMETHING IN IT.

'Well,' said the editor, 'there is but one thing to do, and but one man to do it for his own ends, and that is Stead, of the *Pall Mall Gazette*. You get me the autograph; I will get you an introduction to Stead, and then you must see what you can get him to do.'

---

105   *Sic* in article.

Lipski.

The two men jumped in a cab and drove to Northumberland Street. Mr Stead had gone home, but the editor of *Society* made an appointment for early the next morning. Mr Hayward kept the appointment and succeeded in convincing Mr Stead, who went to work and produced the plea which appeared in the notorious fifth edition of the *Pall Mall Gazette*.

Our readers will remember that Mr Stead spoke of his story as a breach of confidence, asserting that it had been narrated to him by Mr Hayward on the condition that he would not divulge it. If, however, our information is correct this story of Mr Stead was nothing but a journalistic *ruse* invented to give spice to a commonplace attempt to excite public sympathy on behalf of a condemned man.

The result is well known to all, and if any doubt is thrown upon this story of how 'trial by journalism' was obtained, and Lipski was given a week's grace, we must refer them for confirmation to this week's issue of the yellow-covered *Society*, which will appear tomorrow with Lipski's autograph both in English and Russian characters. The condemned man little knew that when he traced those few straggling and scratchy letters which go to form the words Israel Lipski, he was practically singing[106] his own respite, for, if he had not signed it, Mr Hayward would have had no claim on the editor of *Society*, and would never have seen Mr Stead on the subject.

This 'trial by journalism' is, however, no new invention. It was resorted to in many cases by the late Charles Reade, who, with the help of the *Daily Telegraph*, saved more than one life. Odder still, the whole system of 'trial by journalism' was foreshadowed by another novelist, Mr Wilkie Collins, long before it had any existence in fact. We are indebted to the *Bat* for the following very interesting extract:

Fiction, says the *Bat*, is sometimes stranger than truth, or, at any rate, frequently anticipates it. The subjoined, extracted from Mr Wilkie Collins's *Armadale*, Book III, Chapter XV, pp. 519-521, bears a curious analogy to the circumstances attending the respite of the unfortunate Jew, Israel Lipski:

'The verdict was Guilty, as a matter of course; and the judge declared that he agreed with it. ... And she is alive and hearty at the present moment; free to do any mischief she pleases, and to poison, at her own entire convenience, any man, woman, or child that happens to stand in her way.'

'How was she pardoned?' asked Mr Bashwood breathlessly. 'They told me at the time, but I have forgotten. Was it the Home Secretary? If it was, I respect the Home Secretary. I say the Home Secretary was deserving of his place.'

'Quite right, old gentleman!' rejoined Bashwood the younger. 'The Home Secretary was the obedient humble servant of an enlightened free Press – and

---

106 *Sic* in article. Should read: 'signing'.

Appendix X.

he *was* deserving of his place. Is it possible you don't know how she cheated the gallows? If you don't, I must tell you. On the evening of the trial, two or three of the young buccaneers of literature went down to two or three newspaper offices, and wrote two or three heartrending leading articles on the subject of the proceedings in Court. The next morning the public caught light like tinder; and the prisoner was tried over again, before an amateur Court of Justice, in the columns of the newspapers. All the people who had no personal experience whatever on the subject, seized their pens, and rushed (by kind permission of the editor) into print. Doctors who had *not* attended the sick man, and who had *not* been present at the examination of the body, declared by dozens that he had died a natural death. Barristers without business, who had *not* heard the evidence, attacked the jury who had heard it, and judged the judge, who had sat on the bench before some of them were born. The general public followed the lead of the barristers and the doctors, and the young buccaneers who had set the thing going. Here was the Law that they all paid to protect them, actually doing its duty in dreadful earnest! Shocking! Shocking! The British Public rose to protest as one man against the working of its own machinery; and the Home Secretary, in a state of distraction, went to the judge. The judge held firm. He had said it was the right verdict at the time, and he said so still. "But suppose," said the Home Secretary, "that the prosecution had tried some other way of proving her guilty at the trial than the way they did try – what would you and the jury have done then?" Of course it was quite impossible for the judge to say. This comforted the Home Secretary to begin with. And, when he got the judge's consent, after that, to having the conflict of medical evidence submitted to one great doctor; and when the one great doctor took the merciful view, after expressly stating, in the first instance, that he knew nothing practically of the merits of the case, the Home Secretary was perfectly satisfied. The prisoner's death-warrant went into the waste-paper basket; the verdict of the Law was reversed by general acclamation; and the verdict of the newspapers carried the day.'

APPENDIX XI.

Evening News (London), 17 August 1887.

HOW THE LIPSKI RESPITE WAS WORKED.
THE 'VIOLATING-CONFIDENCE' TRICK.
AN INTERVIEW WITH LIPSKI'S SOLICITOR.

In our Special Edition last night we published a story which, if true, throws great doubt upon the statements made by those who got up the agitation in favour of Lipski. It will be remembered that the editor of the *Pall Mall Gazette* stated that, in the interests of humanity, he broke confidence with Mr Hayward, Lipski's solicitor, by publishing what had been privately communicated to him. In order to back up this statement, a letter from Mr Hayward was published in which the writer begged the editor of the *Pall Mall* not to ruin the writer's 'professional standing' by publishing a merely memorised version of what took place at the interview between Mr Hayward and Mr Justice Stephen. Now, why was Mr Hayward so very anxious to suppress the words which he had quoted as the words of Mr Justice Stephen? There could be only one logical reason. It is nonsense to suppose that he went to the *Pall Mall* merely to tell Mr Stead a bit of private information which might amuse him and his family circle, but which he was on no account to publish. Ever since the trial Mr Hayward has been trying to get some one to listen to his story and take up the case. He forwarded pamphlets to every member of the House of Commons, to every member of the Corporation, and to every newspaper in London, and wrote to every editor imploring him to publish his 'facts' proving the innocence of Lipski. His pamphlet contained no 'facts' which did anything of the kind, and so the pamphlet remained unpublished as far as the newspapers went. In the story which we published last night, we showed that Mr Hayward implored the editor of *Society* to take up Lipski's case in return for an autograph of Lipski's, which is published in this week's *Society*. We showed that it was the editor of *Society* who suggested a visit to Mr Stead, of the *Pall Mall*, and actually made an appointment for Mr Hayward to see Mr Stead on the following day at half-past twelve, which appointment Mr Hayward kept. Now, what did Mr Hayward go to the *Pall Mall* for, if not to get his statement published? It is just possible that when he found Mr Stead could not see his 'facts' any clearer than any one else, he, in his excitement, exaggerated Mr Justice Stephen's words. Indeed, we have Mr Justice Stephen's denial that he used the remarks attributed to him. Now, was the reason why Mr Hayward objected to the supposed conversation with Mr Justice Stephen being published because he knew his pious fraud would be discovered? It is just possible; but it

Lipski.

is also just possible that his 'objection' was merely an understanding between himself and Mr Stead, and that all they both desired was a 'boom'.

With these ideas in our mind we sent a representative to call on Mr Hayward and find out exactly what was his idea in going to the *Pall Mall* to tell Mr Stead a story which he was on no account to publish, but which, if published and corroborated by Mr Justice Stephen, would certainly get Lipski liberated. Our representative writes as follows:

I expected to find Mr Hayward a smart young man, full of energy, and with a thorough knowledge of the facts of the whole affair. I was disappointed. I found him an old man, and at once saw he was hardly likely to be able to recall and repeat accurately to Mr Stead what happened at his interview with Mr Justice Stephen. I think this will be borne out by his interview with me, in which he said:

'Now, what is it you want to know from me?'

'I want you to tell me how you came to go to Mr Stead, at the *Pall Mall Gazette* office.'

'Indeed, I hardly remember. Let me see. Oh! somebody made an appointment for me, and I went.'

'Cannot you remember who it was?'

'No! indeed I cannot. You see I have seen so many people, I am quite confused.'

'Did it not arise out of an autograph of Lipski's which you got?'

'I cannot say; it may have done. Did I get an autograph?'

'I fancy so. Did not the editor of *Society* call upon you and ask you to procure him one?'

'I don't remember; he may have. Was it anything to do with the *Jewish World*?'

'No, I fancy not. Did not you ask the editor of *Society* to take up the case for you, and did he not say his paper did not come out till some days after the date set down for the execution?'

'Yes, I fancy there was something of the kind – I will see.'

Mr Hayward then went to the door, and brought in a young man. Taking a copy of *Society* from my pocket I said, offering it to Mr Hayward:

'See, here is an advance copy of *Society* containing the story and Lipski's autograph, which you may recognise.'

'Ah! let me see what he says. He is sure to remember better than I, and I am sure whatever he says is true.'

Mr Hayward then commenced reading *Society*, and the young man addressed me

Appendix XI.

as follows:

'Yes, it was through the editor of *Society* that this whole affair came about, but he did not take Mr Hayward to the *Pall Mall*. After seeing Mr Hayward as you describe, he went off to the *Pall Mall*, and made an appointment for Mr Hayward to see Mr Stead the next day. Then he came back and informed me what he had done, and I told Mr Hayward the next morning.'

'By the way, I did not catch your name?'

'Oh, I don't want my name mixed up in the affair.'

'No,' said Mr Hayward, 'this is my managing clerk – he is a solicitor himself.'

'And now, Mr Hayward,' said I, 'can you tell me what happened? What did you go to the *Pall Mall* for?'

'Why to try and get the whole affair published, to be sure, and save Lipski's life.'

'Then there was no breach of confidence on Mr Stead's part.'

'Oh, no. I can hardly call it breach of confidence. I wanted it done, and I would rather sacrifice my professional reputation than have the man hanged. I'm glad he did it. It was a good thing.'

'Do you mean for him or for Lipski?'

'For both.'

'Then Mr Stead and you thoroughly understood one another?'

'Perfectly. I can say this, I am very sorry that it was done, but I am glad of the results.'

'So is he. But what do you mean by the first part of the sentence?'

'I mean I did not want the conversation of the judge given *in extensor*, but I wanted the matter taken up, and I implored him to do it, for I sent up fifty pieces of paper with the points I wanted noted at the trial, and they never came out.'

'How was that?'

'I can't say, I'm sure. The whole case was in the brief, but not a point was put by the counsel for the defence. I could not get the facts brought out which I wanted brought out. It was scandalous, and I don't care who knows it.'

'And what did you tell Mr Stead?'

'I showed him my pamphlet.'

'Yes, I know; but he said the only convincing thing was what you told him about Mr Justice Stephen. Now, what did you tell him?'

'I said the judge was dead against me at the trial, but I think he is more in my

Lipski.

favour now – but I don't want that published.'

'Those were the words you used to Mr Stead?'

'They were.'

Mr Hayward then proceeded to review points in the case which have already appeared, and to show me how a locked door which has the key inside can be easily opened from the outside by any one possessed of a common button-hook, or a piece of strong wire. Mr Hayward said he had been shown this by a locksmith that morning, and that even he could now do it by himself.

'Think,' said he, 'how much easier it would be for a professional locksmith.' He then showed me how a door, with the key inside, could be locked from the outside. This is done with a piece of ordinary string and a bit of common firewood. There is also another way when the barrel of the key protrudes on the other side of the door.

The object of my interview, however, was to inquire into the facts of Mr Hayward's interview with Mr Stead, and I must confess I fail to reconcile Mr Hayward's ingenious statement with Mr Stead's wild paraphrase in the *Pall Mall*. I cannot understand how, if Mr Hayward merely told Mr Stead, 'the judge was dead against me at the trial, but I think he is more in my favour now,' Mr Stead came to write, 'Mr Justice Stephen had been converted' and 'what makes this conversion all the more remarkable was the whole bearing of the judge. Sir James Fitzjames Stephen has not the reputation of being a very impressionable or soft-hearted man. But "his anxiety, his agony of mind, almost," says Mr Hayward, in describing his interviews, "were obvious." "It would be a terrible thing," he said, "to hang this man, when in reality he may have been half killed by the real murderers, who by that means endeavoured to hide their guilt. Why was not all this," he asked again, "submitted to me before? I cannot tell you what I think. But I can tell you this, that if I were not I, I should heartily wish you success."'

The matter certainly wants clearing up. If the editor of the *Pall Mall Gazette* has merely interfered with the execution of justice in order to work a 'boom' for his paper, it is a very serious thing indeed. It is not the first time Mr Stead has let his impetuosity run away with him, and has excited the public sympathy for nothing better than an advertisement.

[It may interest our readers to know that the whole story, as published by the *Pall Mall Gazette*, was submitted with a view to publication in our columns to one of our representatives, who called upon Mr Hayward, previous to the appearance of the statement in our contemporary. — ED. *E.N.*]

APPENDIX XII.

Mr Buchner's First Statement, 18 August 1887.[107]

Home Office, No. A47465/74.

Date: 18 Augt 1887.

Israel Lipski.

References, &c.: Mr Hayward handed enclosed statement from Mr Buchner as to selling two pennyworth of nitric acid labelled Bell & Co. Camphorated Oil. The man was a foreign Jew. See /82 & /93. Very Pressing.

Minutes:

See direction within to send to Treas^y Sol^r *at once*.

Sent to Treasury Sol^r. HM, 18.8.87.

I confess I regard this story with great suspicion: it seems to me to be just like an alibi which can neither be verified nor disproved and is sprung at the eleventh hour.

This matter has been agitating the Jewish population at the East End for more than two months, and it is incredible that if this had happened it should not previously have been notified either to the prosecution or to the defence.

As contrasted with the evidence in the case, the story is curious both in points of similarity and dissimilarity.

1. The points of similarity are these:
2. The time is about the same.
3. The bottle is exactly like.
4. The label exactly corresponds: 'Camphorated Oil sold by Buchner'.[108]
5. The place of the label on the bottle is the same.
6. The circumstance is thrown in that there was a teaspoonful of oil in the bottle – in itself a most improbable circumstance.
7. The purchaser, as Buchner believes, said he was a stickmaker.

---

107 TNA:PRO HO 144/201/A47465/74.
108 Lushington made a mistake in his hurry to annotate the docket. The label on the bottle found in Miriam Angel's room read, 'Bell & Co. Camphorated Oil'.

Lipski.

On the other hand:

1. The purchaser is said to be a dark man whereas Lipski is fair.
2. The purchaser is said to be a foreign Jew (intended to point to Rosenbloom or Schmuss), and Buchner says he does not know if the man talked English.
3. The quantity sold is two pennyworth not one pennyworth. Hayward's allegation, disproved by Kay and Stevenson, is that one pennyworth or 1 oz would not have sufficed.

GL.

Secretary of State, Home Department.

Left by Mr Hayward with S of S on 18 Aug at 1.30. To be sent at once to Treasury Solicitor to investigate.

GL. 18 Aug 1887.

Copied, 18.8.87.

Mr M. Buchner,
Chemist,
149 Houndsditch.

About end of June, a dark man, rather square built, hair dark brown, a foreign Jew by his face, purchased 2^d of nitric acid (2 oz) in a bottle labelled Bell & Co. Camphorated Oil. I notice the label because the bottle being oily my label would scarcely stick.

There was nearly a teaspoonful of oil left in the bottle which I poured off lest it should spoil the acid. The label was rather high up on the bottle. It was a 2 oz phial, long shape. I believe the man said it was for staining wood or sticks. I am not sure I asked him what it was wanted for. I am not sure that I shd know the man again. I think he had short whiskers coming a little below the ear and slight moustache. I do not think the whole transaction lasted more than a minute.

I do not recollect if he spoke English.

M. Buchner.

APPENDIX XIII.

Mr Buchner's Second Statement, 19 August 1887.[109]

Maximilian Buchner says:

I am a chemist at 149 Houndsditch and have been in business in that neighbourhood for 16 years.

I keep an assistant named Marius Gaziello, an Italian – he is now away for his holiday.

I made my statement to Mr Hayward at his office under these circumstances:

On Tuesday last I read for the first time in the *Daily Telegraph* a resumé of this case in which a description of the bottle was given: 'a long shaped phial with a Camphorated Oil label from Bell & Co. of Commercial Road'. I instantly remembered that I had supplied a man with nitric acid which I had put into a similar bottle for him. I saw also in the resumé Moore's evidence as to the sale of an ounce of nitric acid, and seeing that Dr Kay had said or was reported to have said that more than an ounce had been used I hesitated at first what to do, as I thought the matter hardly of sufficient importance to take notice of, but I consulted some friends who advised me to see some of the persons connected with the case, and I went to Mr Hayward whose address I had seen in the newspaper and told him what I has come about. At first he was disposed to treat any information lightly but when I fully explained the matter to him he said he thought it was most important evidence and took down my statement & I signed it. It was between 11 & 12 when I went to Mr Hayward's and 2 hours or so later, a reporter called upon me from the *Daily Telegraph* and produced to me a copy of my statement to Mr Hayward in the *Evening News*, and he asked me a lot of questions upon it and took my answers down in shorthand.

The copy statement now read to me is a correct statement of what I said to Mr Hayward, and the account in the *Daily Telegraph* is a correct account of what I told the reporter, except that I said I had been in the neighbourhood some 20 years instead of 27 years.

The neighbourhood of Houndsditch is populated chiefly by Jews, and the better half of my customers are Jews, I have more of them than any other chemist as I speak their jargon, Jüdisch, and sell oils, herbs, &c. which English chemists do not keep.

---

[109] TNA:PRO HO 144/201/A47465/93.

Lipski.

I have no means whatsoever of fixing, even approximately, the date when I sold the acid of which I speak. I only think it was in the morning when I made the sale, because I fancy I was not tired, and I am usually tired later in the day as mine is a busy business.

I open at 8. My assistant was not in the shop nor any other customer.

I can't describe the man any more than I have done, as it was so short a time he was in the shop and you don't take such notice of the *minutiae* of the man's features.

I can't say how he was dressed except that he worse a hard felt hat and a dark coloured cut-away coat which was buttoned up. I can't say anything about his tie or collar &c.

I sell nitric acid to small jewellers, stick makers, & cabinet makers, & it is also used as a cold dressing for warts.

It is an article which I sell in small quantities perhaps half a dozen times in a week. We keep no record of the sale. I can't say when I last sold it before the sale I speak of, but I have sold it since in small quantities but I cannot recollect how many times. I sold some last Monday or Tuesday but I cannot say for certain as it is not of sufficient importance to impress itself upon my mind.

My practice when selling this acid is to enquire of the purchaser what he wants it for, and then, if satisfied, I supply it and put upon the bottle a label, 'Poison, nitric acid'. I write these latter words.

Nitric acid is not mentioned in the Pharmacy Act but I put the label on for my own protection.

These acids are free for sale anywhere. Some time ago the police requested us to be careful about supplying these acids in large quantities.

I have given the police today a sample of the acid taken from the bulk from which I sold the 2 oz – I get my supplies from Davy, Yates and Routledge of 64 Park Street, Southwark.

The acid which I sold is known as the 'commercially pure solution' – it is distilled by pouring sulphuric acid on nitre, and it would consequently contain perhaps a mere trace of the sulphuric acid.

The label which I put on the bottle bore my name and was sticking to the bottle, tho' very loosely, when the customer took it away.

The customer was one of a very common type of persons in the East End. I remember that as he turned to leave the shop I noticed that the under and longer hairs in his moustache were of a reddish colour. He was rather pleasing looking and about 24 or 25 years of age. I cannot remember his face or his expression. I

Appendix XIII.

cannot remember what sort of a nose he had – if I saw a number of Jews I could not say if I could recognise him – if I saw one who I thought was the man I should pick him out – but I could not go beyond saying that I thought he was the man.

Camphorated oil is a liniment very commonly used by the Jews and I sell a great deal of it. I know Mess[rs] Bell & Co., the chemists – I believe Dr Kay is the head of the firm. I have often put up medicines in bottles bearing their labels. I cannot say at all whether I have sold any goods by retail in Bell & Co.'s bottles since the sale of the acid.

I agree with the report in the *Lancet* quoted in the *Daily Telegraph* of today, and now read to me, that 'it is doubtful if the quantity of nitric employed in this case can be more than guessed at, for it is so powerfully corrosive and causes such obvious stains that in common parlance a little of it goes a long way'.

I may know Lipski as a customer without knowing him by name. I have never seen the man in custody of that name – but I have heard that he is a tall fair man of slight build. I heard this from the *Pall Mall* reporter yesterday – I have had no end of reporters round. I have sold some of the acid to a reporter.

We keep no record of those sales. My shop is about 10 or 15 minutes' walk from Batty Street.

All chemists and most oilmen in the neighbourhood sell this acid – it is an article in pretty brisk demand among the small craftsmen round about.

(S[d]) M. Buchner.

APPENDIX XIV.

Mr Buchner's Acid, 18 & 19 August 1887.[110]

Chemical Laboratory,
Guy's Hospital,
London, S.E.

August 18th 1887.

Sir,

In the absence of Dr Stevenson I have examined on his behalf three samples of nitric acid received from Inspector John Tunbridge.

The samples were labelled as follows respectively:—

'Nitric Acid, Poison, M Buchner, Dispensing Chemist, 149 Houndsditch, E.C.',

'Acid Nitricum B.P. S.G. 1.420',

'Acid Nitric S.G. 1.360'.

The two latter samples were not marked with the name of the vendor.

I have especially examined the samples for the presence of sulphuric acid and find no trace of that substance in any one of them.

I am, Sir, your obedient servant,

Fred G Hopkins, F.I.C.

Godfrey Lushington Esq, C.B., etc.

Criminal Investigation Department,
Scotland Yard,
19th day of August 1887.

Referring to statement made by M. Buchner, chemist of 149 Houndsditch, I beg to report that as directed by Sir A.K. Stephenson I have this day obtained from Buchner a 2 oz sample of nitric acid, which he said was from the same supply

---

110 TNA:PRO HO 144/201/A47465/93.

Lipski.

as that from which he served the man mentioned in his statement in June last. I then proceeded to Davy, Yates & Routledge, wholesale chemists &c., of 64 Park Street, Southwark, from whom Buchner said he received the acid and on searching their books it was found that during the past twelve months they had supplied Buchner with two different qualities of acid, one on 21st August 1886 and the other on 16th Octr 1886. I obtained samples of each of these acids and took them, together with that obtained from Buchner, to Guy's Hospital, where in the absence of Dr Stevenson they were examined by Mr Hopkins, one of his assistants, who found no trace of sulphuric acid in either sample, and gave a certificate to that effect.

J. Tunbridge, Insp.

To the Treasury Solicitor. John Shore, Supt.

APPENDIX XV.

Standard, 20 August 1887.

THE CONVICT LIPSKI.

MR GRAHAM[111] asked the Home Secretary if it was true that Lipski's solicitor, Mr Hayward, was unable to obtain sight of the bottle labelled 'Camphorated Oil, Ball and Co.[112],' until Thursday' whether, on account of this delay, he would give more time to collect the necessary evidence; and when the Home Office contemplated releasing the unfortunate man from this position of uncertainty.

THE HOME SECRETARY. — The phial in question was taken to Mr Hayward's office on Monday, the 15th, by the Inspector and shown to Mr Hayward's clerk, he himself being absent. The clerk took a sketch of it, and was informed that the phial was in the custody of the Inspector, who would meet Mr Hayward at any time by appointment to show it to him. This message was repeated next morning. Mr Hayward was informed by the Inspector that the police could not part with the phial, but that it could be seen by anybody who desired to see it in the presence of the police. No application has been made by Mr Hayward or anybody for the purpose of identification. On Wednesday, the 17th, Mr Hayward asked the police for leave to take the bottle away to be photographed, and the Inspector refused to give it up for that purpose, and that was probably the incident to which the hon. member referred. On Thursday, the 18th, Mr Hayward complained to me by letter and in person, and I sent for the Inspector, and gave orders that he should have the phial photographed. Mr Hayward has not since made any application to have it photographed. I can hold out no expectation of the respite being further extended.

MR GRAHAM asked a further question, which was quite inaudible in the Gallery.

THE HOME SECRETARY. — As at present advised, I am quite unable to do so. I am giving the most anxious care and consideration to all the materials that have been laid before me, and upon the materials that are before me at present I can hold out no expectation of a further respite.

MR GRAHAM asked whether a petition, signed by one hundred members of Parliament, was about to be presented in favour of the condemned man Lipski, and whether, in view of that fact, the Home Secretary would not reconsider his decision.

---

111 Robert Bontine Cunningham Graham, Member of Parliament for North West Lanarkshire.
112 *Sic* in article.

Lipski.

THE HOME SECRETARY understood that such a petition was in preparation, but he must formally protest against interference with the ordinary course of the administration of justice (hear, hear).

MR CONYBEARE[113] asked whether the right hon. gentleman was aware that the evidence of Mr Brünner[114] in connection with the Lipski trial showed that a bottle precisely corresponding to that found on the scene of the murder had been discovered in the possession of a man not Lipski, and whether that fact was not sufficient to throw such reasonable doubt upon the guilt of the convict as to entitle him to a further respite (oh).

The Home Secretary replied that he had received a report, and was giving it most earnest attention, with most open and impartial mind. More than that he declined to say (hear, hear).

---

[113] Charles Augustus Vansittart Conybeare, Member of Parliament for Camborne.
[114] *Sic* in article. Should read: 'Buchner'.

APPENDIX XVI.

Pall Mall Gazette, 20 August 1887.

A LIFE OF LIPSKI.
BY ONE WHO KNOWS HIM.

Israel Lipski – as he is now known, but whose real name is Lobulsk – is a Polish Jew, and was born in Warsaw in 1865. His father gave him a good Hebrew education in a *chida* – which is a small room, generally on the basement. Lipski is not the name by which this family is known. Israel Lipski has three sisters and two brothers. One of the latter is in the army, and the other is a traveller. Israel when young was very fond of swimming and saved more than one from drowning. When his parents became poor, Israel was apprenticed to the trade of a turner. His master was very fond of him, and the other workmen taking a liking to him, he soon became a favourite in the workshop. When his term of apprenticeship was over his master employed him as a journeyman at a very decent wage, out of which he was able to assist his parents, who were becoming poorer and poorer. But at the age of twenty, he, having already heard of his brother's experience, determined to make his escape from the chance of service in the army. He had sold all he had to turn it into money in order to pay his fare to London. But the difficulty was how to make his escape when the Granetz – the territory between Russia and Germany – was guarded. The gendarmes would not allow any one to pass unless provided with a passport, signed and sealed, and notifying the place of destination. This Israel did not have, and had he applied for one he would have been asked all sorts of questions, and being so near to the age when he must become a soldier, they would have arrested him at once. The difficulty of passing the territory, however, was easily got over. In every town there are smugglers, some of whom make a special business of this sort of thing. Lipski's escape was effected in a very peculiar manner. A miller had occasion to pass the guards with a van load of flour, and Israel being on friendly terms with the miller was placed among the bags and taken over to Germany. From thence he took the train to Hamburg. Walking the streets in the hopes of meeting a countryman among the many Jews in Hamburg, he met a man who, after some conversation, engaged him as a servant in a cattle ship bound for London. Here he arrived penniless. At the docks there are plenty of 'runners,' and among them are agents for 'sweaters.' Israel Lipski was taken to Mr Mark[115] Katz, his late employer. Lodgings were obtained for him, and in a few days he was seen in the workshop.

---

115   *Sic* in article. Should read: 'Marks'.

Lipski.

Having been taught the trade of a turner in Warsaw, it was not difficult to turn to stick-making. Mr Katz found him an energetic workman, and gradually gave him a rise; with it he obtained a good wage. His employer saw that he was a prudent and respectable young man, and after a time Israel was engaged to his sister-in-law, Miss Kate Lyons. Mr Katz gave him another rise in order to enable him to save more money with which to get married early. Israel was now beginning to learn to read and write English, and with the assistance of his sweetheart he managed to read some easy things. The engagement was broken off for a time, but afterwards renewed until his arrest. Business with Mr Katz became slack, and Israel did not earn sufficient to keep himself; he was thus obliged to withdraw money from the savings bank. But this could not last, so Mrs Lyons, the mother of the young woman, advised him to get work for himself. The advice was taken, and Israel withdrew the remainder of his savings and bought some tools for his work. On the second day of his new enterprise the murder of Miriam Angel was committed, and the events which followed are well-known.

APPENDIX XVII.

Lipski's Confession, 21 August 1887.[116]

H.M. Prison Newgate.
Sunday 21 August 1887.

Sir,

I have the honour to enclose the confession of Israel Lipski, under sentence of death for the murder of Miriam Angell[117], taken down this afternoon from the prisoner's lips by the Revd S. Singer, Minister of the St Petersburg Place Synagogue. It was spoken in Jüdisch, the Judeo-German jargon, and translated word by word by Mr Singer. It was read and translated to the prisoner in my presence, he assenting to every statement. We have thought it well to forward a copy of the confession to the Press Assoc^n for publication in the morning's papers before the execution.

I have the honour to be, Sir, your most obedient servant,

Everard S. Milman Esqr,

Governor of H.M. Prisons Holloway & Newgate.

I, Israel Lipski, before I appear before God in judgment, desire to speak the whole truth concerning the crime of which I am accused. I will not die with a lie on my lips. I will not let others suffer even in suspicion for my sin. — I alone was guilty of the murder of Miriam Angel. I thought the woman had money in her room. So I entered, the door being unlocked, & the woman asleep. I had no thought of violating her, & I swear I never approached her with that object, nor did I wrong her in this way. Miriam Angel awoke ~~while I was~~ before I could search about for money & cried out, but very softly. Thereupon, I struck her on the head, & seized her by the neck & closed her mouth with my hand, so that she should not arouse the attention of ~~all~~ those who were about the house. I had long been tired of my life. I had bought ~~some aqua fortis of Mr Moore~~ a pennyworth of *aqua fortis* that

---

116 TNA:PRO HO 144/201/A47465/127.
117 *Sic* in letter.

Lipski.

morning for the purpose of putting an end to myself. Suddenly I thought of the bottle I had in my pocket. I drew it out, & poured some of the contents down her throat. She fainted, & ~~seeing~~ recognising my desperate condition, I took the rest. The bottle was an old one which I had formerly used & it[118] ~~which I [obscured] the oilman~~ was the same as that which I had taken with me to the oil shop. The quantity of *aqua fortis* I took had no effect on me. Hearing the voices of people coming up stairs, I crawled under the bed. The woman seemed already dead. ~~From~~ There was only a very short time from the moment of my entering the room until I was taken away. In the agitation I ~~partly~~ also fainted. I do not know how it was that my arms became abraded. I did not feel it & was not aware of it. As to the door being locked from the inside, I myself did this immediately after I entered the room, wishing not to be interrupted. — I solemnly declare that Rosenbloom & Schmuss knew nothing whatever of the crime of which I have been guilty, & I alone. I implore them to pardon me for having in my despair tried to cast the blame upon them. I also beseech the forgiveness of the bereaved husband. —

~~I acknowledge the justice of the sentence which has been passed upon me.~~ I admit that I have ~~[obscured] rightly and fairly dealt~~ had a fair trial and acknowledge the justice of the sentence that has been passed upon me. I desire to thank Mr Hayward for his efforts on my behalf, as well as all those who have ~~shown me such~~ interested themselves in me during this unhappy time.

~~A gold stud, wh~~ ~~The above is written by Mr Singer at my re~~ This confession is made of my own free will, & is written down by Mr Singer at my request.

May God comfort my loving father & mother, & may He accept my repentance & my death as an atonement for all my sins!

Sunday 21st Augt 1887.

Israel Lipski.

Witness – S. Singer, Minister.

Witness – E.S. Milman, Governor, H.M. Prison, Newgate.

---

118 Added in superscript to maintain the grammar of the sentence after the excision of the reference to the oilman.

APPENDIX XVIII.

Pall Mall Gazette, 22 August 1887.

ALL'S WELL THAT ENDS WELL.

Lipski's confession fortunately removes all doubt that he has been justly accused, justly convicted, and justly executed. He has been hanged, and few criminals ever went to the gallows who better deserved their fate.

In this painful business we have acted from first to last in a manner that was plainly demanded by the responsibilities of the position in which we were placed by the statement made to us by the prisoner's solicitor on Friday week. Those who have imputed to us either in praise or in censure the usurpation of the functions of a Supreme Court of Criminal Appeal are entirely mistaken. We neither merit the praise nor deserve the blame. We never sought in any way to interfere with the course of justice in Lipski's case until Lipski's solicitor assured us solemnly that the judge who tried Lipski had grave doubts as to the justice of the verdict. The proof of this is that until a late edition on Friday week, published after the receipt of Mr Hayward's confidence, we had never said a word in deprecation of the execution of the sentence. We had turned a deaf ear to Mr Hayward's appeal. We had rejected a lengthy plea sent us by one of our contributors urging consideration in Lipski's favour. It was only when Mr Hayward declared that he had been twice summoned to Mr Justice Stephen, and repeatedly assured us that on the second occasion he found the judge in a state of mental distress lest an innocent man should be executed, that we consented to touch the matter at all. Of course, if Mr Hayward was mistaken, we were misled. But, considering the fact that the life of a fellow-creature was left at the mercy of the discredited Minister who had condemned Miss Cass, we had no option left but to take the course which secured for Lipski a week's reprieve.

If Mr Justice Stephen had written a letter to the Home Secretary or the *Times* saying briefly that Mr Hayward was entirely mistaken, the whole matter would have been at an end. But, instead of this clear and explicit disclaimer, all that the Home Secretary could produce, even after all the pressure that must have been brought to bear upon the judge, was a halting and equivocal statement that 'I did not feel so clear and strong in my opinion as you – Mr Matthews – did.' If the judge did not feel certain, then certainly Mr Matthews's opinion was no reason why Lipski should not have the benefit of the doubt. So we pleaded for him day after day, adducing with laborious industry and in painful detail all the evidence

Lipski.

that seemed to us to justify the doubts of the judge. It is no use doing things by halves. If we had to defend the doubts of the judge against the cocksureness of the Home Secretary, we were irresistibly driven into the path we took, and although Lipski's confession releases us from the great doubt which we felt and expressed, it also affords a very remarkable confirmation of some of the criticisms on which we based our appeal for mercy. We do not hesitate to say that if the jury had known that Mr Justice Stephen was altogether mistaken in the theory by which he accounted for the crime, and that the medical experts were entirely at sea in their evidence as to when the murder was committed, they would never have convicted Lipski. The confession proves that they convicted the right man, but it also proves that they convicted him on the wrong evidence. Their conclusion was sound, but their premisses[119] were mistaken. Until Lipski confessed his guilt we had only the mistaken presmisses, the incorrect evidence, and the unsound hypothesis to go upon. Hence our agreement rather with the doubts of the judge than with the certainty of the Minister. Nor do we hesitate to say that it would have been much better if Lipski, although guilty, had been set at liberty than to have hanged him while doubts so grave, which his confession proves to be so well-founded, existed as to the theory of the murder on which the judge summed up and the jury convicted.

It must be a matter of profound relief to all concerned that Lipski's confession exonerates every one else from all complicity in his crime. Schmuss and Rosenbloom, whom he accused, are now explicitly freed from all blame by their accuser; and we heartily rejoice that a suspicion so widespread has been so conclusively dissipated. Mr Matthews has reason to rejoice that he has achieved the solitary success of a ministerial career now fast drawing to a close, and we congratulate him upon the unexpected vindication of the superior accuracy of his opinion on the case to that of Mr Justice Stephen. For our own part we did our level best for a man concerning whose guilt we knew his judge did not feel 'clear and strong;' and although the end has shown that the judge was not justified in his doubts, it would have been unpardonable if we had remained apathetic in face of the uncertainty which existed as to the soundness of the case for the prosecution. The confession at once vindicates the verdict and condemns the hypothesis on which it was obtained.

---

119 *Sic* in article.

Appendix XVIII.

LIPSKI'S CONFESSION.
BY A COMPATRIOT WHO LABOURED ON HIS BEHALF.

The confession made last evening by the criminal who expiated his crime at Newgate to-day is a fitting climax to this most remarkable case – perhaps one of the most remarkable in the annals of crime. For the confession, although a full one, by no means clears up many a mysterious point; and the more it is examined the less it looks like the truth, the whole truth, and nothing but the truth. One thing, however, the confession does – it justifies most absolutely those who since Lipski's condemnation have been arguing for a reprieve. For no one – except, perhaps, Mr Hayward, whom the criminal impressed most wonderfully – no one said Lipski was innocent. It was impossible to say that until some one else was shown to be guilty; and from that the proof was very far. What was said by those who urged his reprieve, and what will be adhered to more strenuously than ever now, was that upon the evidence as presented to the court the last extremity of the law should not be enforced. Two points were of paramount difficulty to overcome – first, as to motive; second, as to how Lipski got under the bed. As to the first, the judge laid out to the jury the theory of lust and attempted outrage; and as to the second, it was explained that he swallowed some acid and then crawled under the bed. Against the theory of outrage there was urged the prisoner's good character, that no attempt was shown, that no struggle was heard and that altogether it was a monstrous assumption. The confession made by the prisoner shows that the judge was wrong and those who dissented from his dictum were right. As to his being under the bed it was urged that he could not have become unconscious – according to medical testimony – either by fear or by the poison he took, and could only have been rendered so by violence administered to him. If, however, no violence was done him he shammed; and if so, there was no reason he should have done so, seeing he could have slipped out of the room, and that it was utterly inconceivable he would remain, as, according to medical evidence he must have done, for two hours in the room with his victim dead above him and the door locked. The confession shows the medical testimony to be all wrong. The woman had been dead but half an hour, or at most three-quarters, when Dr Kay examined her, and Lipski had only just murdered her when he was disturbed by knocking at the door and sought refuge under the bed. So that those were right who said that so far as the evidence went it was more than improbable that Lipski committed the crime. Why such an error in the exact science of forensic medicine should have been made is hard to say. But then the confession hardly clears the point. If Miriam Angel was not murdered till eleven o'clock, why was she in bed at all, seeing that by the evidence she always went to her mother's to breakfast at 9.30 or thereabouts. If on this morning she was ill her husband would have known it, or if she was taken suddenly ill after he left her she would have called Mrs Lipski, the landlady, or one of her fellow-lodgers. And, again, why did Lipski go into her room to rob her on this one day, when for some reason she did not go out,

Lipski.

when he could have gone any other day without encountering her? She may have locked the door when she went out, but then it was shown that the door would yield to very little pressure. The acid question, too, is by no means cleared up. Experts declared that upwards of an ounce was used upon the poor woman, and at least another ounce upon the coat, &c. Lipski says that he had only a pennyworth – which is an ounce. Where did the rest come from? His statement that he had the acid to commit suicide with is utterly incredible. Lipski commit suicide! The man who was just fitting up a workshop – who was busy upon his first business order – who was young and apparently in excellent spirits. Why on earth he of all men should have wanted to commit suicide it is simply impossible to say. Why he should have given Miriam Angel acid after she was stunned and he was able to rob her is a mystery. So are the abrasions on his arms, the burns on his coat, the movements of Schmuss, the obliviousness of Rosenbloom, the disappearance of the sovereign he undoubtedly had the night before the murder, and the breaking open of Mrs Lipski's box when the murderer knew he had but to ask her for anything she had in the way of a loan in order to get it. No less mysterious in face of the confession is Mr Buchner's evidence as to supplying two ounces of acid in the fatal phial, or the strange man in Birmingham – Schmuss's only acquaintance there, who answered so accurately Mr Buchner's description of the purchaser of the acid. The Whitechapel mystery will remain a mystery. Lipski's confession if anything has but deepened it: it is a pity a further respite could not have been given to him after he made his statement, so that he might have been examined on it. That the man deserved to die by his own confession is certain – whether that confession is wholly true is open to grave doubt. Any way, it has effected what perhaps from a public point of view was most desirable, and that is the justification it gives to those who urged that the guilt of the man did not tally with the evidence; and those who have striven in his favour will feel ample reward if the case is the means of an amendment in the law by which capital criminals are sent to their reckoning without proof positive against them so far as, humanly speaking, proof positive can be obtained.

APPENDIX XIX.

Isaac Angel: An Impressionistic Chronology.

The humble memorial of Isaac Angel of 93 Bedford Street, Commercial Road in the County of London, Bootmaker, an Alien, sheweth that your Memorialist is a Subject of Poland (Russia) having been born at Dombrowitz in the County of Warsaw on the 2nd day of October 1866 and that the Names and Nationalities of his parents are Polish Jews: Harris Angel; Dinah Angel.[120]

*

I come from near Warsaw. She came from the same province, not far from Warsaw.[121]

*

Miriam Angel is a native of Kolo (Poland).[122]

*

I have been married to her a twelvemonth next Friday.[123]

*

Have you been about twelve months in England? — Ten months. Longer now: ten months at the time.[124]

*

About a week before Whitsuntide this year, did you go to live at 16 Batty Street, towards the end of May? — Yes.[125]

*

When I went out on Thursday morning, my wife was awake and spoke to me.[126]

*

---

120 TNA:PRO HO 144/724/111470. Memorial for Certificate of Naturalization, September 1903.
121 TNA:PRO CRIM 1/26/5. Evidence given on the first day of the inquest, 29 June 1887.
122 TNA:PRO HO 144/201/A47465/1. Letter from James Monro, Assistant Commissioner of the Metropolitan Police, to the Home Office, 11 July 1887.
123 TNA:PRO CRIM 1/26/5. Evidence given on the first day of the inquest, 29 June 1887.
124 TNA:PRO HO 144/201/A47465/16. Evidence given on the first day of the trial of Israel Lipski, 29 July 1887.
125 Ibid.
126 TNA:PRO CRIM 1/26/5. Evidence given on the first day of the committal proceedings, 2 July 1887.

Lipski.

She had prepared my breakfast overnight. She was lying in bed while I said my prayers. She told me to take what she had prepared overnight for my luncheon, and asked me what she should get for me when I came back.[127]

*

She was in the family way then and was six months advanced in pregnancy.[128]

*

When I went outside, I closed the door by shutting it and leaving the key inside the room.[129]

*

At 11.45 am that morning, a woman came to me. She told me something. I went back to my apartments. I rushed upstairs. I was not permitted to enter my own room. I was dragged in the back room.[130]

*

The removal of the deceased in a coffin, borne on the shoulders of undertaker's men, was carried out amidst remarkable manifestations of grief by a large number of foreign dwellers in the vicinity, by whom Mrs Angel, who is described as a singularly genial young Jewess, was held in great esteem. Fully a thousand persons – mostly women – were in the street at the time the body was brought out. As the coffin proceeded on its way, the murdered woman's husband, a man of small stature, repeatedly wrung his hands, cried, and exclaimed in grief-stricken tones, 'My vife! my vife!'[131]

*

And have you lived at your father's and away from that house from the day this happened to the present time? — Yes.[132]

*

About 7.00 am on 30 June, the Thursday after the murder, I went to the room where it was committed. The door was locked and I was admitted by a P.C. who spoke German. I went to get a chemise and a sheet. My sister Sarah Angel was with me. I took the chemise and sheet out of a box, after which I saw, lying on the bed from which the body of my wife had been removed, a dirty dark-coloured

---

127 TNA:PRO CRIM 1/26/5. Evidence given on the first day of the inquest, 29 June 1887.
128 TNA:PRO CRIM 1/26/5. Evidence given on the second day of the committal proceedings, 9 July 1887.
129 Ibid.
130 TNA:PRO CRIM 1/26/5. Evidence given on the first day of the committal proceedings, 2 July 1887.
131 *Reynolds's Newspaper*, 3 July 1887.
132 TNA:PRO HO 144/201/A47465/16. Evidence given on the first day of the trial of Israel Lipski, 29 July 1887.

Appendix XIX.

neck muffler. This did not belong to me and I had never seen it before. I picked it up and said to the P.C. in Yiddish, 'This handkerchief does not belong to me'. The P.C. shook his head when I spoke to him and I then hung the handkerchief on the bed rail and left the room. I did not again return to the room and never again saw the handkerchief. The handkerchief was folded up for wearing around the neck and had the appearance of having been so worn.[133]

*

Last Thursday, I saw the corpse of my wife in the coffin.[134]

*

At the adjournment of the inquest, the body was conveyed to 40 Grove Street, where the mother-in-law lives, and from that house the funeral procession started at 12.00 pm on Thursday for West Ham cemetery, the burial taking place in accordance with the Hebrew rites. Long before the hearse, mourning coach and private carriage left 40 Grove Street, the narrow thoroughfares adjacent were thronged by an almost impassable crowd.[135]

*

Sarah Angel, sister to the above, says: On the following Sunday, 3 July, I went to the room with my brother Davis to fetch away Isaac's things. We had the key and admitted ourselves. Mrs Lipski entered the room with us. I went to clear the bed and then saw the handkerchief still hanging on the bed rail where Isaac had put it on the Thursday. I said, 'This is no good to us. We will leave it.' Mrs Lipski then began to cry, put both hands up to her face and said, 'Dear me, that is the murderer's handkerchief'. We took everything out of the room except an old straw mattress and the handkerchief. The latter was lying on the mattress when we left. The key was handed to Mrs Lipski. I have never been to the room since and had not since seen the handkerchief. On the following day, Mrs Lipski sent for us to remove the mattress but we declined to do so. She then emptied it herself and sent us the canvas cover, but no handkerchief was with it.[136]

*

Mrs Lipski says: I was in the room when it was cleared by Sarah Angel and her brother. They never showed any handkerchief to me and I did not see one. It is untrue that I cried and said, 'Dear me, that is the murderer's handkerchief'. I know nothing about any handkerchief and when they left the room the only thing left therein was a straw mattress. I am sure there was nothing else. A day or two

---

133 TNA:PRO HO 144/201/A47465/16. Report of Inspector Tunbridge, 18 August 1887.
134 TNA:PRO CRIM 1/26/5. Evidence given on the first day of the committal proceedings, 2 July 1887.
135 *Lloyd's Weekly Newspaper*, 3 July 1887.
136 TNA:PRO HO 144/201/A47465/16. Report of Inspector Tunbridge, 18 August 1887.

Lipski.

afterwards, as the Angels would not fetch the mattress away, I emptied it into the dung pit at the cowsheds, and sent the cover round to the Angels. There was no handkerchief on the mattress when I took it away to empty.[137]

*

P.C. Frank Ludwig, 273H, says: I was in charge of the room on 30 June when Angel and his sister called to fetch a chemise from the room. I admitted them and they took what they wanted from a box. They spoke to me, but I could only imperfectly understand what they said. I did not hear them say anything about a handkerchief, nor did I notice Angel with one in his hand or anywhere about the room. I had no occasion to examine anything in the room and I am not prepared to say there was no handkerchief in the room. I was the only officer about the room who could speak German.[138]

*

Mrs Sarah Katz, wife of Mark Katz, 3 Watney Passage, stick maker, when called upon with reference to query no. 9 said in respect to a handkerchief: About a year ago I bought a silk handkerchief from a shop in the Commercial Road. I think I paid 2s 10½d for it. I bought it to wear round my neck but it was not long enough to tie into bows in front. It was a reddish coloured one. Some time afterwards I sold it to Lipski for 3s, I think. I never saw him wear it round his neck.[139]

*

At the Thames Police Court yesterday, Mrs Lipski, the landlady of 16 Batty Street, Commercial Road, the house in which Lipski murdered Mrs Angel, again attended and complained about Angel, the husband of the dead woman. Mr Lushington[140] issued a warrant, and in the evening Isaac Angel was brought up, charged with assaulting Mrs Lipski. Mrs Lipski stated that on Saturday last, at 5.00 pm, the defendant came to the house in company with his two brothers. The latter knocked her down, and the defendant then kicked her in the stomach and on the legs. His brothers pulled him away, or he would have kicked her to death. Defendant said, 'I will not rest till I have killed you'. Sophie Woodensdein said she was standing with complainant when defendant and his brothers came up, knocked her down, and kicked her, saying in Yiddish, 'I will do for you as you have done for my wife'. Another witness said a large crowd assembled and smashed all the windows. Leah Levy, of 16 Batty Street, said that, on Saturday, defendant came to the house, caught the prosecutrix, threw her to the ground, and then kicked her on the leg. He also kicked witness. Mr Lushington remanded

---

137   TNA:PRO HO 144/201/A47465/16. Report of Inspector Tunbridge, 18 August 1887.
138   Ibid.
139   Ibid. 'Mark Katz' *sic* in report; should read, 'Marks Katz'.
140   Franklin Lushington, Metropolitan Police Magistrate to the Thames Police Court.

Appendix XIX.

Angel for the attendance of an interpreter.[141]

*

Isaac Angel, boot rivetter, living in Grove Street, Whitechapel, was charged on a warrant with assaulting Leah Lipski, living at 16 Batty Street, Commercial Road East. The prisoner is the husband of the Jewess Miriam Angel, who was murdered by Israel Lipski, and Leah Lipski is the landlady of the house in Batty Street. The prosecutrix stated that at 5.00 pm on Saturday afternoon, the prisoner and his two brothers went to 16 Batty Street. The brothers knocked her down, and the prisoner kicked her. In answer to Mr Lushington, the prosecutrix said that after the prisoner had assaulted her, his two brothers took him away or he would have killed her. At the time of the attack he said, 'I'll do for you the same as you have done for my wife'. On the previous Monday, the prisoner's brothers broke the shutters and windows, and shouted out, 'Lipski, Lipski'. Mrs Rubenstein said she saw a mob in Batty Street, and spoke to Mrs Lipski. The prisoner came along with his two brothers, knocked her down, and the brothers kicked her. Clara Fossner, of Brunswick Place, Backchurch Lane, said she saw the prisoner throw Mrs Lipski down and kick her. Henry Matthews, 212H, said that on Saturday, seeing a crowd, he went and stood opposite number 16. The prisoner and two other men came down the street from Commercial Road, and he saw them speak to a man, who made a feint at Angel as if to strike him. He was a tall young man, and wore a cap. No complaint was made to him of any assault being committed, and he saw the prisoner go away. Elizabeth Lucas, 27 Batty Street, said at 6.00 pm on Saturday evening she saw the prisoner come down Batty Street, and a man made an attempt to strike him, and a woman with a baby took him away. Mr Lushington said the women had contradicted themselves as to the details, but he could not doubt there was some squabble about this murder. Everybody had great compassion for the prisoner, but he must not annoy the landlady. A great deal of annoyance and damage had been caused, and he bound him over to keep the peace for six months.[142]

*

1891 England Census: 66 Bedford Street, London.

> Isaac Angel, head, married, 25 years of age, bootmaker / laster, employed, born in Poland.
> Jane Angel, wife, married, 21 years of age, no occupation, born in Poland.[143]

*

---

141 *Pall Mall Gazette*, 25 August 1887.
142 *Evening Standard*, 26 August 1887.
143 TNA:PRO Census Returns of England and Wales, 1891, RG12/p300/f98/p16.

Lipski.

1901 England Census: 91 Bedford Street, London.

> Isaac Angel, head, married, 35 years of age, boot-laster, working on own account at home, born Russia (Poland).
>
> Jane Angel, wife, married, 32 years of age, no occupation, born in Russia (Poland).
>
> Abraham Angel, son, 10 years of age, born in London.
>
> Jack Angel, son, 8 years of age, born in London.
>
> Morris Angel, son, 6 years of age, born in London.
>
> Mary Angel, daughter, 4 years of age, born in London.
>
> Reuben Angel, son, 3 years of age, born in London.[144]

*

Your Memorialist is a married man and has six children under age residing with him:

> Abraham Angel – 11 years and 10 months;
>
> Alexander Angel – 10 years and 4 months;
>
> Morris Angel – 8 years and 10 months;
>
> Mary Angel – 6 years and 10 months;
>
> Reuben Angel – 5 years and 10 months;
>
> Rosey Angel – 5 months.[145]

*

Your Memorialist's settled place of business is at 93 Bedford Street, Commercial Road, in the County of London.[146]

*

Your Memorialist has for five years within the period of the eight years last past resided within the United Kingdom, viz., from March 1892 to August 1901 at 91 Bedford Street in the County of London aforesaid; from August 1901 to August 1903 at 93 Bedford Street, same county.[147]

*

Your Memorialist seeks to obtain the rights and capacities of a natural born British Subject from a desire to obtain the privileges of an English citizen for himself and children including the right to vote and acquire property. Your

---

144 TNA:PRO Census Returns of England and Wales, 1901, RG13/p326/f12/p13.
145 TNA:PRO HO 144/724/111470. Memorial for Certificate of Naturalization, September 1903.
146 Ibid.
147 Ibid.

Appendix XIX.

Memorialist humbly prays that a Certificate of Naturalization may be granted to him in pursuance of the Statute 33 Victoria, Cap. 14, intituled 'An Act to amend the Law relating to the legal condition of Aliens and British Subjects'.[148]

*

And whereas I have inquired into the circumstances of the case, and have received such evidence as I have deemed necessary for proving the truth of the allegations contained in such Memorial, so far as the same relate to the Memorialist:

Now, in pursuance of the authority given to me by the said Acts, I grant to the aforesaid Isaac Angel this Certificate, and declare that he is hereby naturalized as a British Subject, and that, upon taking the Oath of Allegiance, he shall in the United Kingdom be entitled to all political and other rights, powers, and privileges, and be subject to all obligations, to which a natural-born British Subject is entitled or subject in the United Kingdom. ...

In witness whereof I have hereto subscribed my Name this 29th day of March 1904.

Home Office, London.
A. Akers Douglas.[149]

*

Oath of Allegiance.

I, Isaac Angel, do swear that I will be faithful and bear true allegiance to His Majesty King Edward, His Heirs and Successors, according to law. So help me God.

(Signature of Alien): I. Angel.

Sworn and subscribed this 5th day of April 1904 before me
(Signature) H. M. Gowing
A Commissioner for Oaths.
Address: 41 Finsbury Pavement, London, E.C.[150]

*

1911 England Census: 11 Station Road, Finsbury Park, London.

> Isaac Angel, head, 45 years of age, married, bootmaker, employer working at home, born in Russia, Naturalized British Subject.
>
> Jane Angel, wife, 40 years of age, married 22 years, eight children born alive to the present marriage, six children still living, two children who have died, no occupation, born in Russia.

---

148 TNA:PRO HO 144/724/111470. Memorial for Certificate of Naturalization, September 1903.
149 TNA:PRO HO 334/37/14290. Certificate of Naturalization to an Alien, April 1904.
150 Ibid.

Lipski.

Henry Angel, brother, 37 years of age, single, tailor, employer, born in Russia, Naturalized British Subject.

Abraham Angel, son, 19 years of age, single, furrier, worker, born in Stepney, London.

Alexander Angel, son, 17 years of age, single, clerk, worker, born in Stepney, London.

Maurice Angel, son, 16 years of age, single, tailor, apprentice, born in Stepney, London.

Miriam Angel, daughter, 14 years of age, attending school, born in Stepney, London.

Robert Angel, son, 13 years of age, attending school, born in Stepney, London.

Rose Angel, daughter, 7 years of age, born in Stepney, London.[151]

*

Angel, Isaac of 2 Princess Road, Stoke Newington, Middlesex, died 13 August 1935; probate London, 3 January [1936], to Abraham Angel, furrier, and Alexander Jack Angel, commercial clerk. Effects £2768 3s 9d.[152]

*

My grandfather, Isaac Angel, was a gentle, sweet man and one could never imagine him starting his life in a new country with such a traumatic episode and no outward effects – but there was never any evidence of it. After the death of his wife, he sent to Poland for her next younger sister (as was the Jewish custom) and she, Jane, was his second wife, my grandmother. My father, Abraham, was the first born of that union.

They had six children: Abe (my father), Miriam (always known as Mary), Rose, Jack, Reuben and Morrie. Abe, Jack and Reub were the only ones who married. Mary was a well-known schoolteacher in a Jewish school in the East End; most of the rest of the family were in the shoe business.

My grandfather, Isaac, was involved with the local synagogue (Finsbury Park). It was actually opposite their house in Princess Road.

I spent a great deal of my childhood in their home. There was never any hint of the murder. It was never mentioned. It was a total, absolute secret.[153]

---

151 TNA:PRO Census Returns of England and Wales, 1911, RG14/p840.
152 Principal Probate Registry, *Calendar of the Grants of Probate and Letters of Administration made in the Probate Registries of the High Court of Justice in England.*
153 Valerie Angel-Newstead to the editor, 28 August 2017.

Isaac and Jane Angel

Courtesy Valerie Angel-Newstead

Isaac Angel
Courtesy Valerie Angel-Newstead

INDEX.

Abberline, Inspector Frederick, 2, 42–3
Akers Douglas, Aretas, 201
Angel, Davis (Isaac's brother), 197
Angel, Dinah (Isaac's mother), 5, 11, 195; evidence at trial, 90–1
Angel, Isaac: birth and family background, 195; marriage to Miriam, 195; resident at Batty Street, 1; actions on day of murder, 5, 195–6; distraught, 196; moves out of Batty Street, 86, 196; collects items from apartment, 196–7, 198; views wife's body, 197; evidence at trial, 54–7; charged with assaulting Mrs Lipski, 198–9; second marriage and family, 202; Census returns (1891, 1901), 199–200; becomes British citizen by naturalization, 200–1; Census return (1911), 201–2; death and probate, 202
Angel, Jane (Isaac's second wife), 202
Angel, Miriam: birth, 195; marriage to Isaac, 195; resident at Batty Street, 1; breakfast routine, 5; borrows money to pay rent, 86; last hours, 5, 54–5, 195–6; body discovered, 11; examined at scene, 12, 100–1, 120–1; body removed from house, 196; post mortem, 122–4; inquest, 17, 24; no evidence of rape or attempted rape, 24; as victim of sex crime, 42; funeral procession and burial, 43, 197; L admits killing, 37
Angel, Sarah (Isaac's sister), 196, 197, 198
Angel-Newstead, Valerie (Isaac's granddaughter), 202
anti-semitism, 3, 26, 42–3
aqua fortis see nitric acid
Arbour Square Police Station, 114
Armstrong, Eliza, 26

Bangladeshis: as immigrants, 3
Barsuch, Emil, 34, 35, 74, 77n
Batty Gardens, 1
Batty Street, No 1 (vestmaker shop), 4
Batty Street, No 16 (murder house): description, 50–2, 55; location, 52–3; residents, 1; morning of murder, 5–6, 195–6; L's bedroom workshop, 6–7, 8, 9–10; body discovered, 11; murder scene, 12, 100–2, 121; crowds gather outside, 12, 13–14; L found unconscious under bed, 12–13, 96–7, 103–4, 105, 121–2; L arrested and taken from house, 13–14, 105; police search room, 106–8, 112–13; body removed, 196; handkerchief clue, 196–8; room clearance, 197–8; alleged attempted robbery at, 31, 159;

new tenants, 86; fracas and alleged assault of Mrs Lipski, 198–9; *see also* door lock
Batty Street, No 19 (boot and shoe repair shop), 52, 110–11
Baxter, Wynne, 2, 17
Berner Street, 42
Bitten, Sgt George, 88–9, 92; evidence at trial, 50–4, 89–90, 131–2
Booth, Charles, 2, 4
Bovill Smith, W., 19
Bowen-Rowlands, Ernest, 33, 38
Bresler, Fenton: *Reprieve: A Study of a System*, 30
Buchner: first statement (18 August 1887), 31–2, 177–8; besieged by journalists, 33; second statement (19 August 1887), 179–81; evidence immaterial, 32, 33, 183–4
business card, Lipski's, 41, 113 & n

Calvert, Dr William, 15, 21, 27, 146; evidence at trial, 125–7
Cameron, Mr (locksmith), 146–7
'Case of Israel Lipski now lying under Sentence of Death, The' (Hayward), 141–7
child sexual abuse, 25–6
Collins, Wilkie: *Armadale*, 170–1
Conybeare, Charles, 186

David (Tartakowski's roommate), 35–6
Diomed (shopkeeper), 12
door lock: recently fitted, 59–60, 108–9; working condition, 27, 56, 86, 146–7, 160; forced, 84; Piper examines, 12, 102–3, 109–10; police inspect, 112; Rosenbloom accused of tampering, 27–8; removed, 86, 87–9
Dougal, Samuel Herbert, 19
Dyke, Philip, 29
Dywein, Harris, 12, 14; evidence at trial, 94–100; interviewed by *Pall Mall Gazette*, 33

East End: and anti-semitism, 3, 26, 42–3; immigration from Eastern Europe, 2–3; sweated labour, 3–4, 41
Elliott, George, 19
employment, 3–4
Evening News (London), 169–71, 173–6
Evening Standard (London), 2, 26, 58n, 185–6, 199

Final, Inspector David: takes statement from L,

203

Index.

16, 20, 113–14, 118–19; charges L with murder, 17, 114, 119; evidence at trial, 112–16, 118–19; Special Report (10 August 1887), 149–50; collects articles for scientific testing, 154, 158; interviews Barsuch, 34

Finsbury Park Synagogue, 202

Fishman, William, 2

Fossner, Clara, 199

Friedland, Martin: *The Trials of Israel Lipski*, 3, 17–19, 22, 23, 24, 26, 32–3, 37

Gartner, Lloyd P., 2, 3, 4

Geoghegan, Gerald, 17–19, 21, 22

Gover, Dr R.M., 151–2

Graham, Robert Cunningham, 185

Graham-Campbell, R. F., 19

Grove Street, Whitechapel, 11, 53, 197

Harrison, Sister (of London Hospital), 15

Hayward, John: jobbing solicitor, 17; briefs defence counsel, 20–1; submits first petition, 27, 139–41; publishes pamphlet outlining L's defence, 141–7; meets with Mr Justice Stephen, 27–8, 162–3; implicates Rosenbloom, 27–8; hamstrung by L's statement, 28; introduced to Stead, 28, 169–70, 173–6; disclosures to *Pall Mall Gazette*, 29–30, 38, 161–5; submits second petition, 31, 159–60; forwards Buchner evidence to Home Office, 31, 33; complains evidence withheld, 185; knowledge of adulterated acid report, 32–3, 158; and Barsuch's allegations, 34; notified commutation refused, 36; interviewed by *Evening News*, 173–6

Hebrew Dramatic Theatre, Prince's Street, 2

Home Office *see* Akers Douglas, Aretas; Lushington, Godfrey; Matthews, Henry

Hopkins, Frederick, 183–4

Houndsditch Murders (1910), 3

House of Commons: exchanges on Lipski case, 36, 185–6

Hutton, Arthur, 19

Illustrated Police News, 17

Inwood, PC Alfred: evidence at trial, 106–8

Jack the Ripper, 2, 4, 14, 42

Jacobs, Mrs (resident at Batty Street), 88, 92

Jacoby, Myer, 42

Jews: and anti-semitism, 3, 26, 42–3; employment, 3–4; Hebrew Dramatic Theatre, 2; immigration from Eastern Europe, 2–3; reaction to Lipski case, 35; workers' rights and unionisation, 41

Karamelli, Mr (court interpreter), 20, 22

Katz, Marks, 6, 36, 187–8

Katz, Sarah, 6, 36, 198

Katz's factory, Watney Passage, 6, 7, 36

Kay, Dr John: called to crime scene, 12–14, 95–7; post mortem on Miriam Angel, 122–4; analyses semen-like substance, 24; evidence at trial, 24, 120–5

Kean, PC William, 13, 14

Laister, Joseph, 3, 26

Langham, Samuel, 38

Lansdowne, Inspector Andrew, 33–4

Lee's oil shop, Backchurch Lane, 7, 10, 53, 67, 128

Leib (Tartakowski's roommate), 35–6

Leman Street Police Station, 14–15, 112

Levy, Leah: resident at Batty Street, 1; actions on day of murder, 5, 11; evidence at trial, 91–2; witness at Isaac Angel assault case, 198; belongings allegedly ransacked, 31

'Lipski': as derogatory epithet, 42–3

Lipski, Fanny, 2

LIPSKI, ISRAEL (*formerly* Lobulsk):

Before the trial: birth and early life in Poland, 1, 187; emigrates to London, 1–2, 187; resident at Batty Street, 1, 58 & n; adopts surname Lipski, 2; physical description, 17, 40; employed as stick maker, 6, 187–8; engaged to Kate Lyons, 6, 188; starts own business from Batty Street, 6–7, 8, 188; pawns silver Geneva watch, 87, 113; borrows money from Mrs Lyons, 6, 130–1; hires staff, 6–7, 8, 9, 73–4, 77, 80; in back yard at Batty Street, 5, 58–9; visits Schmidt's general store, 7, 74–5; returns to Batty Street, 7; buys acid from Lee's oil shop, 10, 128–9; purchases sponge, 10–11; returns again to Batty Street, 10, 110; found unconscious under bed, 12–13, 96–7, 103–4, 105, 121–2; Dr Kay revives, 13, 97–8, 121, 125; medical opinion on L's state of insensibility, 125, 151–2; arrested and taken to Dr Kay's surgery, 13–14, 97, 105 & n; at Leman Street Police Station, 14–15, 112; admitted to London Hospital, 15, 125–7; gives account to Kate Lyons, 15; statement to police, 16, 20, 113–14, 118–19; frames Rosenbloom and Schmuss, 15, 16, 21, 118–19, 145; identified by Charles Moore, 129–30, 144, 149–50; charged with murder, 17, 114, 119; committal proceedings, 17; Old Bailey trial (*see* trial)

After the trial: date fixed for execution, 20; in Newgate Prison, 161; first petition for

204

Index.

clemency, 27, 139–41; second petition, 31, 159–60; death sentence respited for one week, 30, 167; commutation refused, 36; confession, 36–7, 189–90; execution, 38; inquest and burial, 38; unanswered questions, 38–9; character, 40, 59; *ennui* and spiritual vacuity, 40–1; political sympathies, 41; grandiose delusions, 41; possible mental disorder, 42; death as act of martyrdom, 42; motive for murder, 22–5, 40, 132–3, 144

Lipski, Leah (Mrs Lipski): resident at Batty Street, 1; integrated into British life, 2; actions on day of murder, 5, 9; L approaches for loan, 6; forces bedroom door, 11; finds body, 11; fetches doctor, 85; and clearance of room, 197–8; evidence at trial, 81–9; visits L in prison, 161; alleges assault by Isaac Angel, 198–9; belongings allegedly ransacked, 31

Lipski, Philip: resident at Batty Street, 1, 58 & n; integrated into British life, 2; testifies at Hebrew Dramatic Theatre inquest, 2; actions on day of murder, 5; evidence at trial, 57–60

Lloyd's Weekly Newspaper, 132–3, 197

London Hospital: L treated at, 15, 125–7; Kate Lyons visits, 15; L interviewed by police at, 16, 113–14; L identified by Charles Moore at, 129–30, 144, 149–50

Lucas, Elizabeth, 199

Ludwig, PC Frank, 196–7, 198

Lushington, Franklin, 198, 199

Lushington, Godfrey: analysis of L's motives, 22–3; and Stevenson's report, 32–3; writes to Hayward advising no commutation, 36; minutes and annotations, 40, 151, 153; assessment of Buchner's first statement, 177–8

'lust' as motive theory, 22–5, 133, 144

Lyons, Hannah (Kate's mother): possibly encourages L to work for himself, 6, 188; lends money to L, 6; visits L in hospital, 15; evidence at trial, 130–1

Lyons, Kate: engaged to L, 6, 188; visits L in hospital, 15; expedites police interview of L, 15–16; besieged, 33–4; L's relationship with, 41; visits L in prison, 161

'Maiden Tribute of Modern Babylon' affair (1885), 25–6

Marcolescu, Maurice, 35–6

Masset, Louise, 19

Mathews, Charles: prosecution counsel, 19; examinations (Sgt Bitten, 50–3, 131–2; Isaac Angel, 54–7; Richard Pittman, 66–9; Isaac Schmuss, 76–9; Leah Lipski, 81–5; Dinah Angel, 90–1; Rachel Rubenstein, 92–3; Harris Dywein, 94–8; PC Sach, 104–6; Charles Peters, 108–9; Thomas Warwick, 110–11; Inspector Final, 112–14; Dr Calvert, 125–6; Hannah Lyons, 130–1)

Matthews, Henry (Home Secretary): target of Stead's vehemence, 26, 28, 36; receives first petition, 27; receives second petition, 31; grants respite of one week, 30, 167; answers questions in House of Commons, 36, 185–6; dismisses Barsuch's story, 34; refuses commutation, 36; further considers L's case, 36; reaction to L's confession, 38

Matthews, PC Henry, 199

McArthur, A. W., 139, 148

McIntyre, A.: qualities and experience as lawyer, 17; defence counsel, 18–19; cross-examinations (Sgt Bitten, 53–4, 89–90; Isaac Angel, 57; Philip Lipski, 59–60; Simon Rosenbloom, 63–6; Richard Pittman, 69–71, 73; Mark Schmidt, 76; Isaac Schmuss, 79–80; Leah Lipski, 85–7; Dinah Angel, 91; Leah Levy, 92; Rachel Rubenstein, 93; Harris Dywein, 98–100; William Piper, 104, 109–10; PC Sach, 106; PC Inwood, 108; Charles Peters, 109; Thomas Warwick, 111; Inspector Final, 114–16; Henry Smaje, 117–18; Dr Kay, 124–5; Dr Calvert, 126–7; Thomas Redmayne, 127; Charles Moore, 129–30; Hannah Lyons, 131); closing speech, 40, 132–3; reflects on Lipski case, 20–1, 22

memorial from Members of Parliament, 36

Milman, Everard S., 49n, 133n, 189

Moore, Charles: sells nitric acid to L, 10, 128–9; stock of nitric acid adulterated, 32–3, 158; identifies L at hospital, 129–30, 144, 149–50; evidence at trial, 128–30

Moses, Mr (vestmaker), 4

Muir, Richard, 19

necrophilia, 23

Newgate Prison, 19, 38, 42, 161, 189

nitric acid: used in stick making trade, 75–6; L procures, 10, 128–9; in Miriam Angel case, 101–2, 120, 123–4; bottle located at scene, 14, 98, 103; and injuries to L, 122, 126–7; not sufficient to cause unconsciousness, 125, 152; Stevenson's analysis and reports, 27, 30, 32–3, 153–5, 157–8; Buchner's evidence, 31–2, 177–8, 179–81; Hopkins's report, 183–4

Old Bailey, 18; offence statistics, 24–5; *see also* trial

Pall Mall Gazette: Stead's editorship, 25–6;

205

Index.

publishes anti-semitic material, 3, 26; raises questions about Lipski trial, 25, 27, 137; alleges 'conversion' of Mr Justice Stephen, 29–30, 161–5; and 'trial by journalism', 30–1, 169–70, 173–6; interviews Harris Dywein, 33; publicises Buchner's evidence, 31–2; publishes Barsuch's allegations, 34; attacks Matthews, 36; on L's execution, 38; declares Rosenbloom and Schmuss blameless, 38; highlights unresolved issues surrounding case, 38–40; reports Isaac Angel assault case, 198–9; 'A Life of Lipski By One Who Knows Him', 1, 187–8; 'All's Well That Ends Well', 191–4

Peters, Charles, 59–60; evidence at trial, 108–9

petitions for clemency: first (6 August 1887), 27, 139–41; second (13 August 1887), 31, 159–60

Phillips, Dr George Bagster, 14–15, 112

Piper, William: called to crime scene, 11; examines bedroom door lock, 12; evidence at trial, 100–4, 109–10

Pittman, Annie (Richard's mother): evidence at trial, 73

Pittman, Richard: immaturity, 7; L hires, 7–8; helps L provision new business, 8, 128; actions on day of murder, 8, 9–10; evidence at trial, 66–73; as weak and unreliable witness, 8, 22

Poland, 1, 195

Poland, Harry: prosecution counsel, 19; opening speech, 49–50; examinations (Philip Lipski, 57–9; Simon Rosenbloom, 60–3; Mark Schmidt, 73–6; Steva Tartakowski, 80–1; Leah Levy, 91–2; Samuel Spiers, 93–4; William Piper, 100–4; PC Inwood, 106–8; Henry Smaje, 116–17; Inspector Final, 118–19; Dr Kay, 24, 120–4; Thomas Redmayne, 127; Charles Moore, 128–9); re-examinations (Richard Pittman, 71–3; Mark Schmidt, 76; Leah Lipski, 87–8, 88n; Sgt Bitten, 89; Thomas Warwick, 111; Dr Calvert, 127); closing speech, 132; meets with Mr Justice Stephen, 162, 163; reflects on Lipski case, 26, 33

Rabinowitz, Nathan, 9, 21–2, 34, 79

Redmayne, Thomas, 15; evidence at trial, 127

Reynolds's Newspaper, 196

Robinski, Shmuel, 74n, 76, 77n, 78, 79

Rosenbloom, Simon: L hires, 6–7; actions on day of murder, 7, 8, 9; at murder scene, 12, 13; framed by L, 15, 16, 21, 118–19, 145; honest character, 22; implicated by Hayward, 27–8; evidence at trial, 60–6; supposed weight loss since murder, 33; re-employed by Marks Katz, 36; L exonerates, 37; declared blameless by *Pall Mall Gazette*, 38

Rubenstein, Marks, 2

Rubenstein, Rachel (*née* Lipski), 1, 5–6, 86–7; evidence at trial, 92–3; witness at Isaac Angel assault case, 199

Sach, PC Arthur, 13–14; evidence at trial, 104–6

Schacher (Tartakowski's roommate), 35–6

Schmidt, Mark, 7, 78; evidence at trial, 73–6

Schmidt's general store, Backchurch Lane, 7, 9, 53, 73–5, 76–7, 78, 80

Schmuss, Isaac: as locksmith, 27; L hires, 9; actions on day of murder, 9; framed by L, 16, 21, 118–19, 145; in Birmingham after murder, 21–2; honest character, 22; evidence at trial, 76–80; unsubstantiated allegations against, 34; menaced to give false information, 34–5; L exonerates, 37; declared blameless by *Pall Mall Gazette*, 38

Schwartz, Israel, 42

sensation journalism, 26

Siege of Sidney Street (1911), 3

Sims, Francis, 17, 53

Singer, Simeon, 42, 189

Smaje, Henry, 16, 113–14; evidence at trial, 116–18, 119 & n

Society (penny paper), 28, 169–70, 173, 174–5

Solomons, Philip, 42

Spiers, Samuel, 6; evidence at trial, 93–4

St George in the East, Whitechapel, 2

Stead, W.T.: personality, 25; journalistic approach, 25–6; introduced to L's solicitor, 28, 169–70, 173–6; agitates around Lipski case, 28–30, 31–2, 33, 39–40; denounced by Mr Justice Stephen, 29; *see also Pall Mall Gazette*

Stephen, Sir James Fitzjames (Mr Justice): reputation and mental state, 19; tries Lipski case, 19; intervenes in proceedings (layout of Miriam Angel's bedroom, 52; acid stains on L's clothes, 56; stick making, 65, 128; Simon Rosenbloom's evidence, 66; Richard Pittman's evidence, 70, 71, 72–3; Leah Lipski's evidence, 84–5, 86, 87–8 & n, 89; Harris Dywein's evidence, 96–7, 98; William Piper's evidence, 102; PC Sach's evidence, 106; landlord's evidence, 109; Inspector Final's evidence, 119 & n; Dr Kay's evidence, 125; Thomas Redmayne's evidence, 127); summing-up, 133–4; passes death sentence, 134; and 'lust' theory, 22, 23–5; meets with Hayward, 27–8, 162–3; report to Home Office, 28; alleged 'conversion', 29–30, 161–5; advocates respite of one week, 30; urges sharing of Stevenson's evidence with defence, 32; dismisses Barsuch's story, 34; further considers L's case, 36;

Index.

reaction to L's confession, 38
Stephenson, A. K., 36, 183
Stevenson, Dr Thomas: analyses acid burns, 27, 153–5; reports on composition of acid, 30, 32–3, 157–8
Stride, Elizabeth, 42
sweated labour, 3–4, 41

Tartakowski, Steva, 9, 35–6, 74n, 76–7; evidence at trial, 80–1
Thames Police Court, 17, 198–9
Thick, Sgt William, 113, 149, 150
Times, The, 19, 23, 49–50, 133–4
trial: bench and legal teams, 17–19; arraignment, 19–20; opening speech for prosecution, 49–50; first day, 50–111; second day, 112–32; closing speech for prosecution, 132; closing speech for defence, 132–3; judge's summing-up, 133–4; verdict and sentence, 20, 134; defence hamstrung, 20–1, 28; concerns about fairness of trial, 22–5; claims of inaccurate interpreting, 22; jury possibly misdirected by judge's remarks on motive, 22, 23–5, 144
'trial by journalism', 30–1, 169–70, 173–6
Tunbridge, Inspector John: questions Pittman, 8; investigates attempted robbery at Batty Street, 31; investigates handkerchief clue, 196–8; traces Buchner's acid, 183–4

Valetta, J. P., 19
Vestry Hall, St George in the East, 17

Warwick, Thomas, 10; evidence at trial, 110–11
Watson, Basil, 19
Webb, Sydney and Beatrice, 4
West Ham Cemetery, 43, 197
White, PC Arthur, 13–14, 15
Woodensdein, Sophie, 198

NOTABLE BRITISH TRIALS SERIES.

Trial	Date of Trial(s)	Editor(s)	Volume No.
Mary Queen of Scots	1586	A. Francis Steuart	30
Guy Fawkes	1605-1606	Donald Carswell	61
King Charles I	1649	J. G. Muddiman	43
The Bloody Assizes	1685	J. G. Muddiman	48
Captain Kidd	1701	Graham Brooks	51
Jack Sheppard	1724	Horace Bleackley	59
Captain Porteous	1736	William Roughead	9
The Annesley Case	1743	Andrew Lang	16
Lord Lovat	1747	David N. Mackay	14
Mary Blandy	1752	William Roughead	22
James Stewart	1752	David N. Mackay	6
Eugene Aram	1759	Eric R. Watson	19
Katherine Nairn	1765	William Roughead	38
The Douglas Cause	1761-1769	A. Francis Steuart	8
Duchess of Kingston	1776	Lewis Melville	42
Deacon Brodie	1788	William Roughead	5
The 'Bounty' Mutineers	1792	Owen Rutter	55
Abraham Thornton	1817	Sir John Hall, Bt.	37
Henry Fauntleroy	1824	Horace Bleackley	34
Thurtell and Hunt	1824	Eric R. Watson	26
Burke and Hare	1828	William Roughead	27
James Blomfield Rush	1849	W. Teignmouth Shore	45
William Palmer	1856	Eric R. Watson	15
Madeleine Smith	1857	A. Duncan Smith (first edition)	
		F. Tennyson Jesse (second edition)	1
Dr Smethurst	1859	L. A. Parry	53
Mrs M'Lachlan	1862	William Roughead	12
Franz Müller	1864	H. B. Irving	13
Dr Pritchard	1865	William Roughead	3
The Wainwrights	1875	H. B. Irving	25
The Stauntons	1877	J. B. Atlay	11
Eugène Marie Chantrelle	1878	A. Duncan Smith	4
Kate Webster	1879	Elliott O'Donnell	35

Notable British Trials Series.

City of Glasgow Bank Directors	1879	William Wallace	2
Charles Peace	1879	W. Teignmouth Shore	39
Dr Lamson	1882	H. L. Adam	18
Adelaide Bartlett	1886	Sir John Hall, Bt.	41
Israel Lipski*	1887	M. W. Oldridge	84
Mrs Maybrick	1889	H. B. Irving	17
John Watson Laurie	1889	William Roughead	57
The Baccarat Case	1891	W. Teignmouth Shore	56
Thomas Neill Cream	1892	W. Teignmouth Shore	31
Alfred John Monson	1893	J. W. More	7
Oscar Wilde	1895	H. Montgomery Hyde	70
William Gardiner	1903	William Henderson	63
George Chapman	1903	H. L. Adam	50
Samuel Herbert Dougal	1903	F. Tennyson Jesse	44
The 'Veronica' Mutineers	1903	Prof. G. W. Keeton and John Cameron	76
Adolf Beck	1904	Eric R. Watson	33
Robert Wood	1907	Basil Hogarth	65
Oscar Slater	1909-1928	William Roughead	10
Hawley Harvey Crippen	1910	Filson Young	24
John Alexander Dickman	1910	S. O. Rowan-Hamilton	21
Steinie Morrison	1911	H. Fletcher Moulton	28
The Seddons	1912	Filson Young	20
George Joseph Smith	1915	Eric R. Watson	29
Sir Roger Casement	1916	George H. Knott (first and second editions)	
		H. Montgomery Hyde (third edition)	23
Harold Greenwood	1920	Winifred Duke	52
Field and Gray	1920	Winifred Duke	67
Bywaters and Thompson	1922	Filson Young	32
Ronald True	1922	Donald Carswell	36
Herbert Rowse Armstrong	1922	Filson Young	40
Jean Pierre Vaquier	1924	R. H. Blundell	47
John Donald Merrett	1927	William Roughead	46
Browne and Kennedy	1927	W. Teignmouth Shore	49
Benjamin Knowles	1928	Albert Lieck	60
Sidney Harry Fox	1930	F. Tennyson Jesse	62
Alfred Arthur Rouse	1931	Helena Normanton	54
The Royal Mail Case	1931	Collin Brooks	58

Notable British Trials Series.

Jeannie Donald . . . . .1934. . . . . .J. G. Wilson. 79
Rattenbury and Stoner. . . . . .1935. . . . . .F. Tennyson Jesse 64
Buck Ruxton . . . . .1936. . . . . .Prof. H. Wilson. 66
Frederick Nodder. . . . . .1937. . . . . .Winifred Duke. 72
Patrick Carraher. . . . . .1938-1946 . . . . .George Blake 73
Peter Barnes and Others . . . . .1939. . . . . .Letitia Fairfield. 77
August Sangret . . . . .1943. . . . . .MacDonald Critchley 83
William Joyce . . . . .1945. . . . . .J. W. Hall. 68
Neville George Cleveley Heath. . . .1946. . . . . .MacDonald Critchley 75
Ley and Smith. . . . . .1947. . . . . .F. Tennyson Jesse 69
James Camb. . . . . .1948. . . . . .G. Clark. 71
Peter Griffiths . . . . .1948. . . . . .George Godwin. 74
John George Haigh . . . . .1949. . . . . .Lord Dunboyne. 78
Evans and Christie. . . . . .1950 & 1953. . . .F. Tennyson Jesse 82
John Thomas Straffen . . . . .1952. . . . . .Letitia Fairfield and Eric P. Fullbrook. . 80
Craig and Bentley . . . . .1952. . . . . .H. Montgomery Hyde. 81

* New series.

In preparation:
No. 85: Louise Masset (ed. Kate Clarke)
No. 86: Percy Lefroy Mapleton (ed. Adam Wood)

www.ingramcontent.com/pod-product-compliance
Lightning Source LLC
Chambersburg PA
CBHW062158080426
42734CB00010B/1734